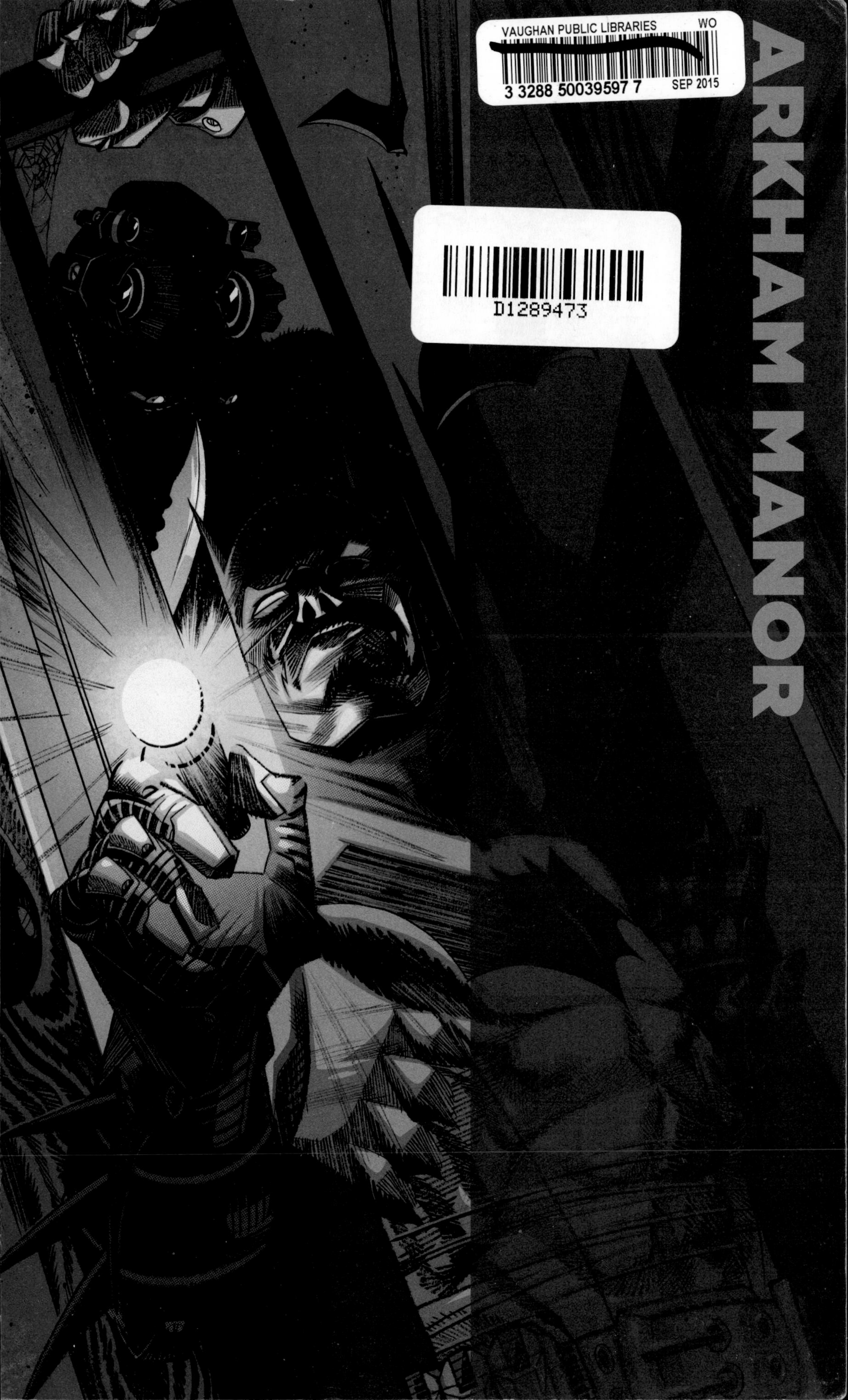
ARKHAM MANOR

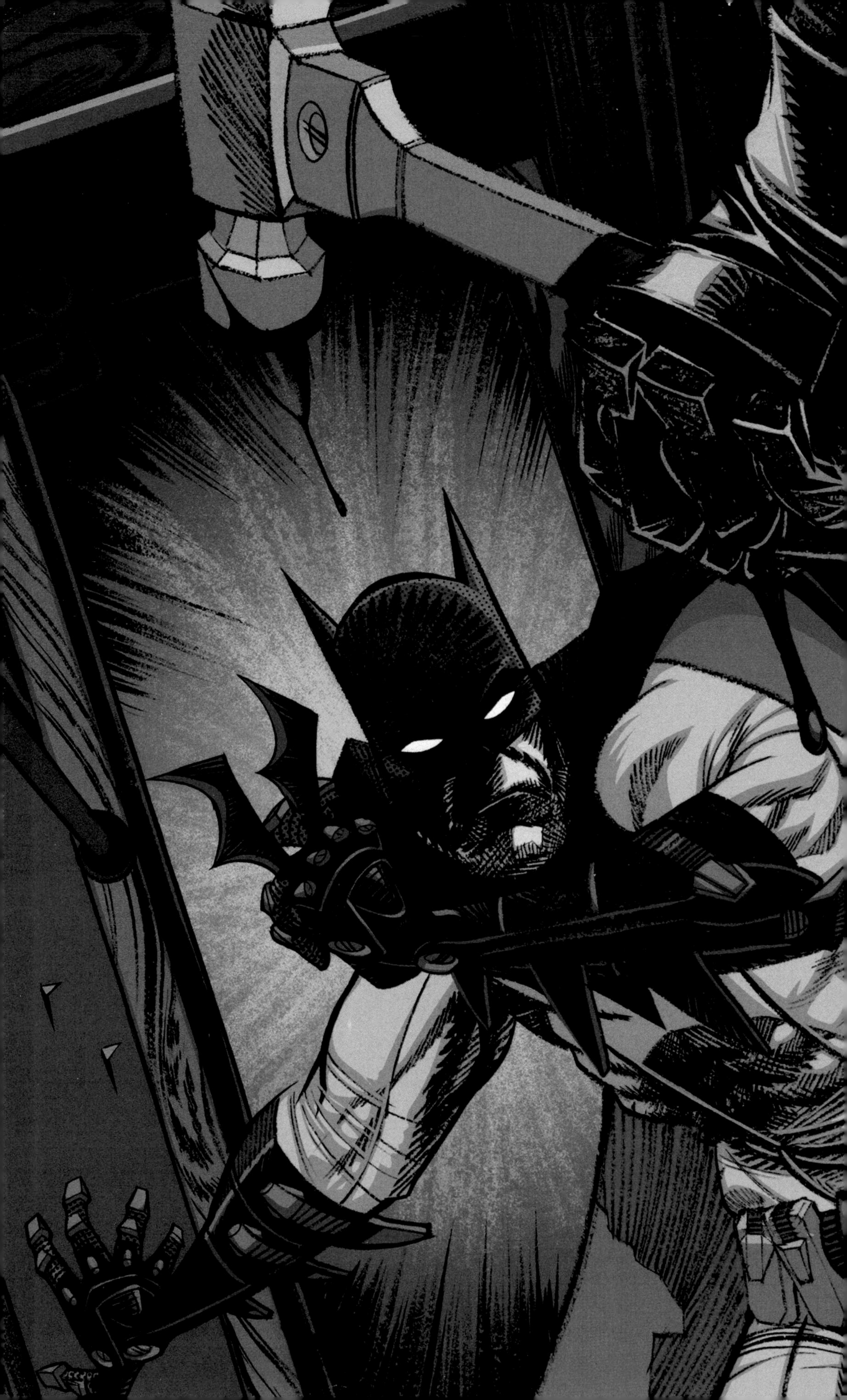

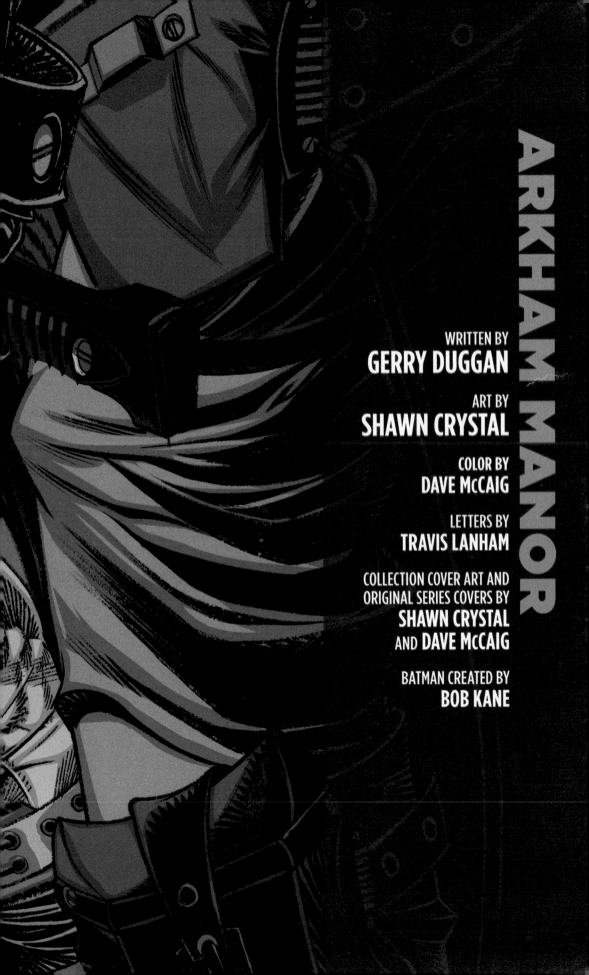

ARKHAM MANOR

WRITTEN BY
GERRY DUGGAN

ART BY
SHAWN CRYSTAL

COLOR BY
DAVE McCAIG

LETTERS BY
TRAVIS LANHAM

COLLECTION COVER ART AND
ORIGINAL SERIES COVERS BY
SHAWN CRYSTAL
AND **DAVE McCAIG**

BATMAN CREATED BY
BOB KANE

MARK DOYLE Editor – Original Series
MATT HUMPHREYS Assistant Editor – Original Series
SCOTT NYBAKKEN Editor
ROBBIN BROSTERMAN Design Director – Books
CURTIS KING JR. Publication Design

BOB HARRAS Senior VP – Editor-in-Chief, DC Comics

DIANE NELSON President
DAN DIDIO and JIM LEE Co-Publishers
GEOFF JOHNS Chief Creative Officer
AMIT DESAI Senior VP – Marketing & Franchise Management
AMY GENKINS Senior VP – Business & Legal Affairs
NAIRI GARDINER Senior VP – Finance
JEFF BOISON VP – Publishing Planning
MARK CHIARELLO VP – Art Direction & Design
JOHN CUNNINGHAM VP – Marketing
TERRI CUNNINGHAM VP – Editorial Administration
LARRY GANEM VP – Talent Relations & Services
ALISON GILL Senior VP – Manufacturing & Operations
HANK KANALZ Senior VP – Vertigo & Integrated Publishing
JAY KOGAN VP – Business & Legal Affairs, Publishing
JACK MAHAN VP – Business Affairs, Talent
NICK NAPOLITANO VP – Manufacturing Administration
SUE POHJA VP – Book Sales
FRED RUIZ VP – Manufacturing Operations
COURTNEY SIMMONS Senior VP – Publicity
BOB WAYNE Senior VP – Sales

DC Comics, 4000 Warner Blvd., Burbank, CA 91522
A Warner Bros. Entertainment Company
Printed by RR Donnelley, Owensville, MO, USA. 6/19/15.
ISBN: 978-1-4012-5458-2
First Printing.

Library of Congress Cataloging-in-Publication Data

Duggan, Gerry, author.
Arkham Manor. / Gerry Duggan, Shawn Crystal.
pages cm
ISBN 978-1-4012-5458-2 (paperback)
1. Graphic novels. I. Crystal, Shawn, illustrator. II. Title.
PN6728.A73D84 2015
741.5'973—dc23
2015007192

SUSTAINABLE FORESTRY INITIATIVE

Certified Chain of Custody
20% Certified Forest Content,
80% Certified Sourcing
www.sfiprogram.org
SFI-01042
APPLIES TO TEXT STOCK ONLY

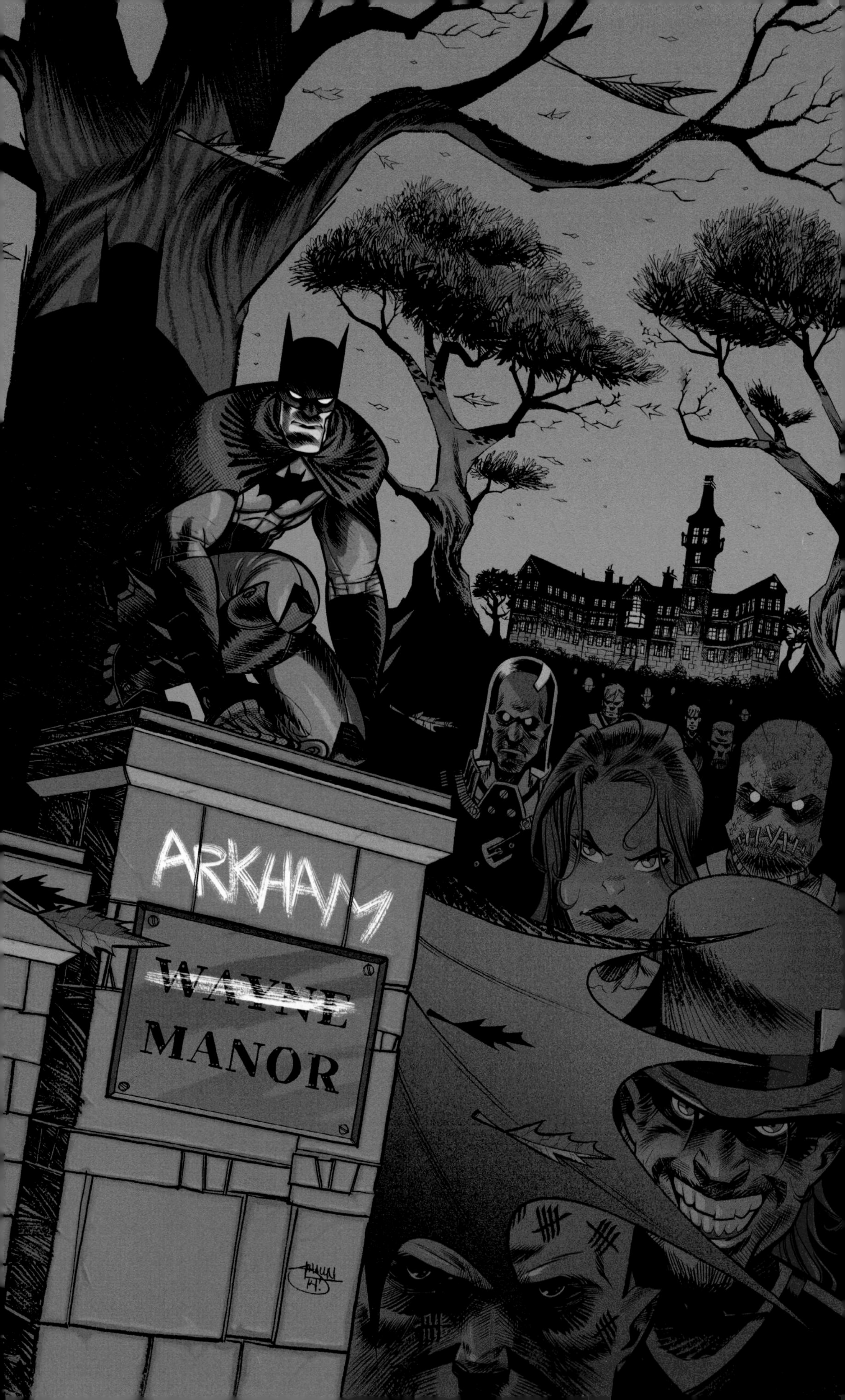
ARKHAM
WAYNE
MANOR

Variant cover art for issue #1 by **ERIC CANETE**

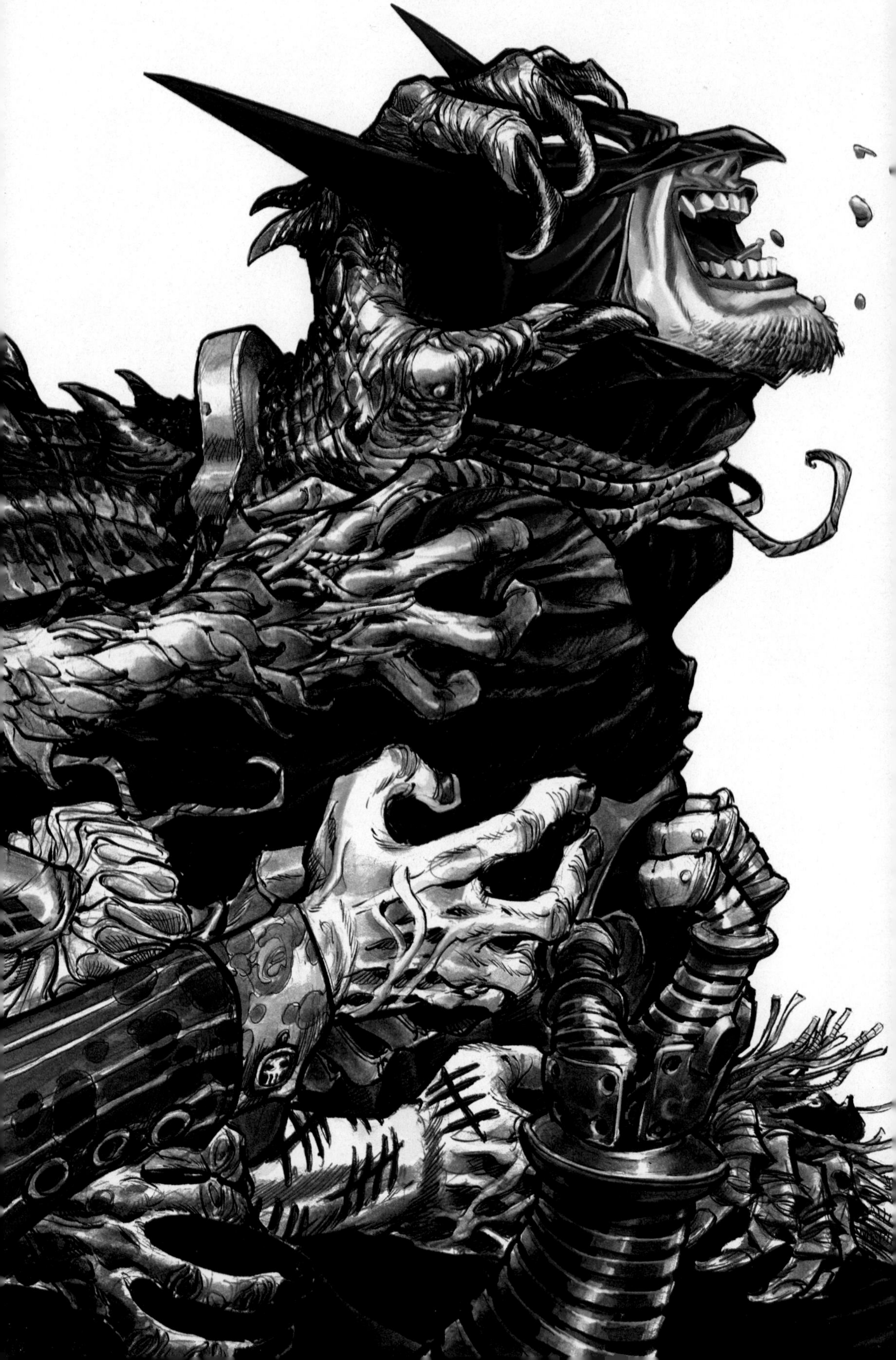

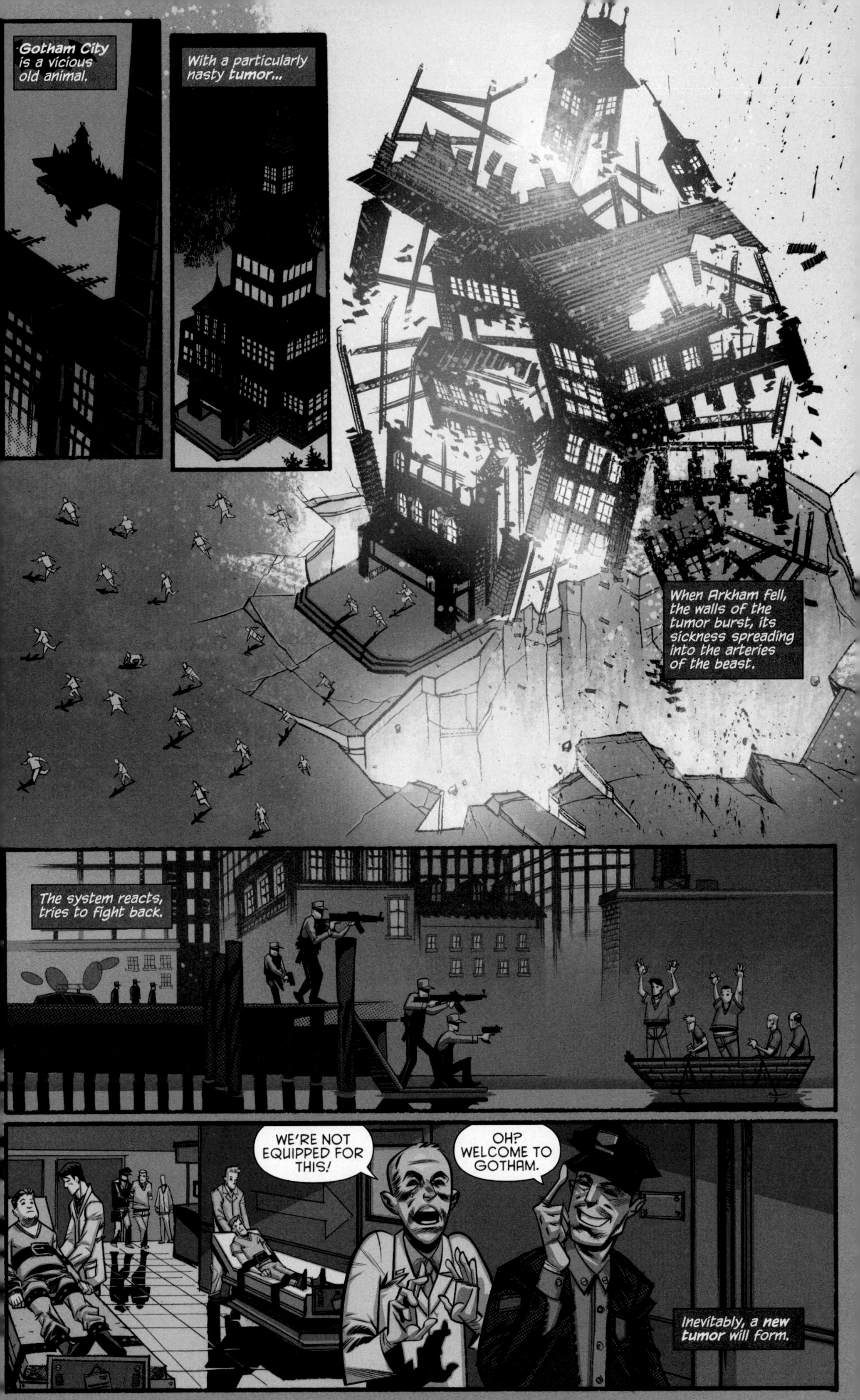
Gotham City is a vicious old animal.
With a particularly nasty tumor...
When Arkham fell, the walls of the tumor burst, its sickness spreading into the arteries of the beast.
The system reacts, tries to fight back.
WE'RE NOT EQUIPPED FOR THIS!
OH? WELCOME TO GOTHAM.
Inevitably, a new tumor will form.

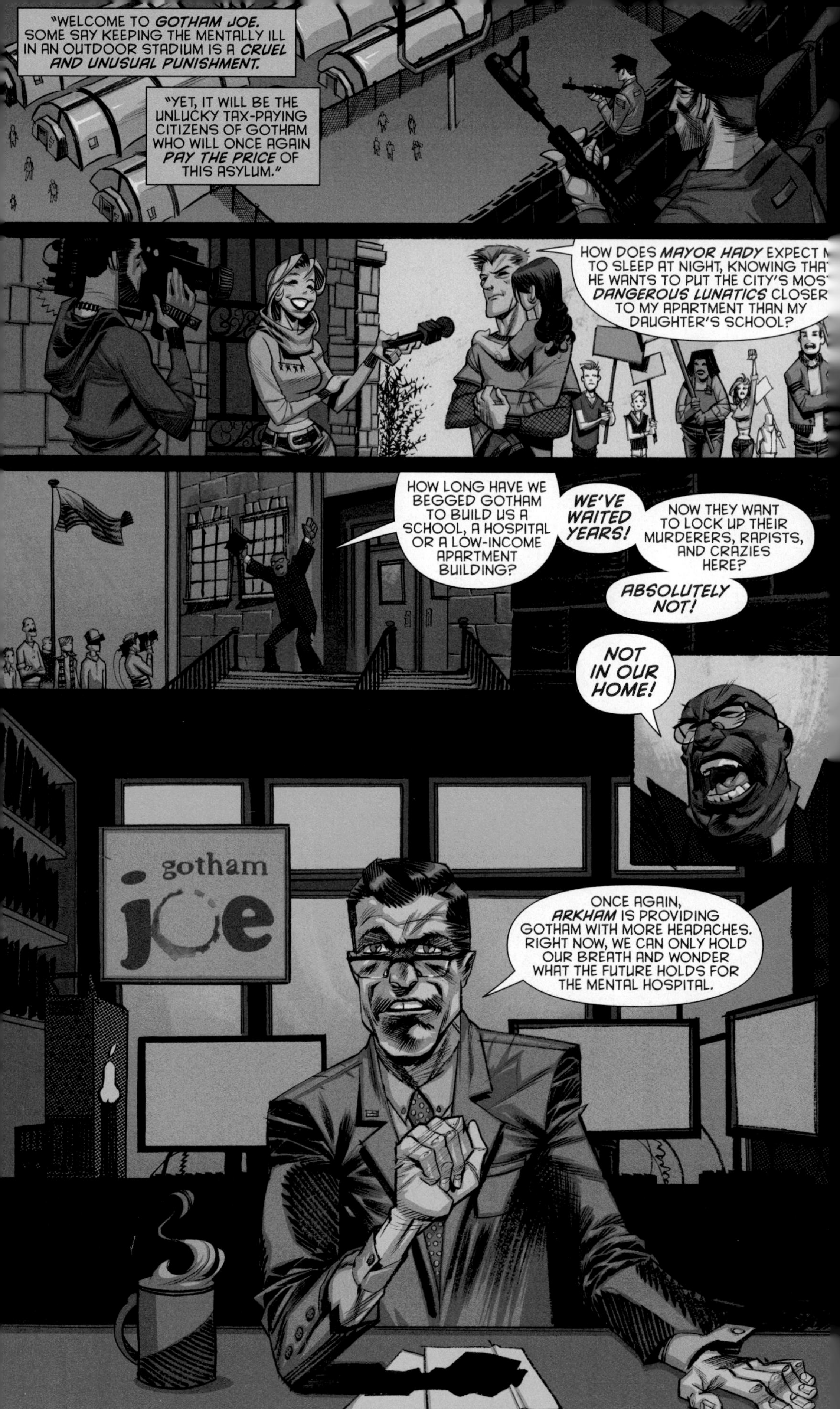

"WELCOME TO GOTHAM JOE. SOME SAY KEEPING THE MENTALLY ILL IN AN OUTDOOR STADIUM IS A CRUEL AND UNUSUAL PUNISHMENT.
"YET, IT WILL BE THE UNLUCKY TAX-PAYING CITIZENS OF GOTHAM WHO WILL ONCE AGAIN PAY THE PRICE OF THIS ASYLUM."
HOW DOES MAYOR HADY EXPECT M TO SLEEP AT NIGHT, KNOWING THAT HE WANTS TO PUT THE CITY'S MOST DANGEROUS LUNATICS CLOSER TO MY APARTMENT THAN MY DAUGHTER'S SCHOOL?
HOW LONG HAVE WE BEGGED GOTHAM TO BUILD US A SCHOOL, A HOSPITAL OR A LOW-INCOME APARTMENT BUILDING?
WE'VE WAITED YEARS!
NOW THEY WANT TO LOCK UP THEIR MURDERERS, RAPISTS, AND CRAZIES HERE?
ABSOLUTELY NOT!
NOT IN OUR HOME!
gotham joe
ONCE AGAIN, ARKHAM IS PROVIDING GOTHAM WITH MORE HEADACHES. RIGHT NOW, WE CAN ONLY HOLD OUR BREATH AND WONDER WHAT THE FUTURE HOLDS FOR THE MENTAL HOSPITAL.

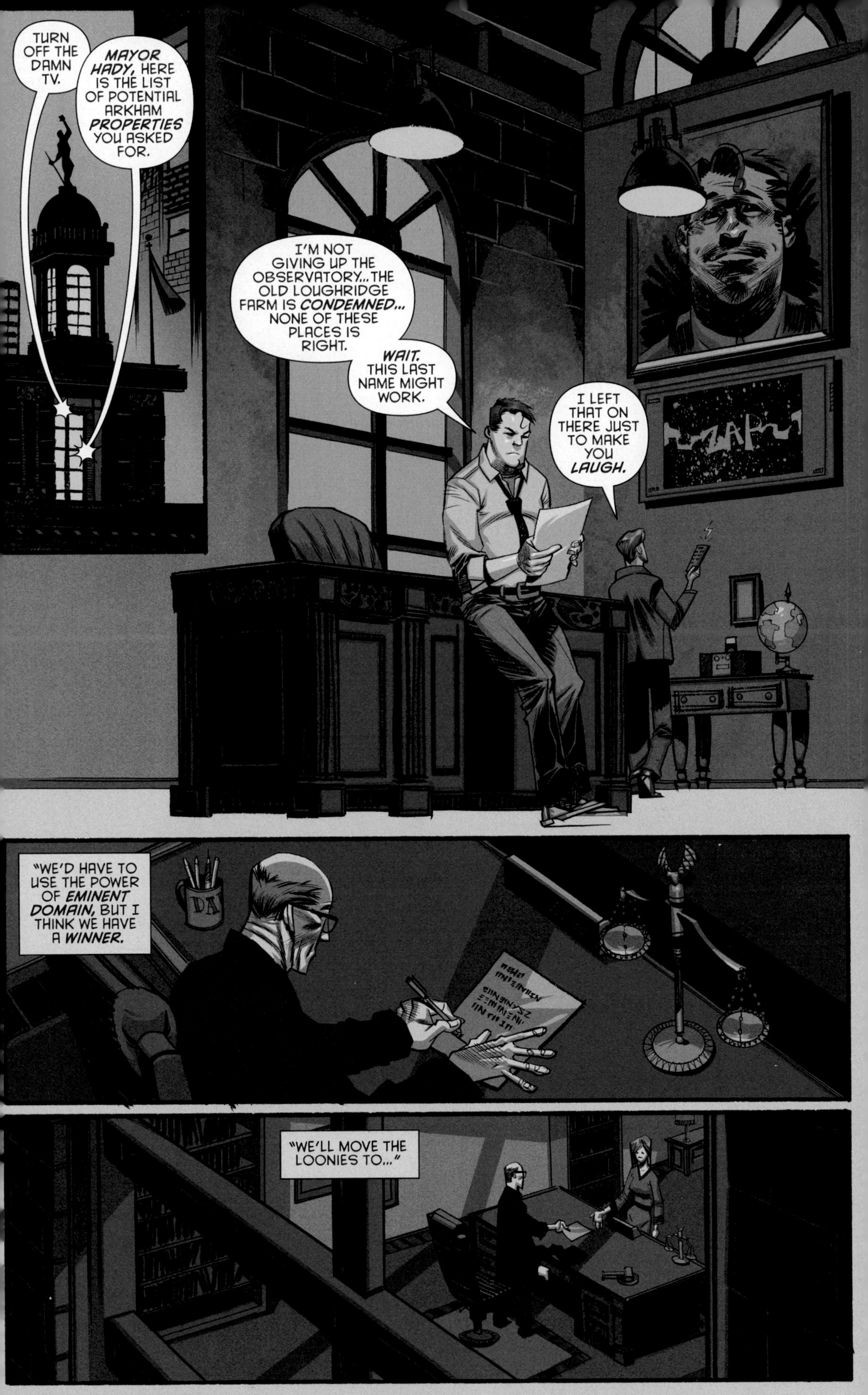
TURN OFF THE DAMN TV.
MAYOR HADY, HERE IS THE LIST OF POTENTIAL ARKHAM PROPERTIES YOU ASKED FOR.
I'M NOT GIVING UP THE OBSERVATORY... THE OLD LOUGHRIDGE FARM IS CONDEMNED... NONE OF THESE PLACES IS RIGHT.
WAIT. THIS LAST NAME MIGHT WORK.
I LEFT THAT ON THERE JUST TO MAKE YOU LAUGH.
ZAP
"WE'D HAVE TO USE THE POWER OF EMINENT DOMAIN, BUT I THINK WE HAVE A WINNER.
DA
"WE'LL MOVE THE LOONIES TO..."

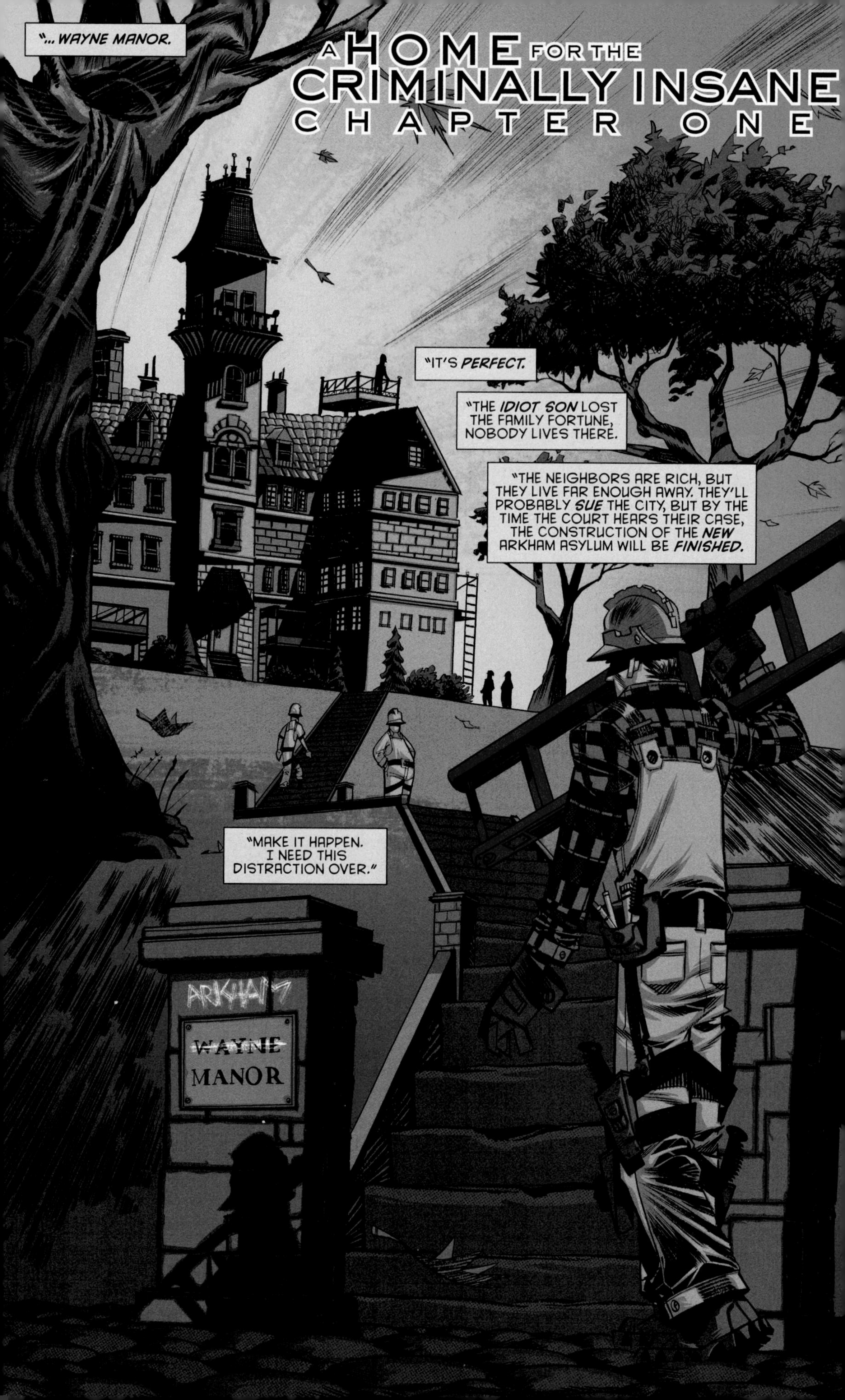
"...WAYNE MANOR.
A HOME FOR THE CRIMINALLY INSANE
CHAPTER ONE
"IT'S PERFECT.
"THE IDIOT SON LOST THE FAMILY FORTUNE, NOBODY LIVES THERE.
"THE NEIGHBORS ARE RICH, BUT THEY LIVE FAR ENOUGH AWAY. THEY'LL PROBABLY SUE THE CITY, BUT BY THE TIME THE COURT HEARS THEIR CASE, THE CONSTRUCTION OF THE NEW ARKHAM ASYLUM WILL BE FINISHED.
"MAKE IT HAPPEN. I NEED THIS DISTRACTION OVER."
ARKHAM
WAYNE
MANOR

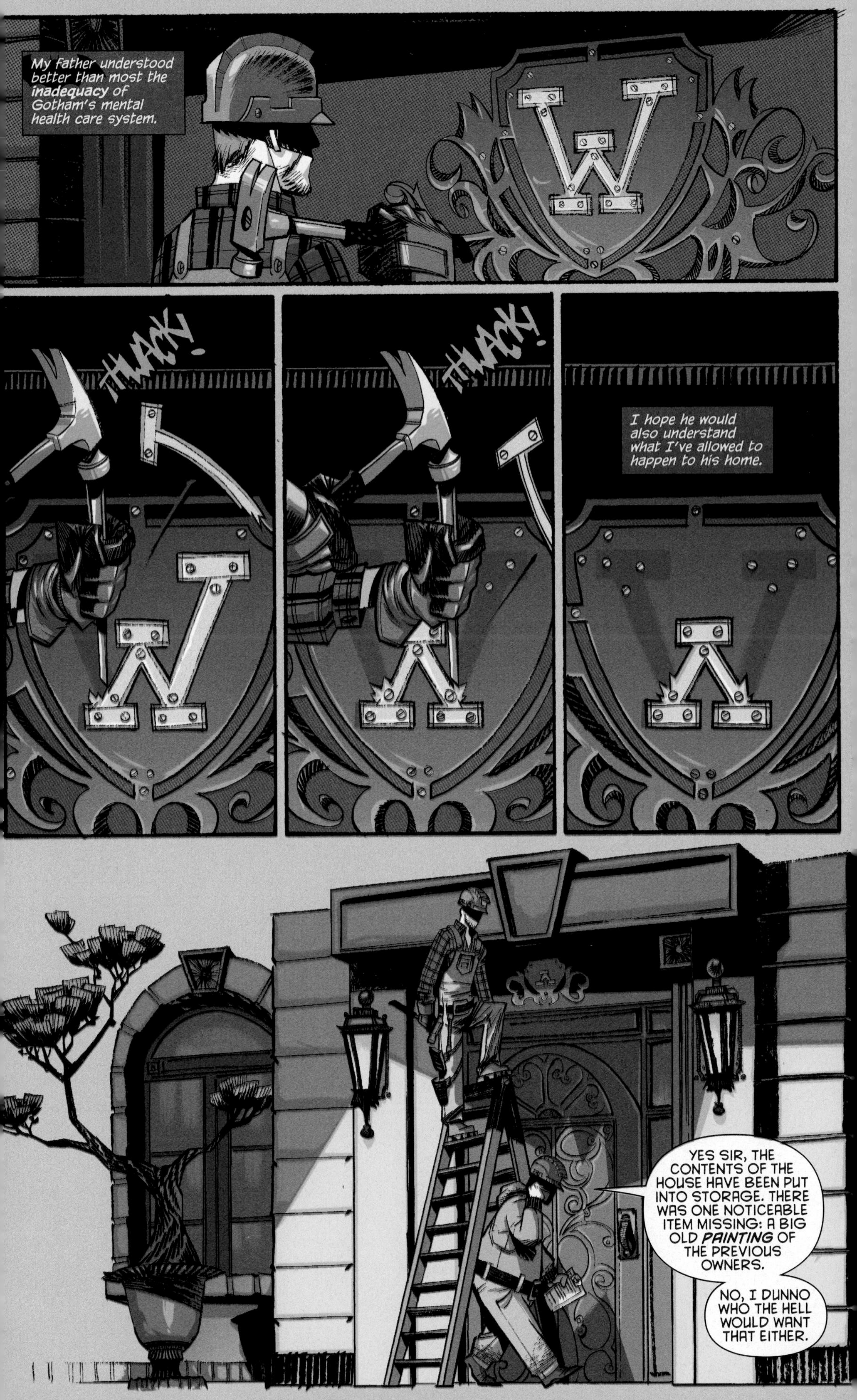

My father understood better than most the *inadequacy* of Gotham's mental health care system.
THACK!
THACK!
I hope he would also understand what I've allowed to happen to his home.
YES SIR, THE CONTENTS OF THE HOUSE HAVE BEEN PUT INTO STORAGE. THERE WAS ONE NOTICEABLE ITEM MISSING: A BIG OLD *PAINTING* OF THE PREVIOUS OWNERS.
NO, I DUNNO WHO THE HELL WOULD WANT THAT EITHER.

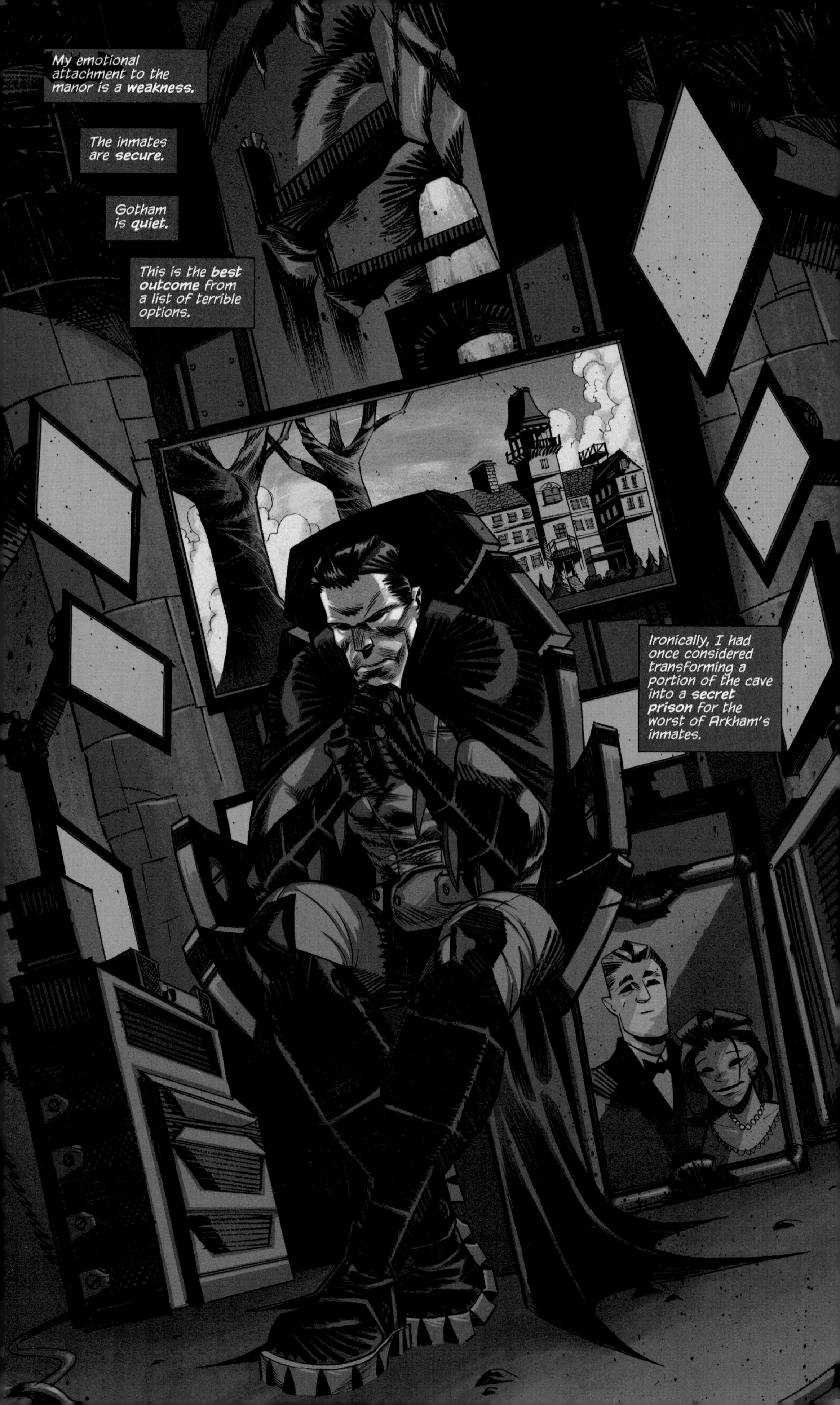
My emotional attachment to the manor is a **weakness.**
The inmates are **secure.**
Gotham is **quiet.**
This is the **best outcome** from a list of terrible options.
Ironically, I had once considered transforming a portion of the cave into a **secret prison** for the worst of Arkham's inmates.

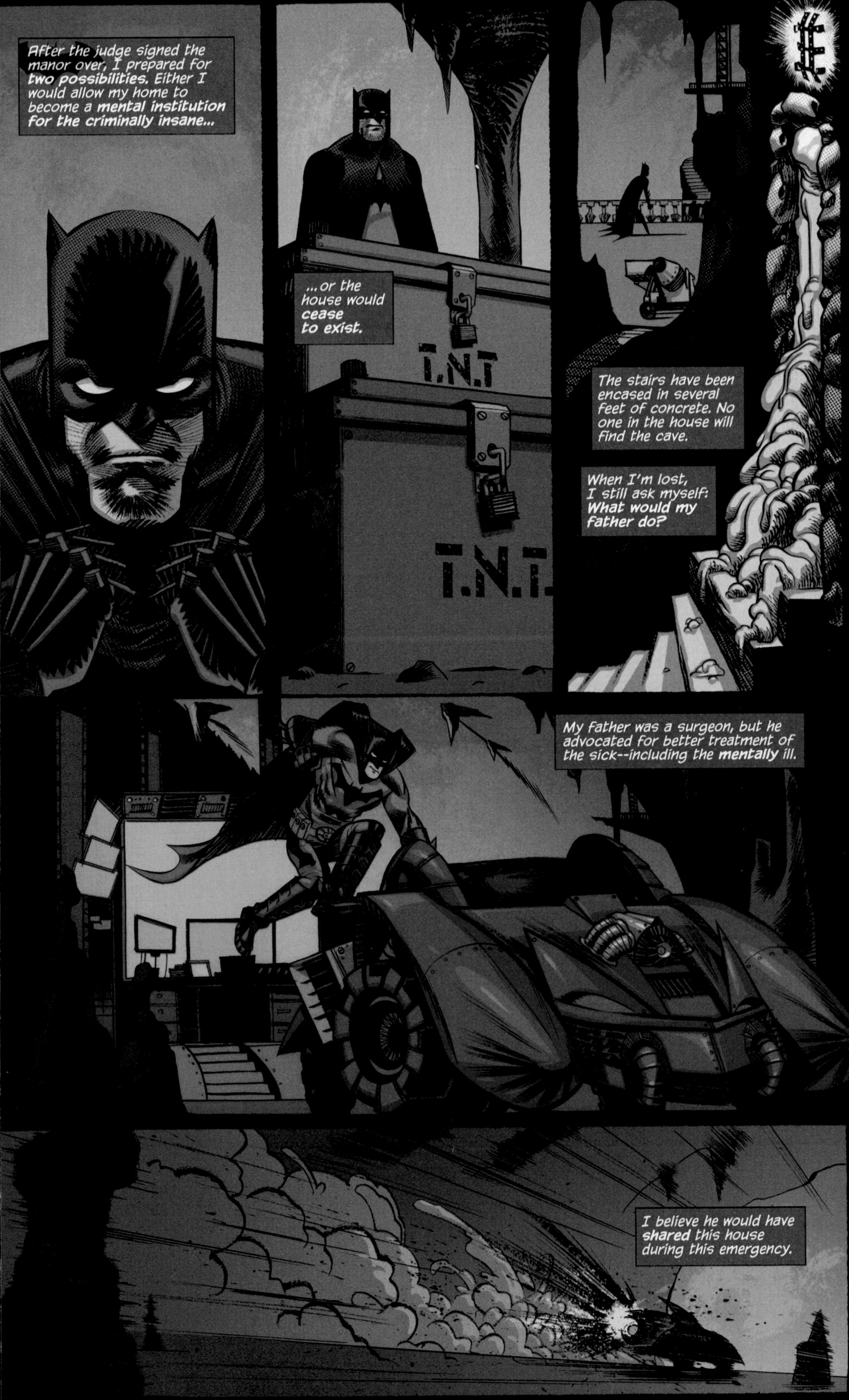
After the judge signed the manor over, I prepared for **two possibilities.** Either I would allow my home to become a **mental institution for the criminally insane...**
...or the house would **cease to exist.**
T.N.T
T.N.T.
The stairs have been encased in several feet of concrete. No one in the house will find the cave.
When I'm lost, I still ask myself: **What would my father do?**
My father was a surgeon, but he advocated for better treatment of the sick--including the **mentally** ill.
I believe he would have **shared** this house during this emergency.

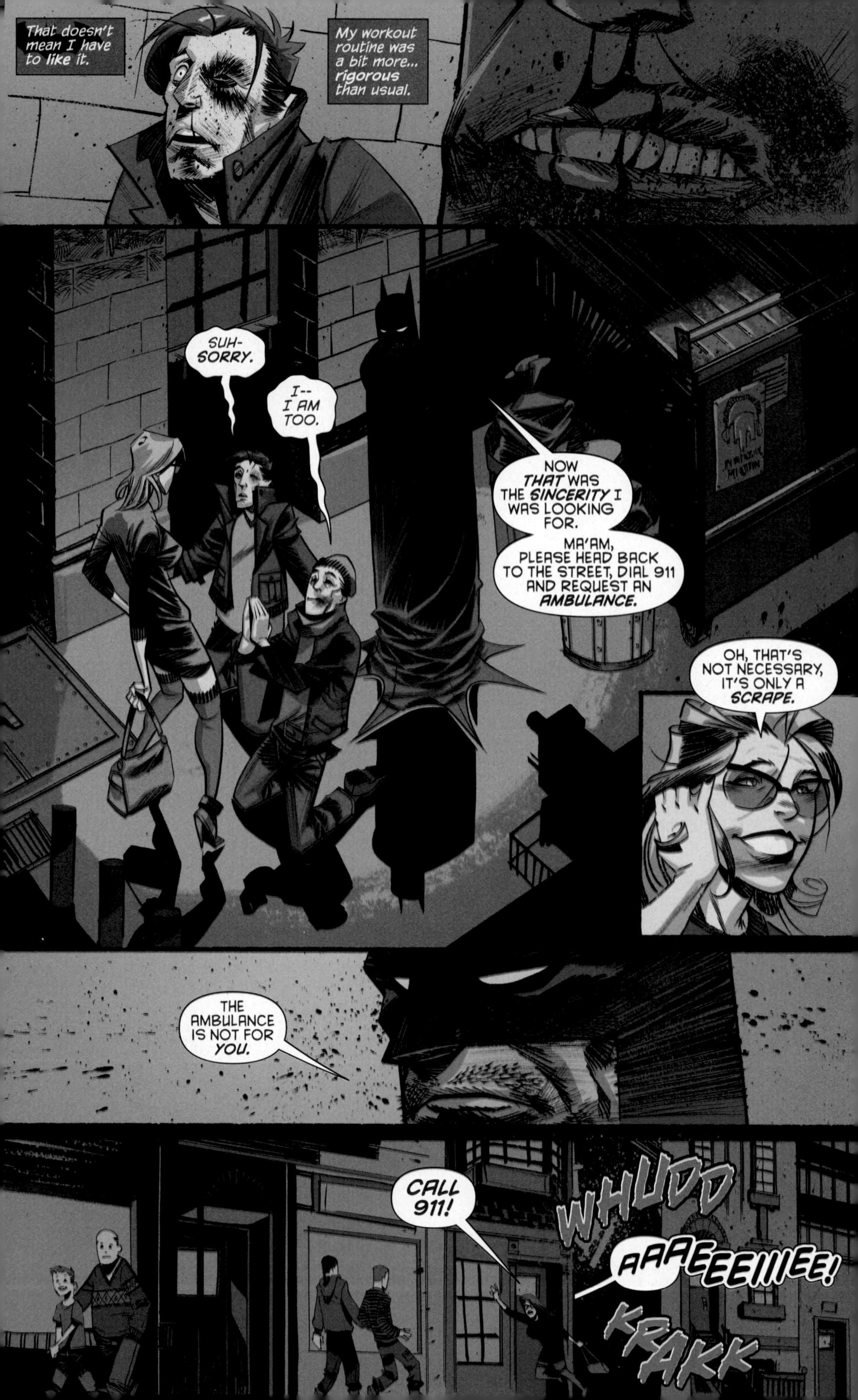
That doesn't mean I have to like it.
My workout routine was a bit more... rigorous than usual.
SUH-SORRY.
I-- I AM TOO.
NOW THAT WAS THE SINCERITY I WAS LOOKING FOR.
MA'AM, PLEASE HEAD BACK TO THE STREET, DIAL 911 AND REQUEST AN AMBULANCE.
OH, THAT'S NOT NECESSARY, IT'S ONLY A SCRAPE.
THE AMBULANCE IS NOT FOR YOU.
CALL 911!
WHUDD
AAAEEEIIIIEE!
KRAKK

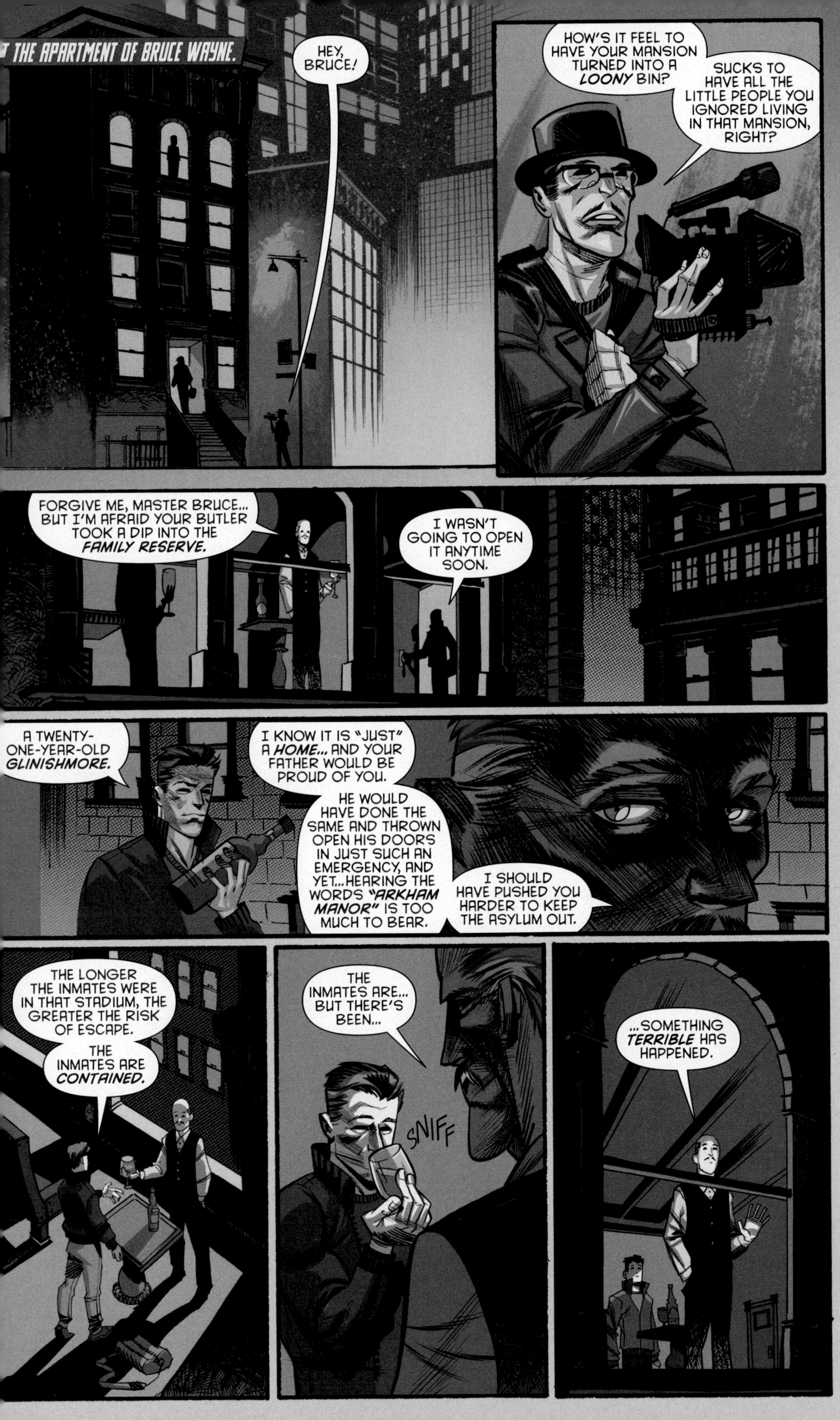

THE APARTMENT OF BRUCE WAYNE.
HEY, BRUCE!
HOW'S IT FEEL TO HAVE YOUR MANSION TURNED INTO A LOONY BIN?
SUCKS TO HAVE ALL THE LITTLE PEOPLE YOU IGNORED LIVING IN THAT MANSION, RIGHT?
FORGIVE ME, MASTER BRUCE... BUT I'M AFRAID YOUR BUTLER TOOK A DIP INTO THE FAMILY RESERVE.
I WASN'T GOING TO OPEN IT ANYTIME SOON.
A TWENTY-ONE-YEAR-OLD GLINISHMORE.
I KNOW IT IS "JUST" A HOME... AND YOUR FATHER WOULD BE PROUD OF YOU.
HE WOULD HAVE DONE THE SAME AND THROWN OPEN HIS DOORS IN JUST SUCH AN EMERGENCY, AND YET...HEARING THE WORDS "ARKHAM MANOR" IS TOO MUCH TO BEAR.
I SHOULD HAVE PUSHED YOU HARDER TO KEEP THE ASYLUM OUT.
THE LONGER THE INMATES WERE IN THAT STADIUM, THE GREATER THE RISK OF ESCAPE.
THE INMATES ARE CONTAINED.
THE INMATES ARE... BUT THERE'S BEEN...
SNIFF
...SOMETHING TERRIBLE HAS HAPPENED.

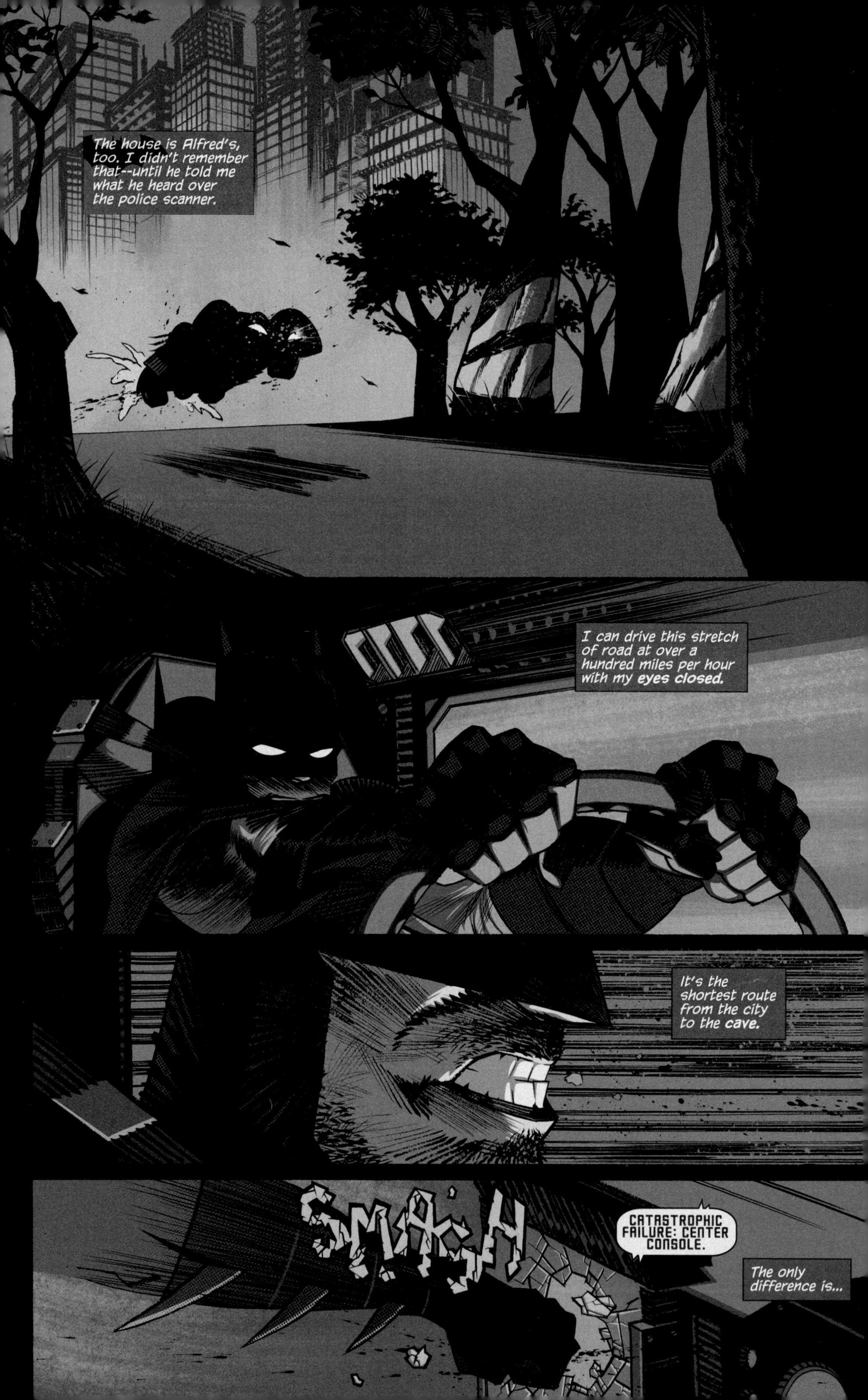
The house is Alfred's, too. I didn't remember that--until he told me what he heard over the police scanner.
I can drive this stretch of road at over a hundred miles per hour with my eyes closed.
It's the shortest route from the city to the cave.
SMASH
CATASTROPHIC FAILURE: CENTER CONSOLE.
The only difference is...

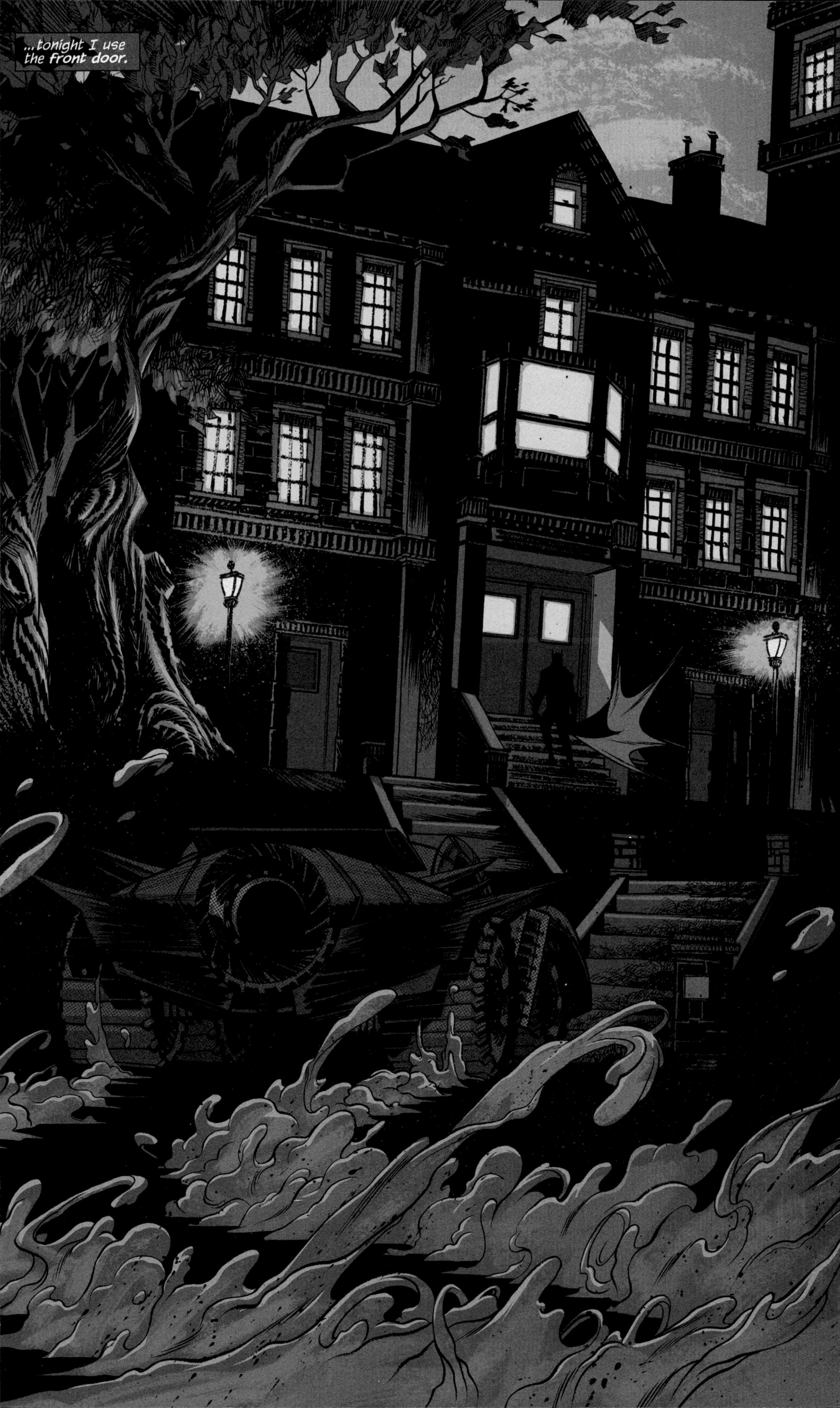
...tonight I use the front door.

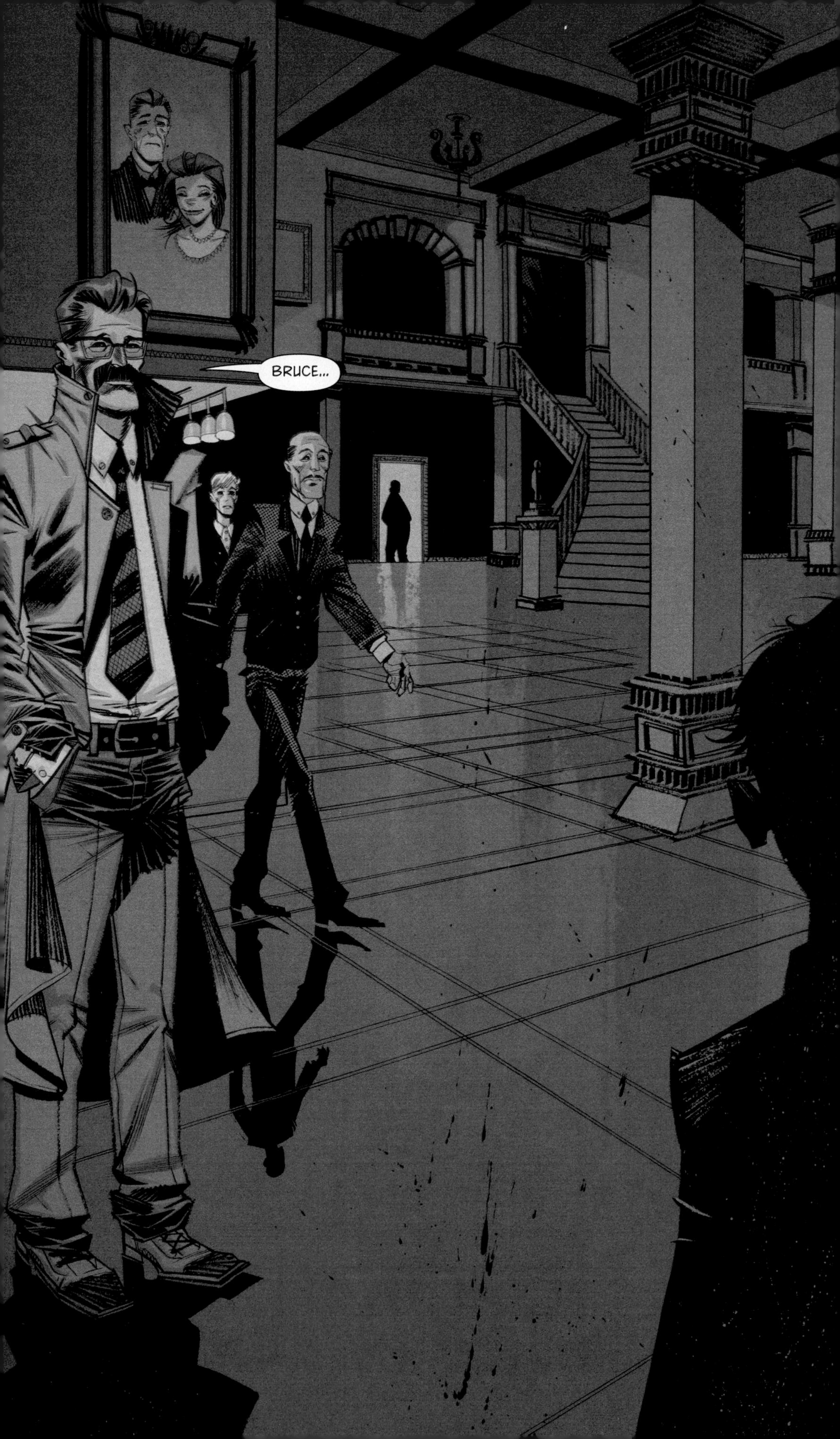
BRUCE...

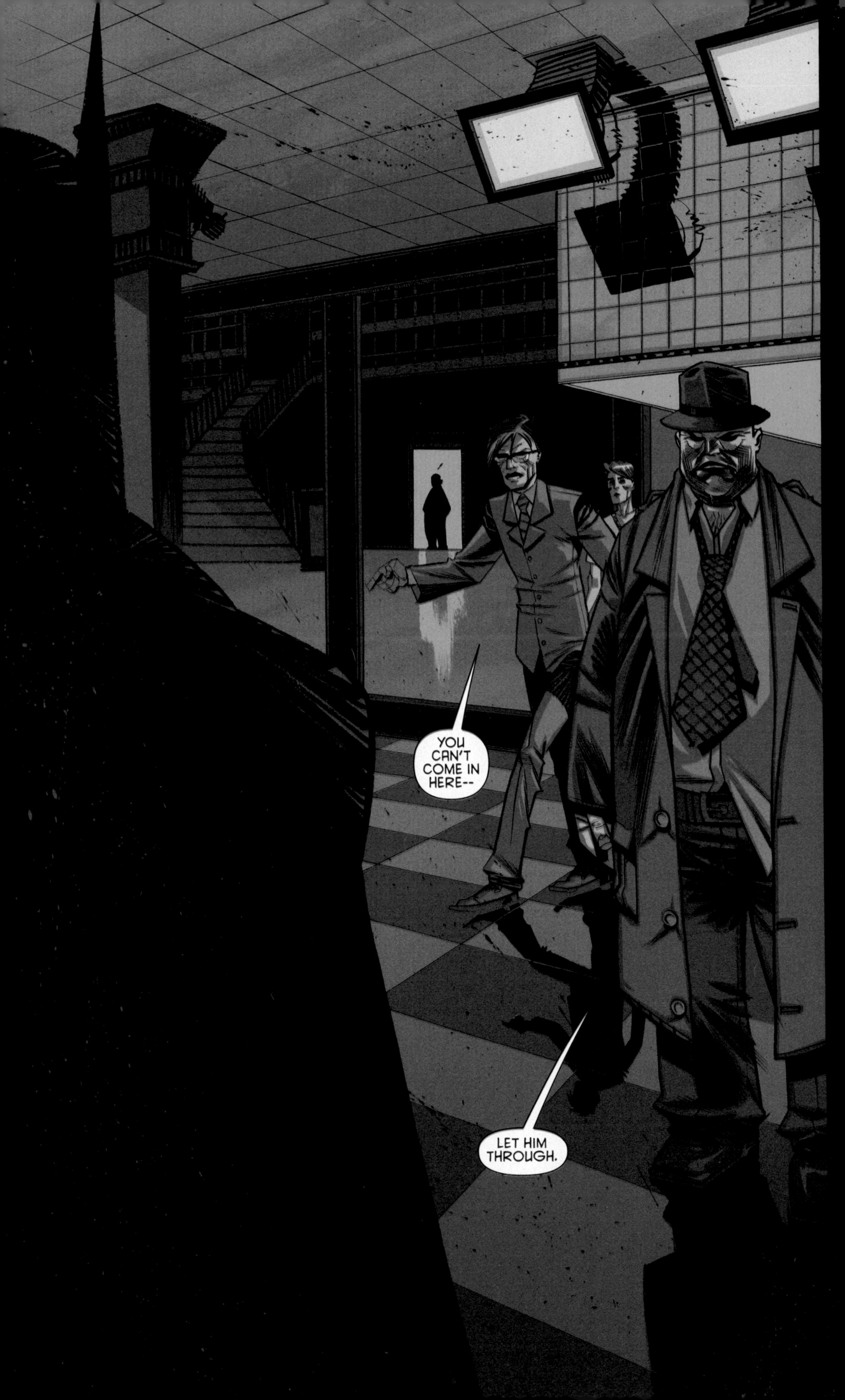
YOU CAN'T COME IN HERE--
LET HIM THROUGH.

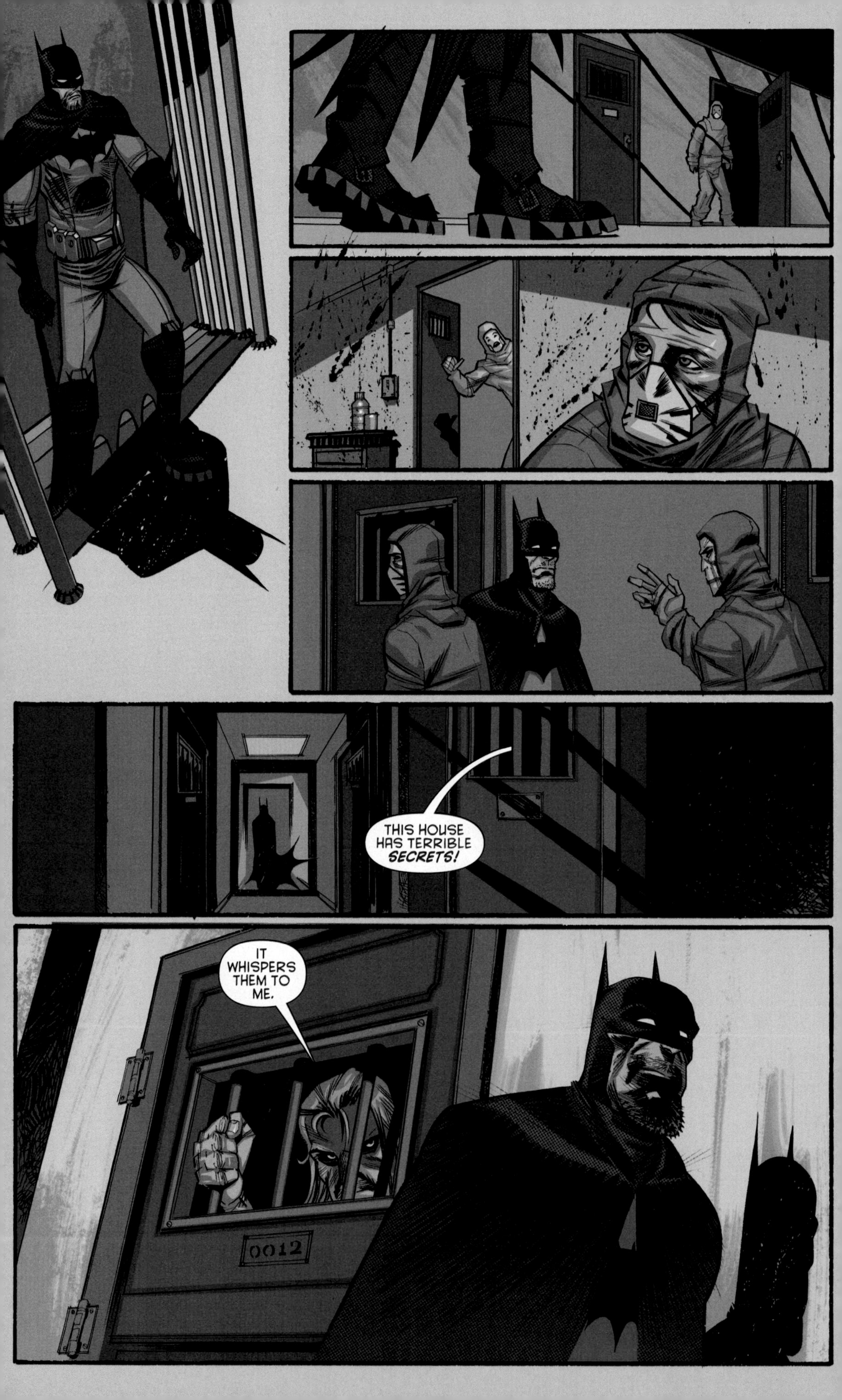
THIS HOUSE HAS TERRIBLE SECRETS!
IT WHISPERS THEM TO ME.
0012

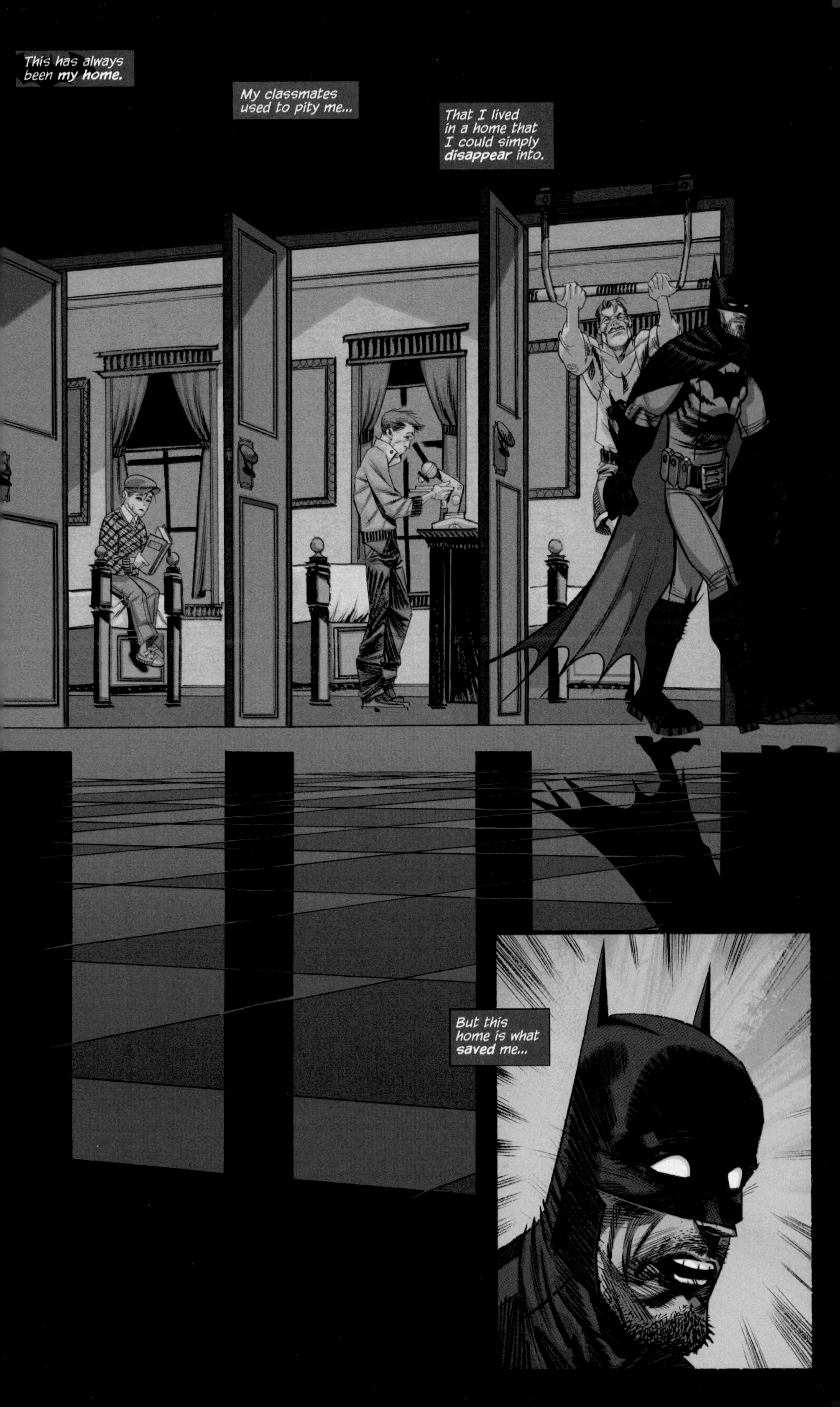
This has always been my home.
My classmates used to pity me...
That I lived in a home that I could simply disappear into.
But this home is what saved me...

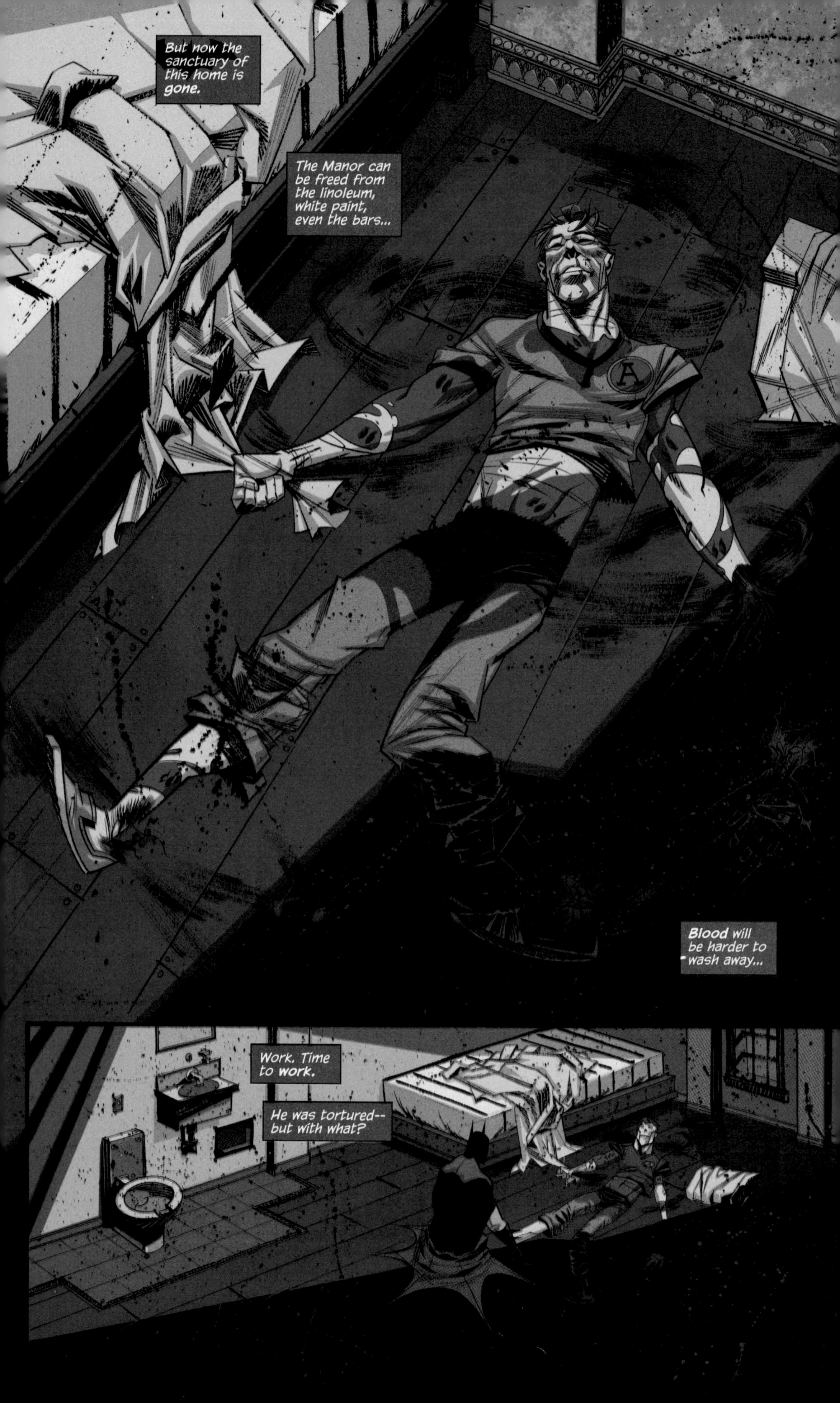

But now the sanctuary of this home is gone.
The Manor can be freed from the linoleum, white paint, even the bars...
Blood will be harder to wash away...
Work. Time to work.
He was tortured--but with what?

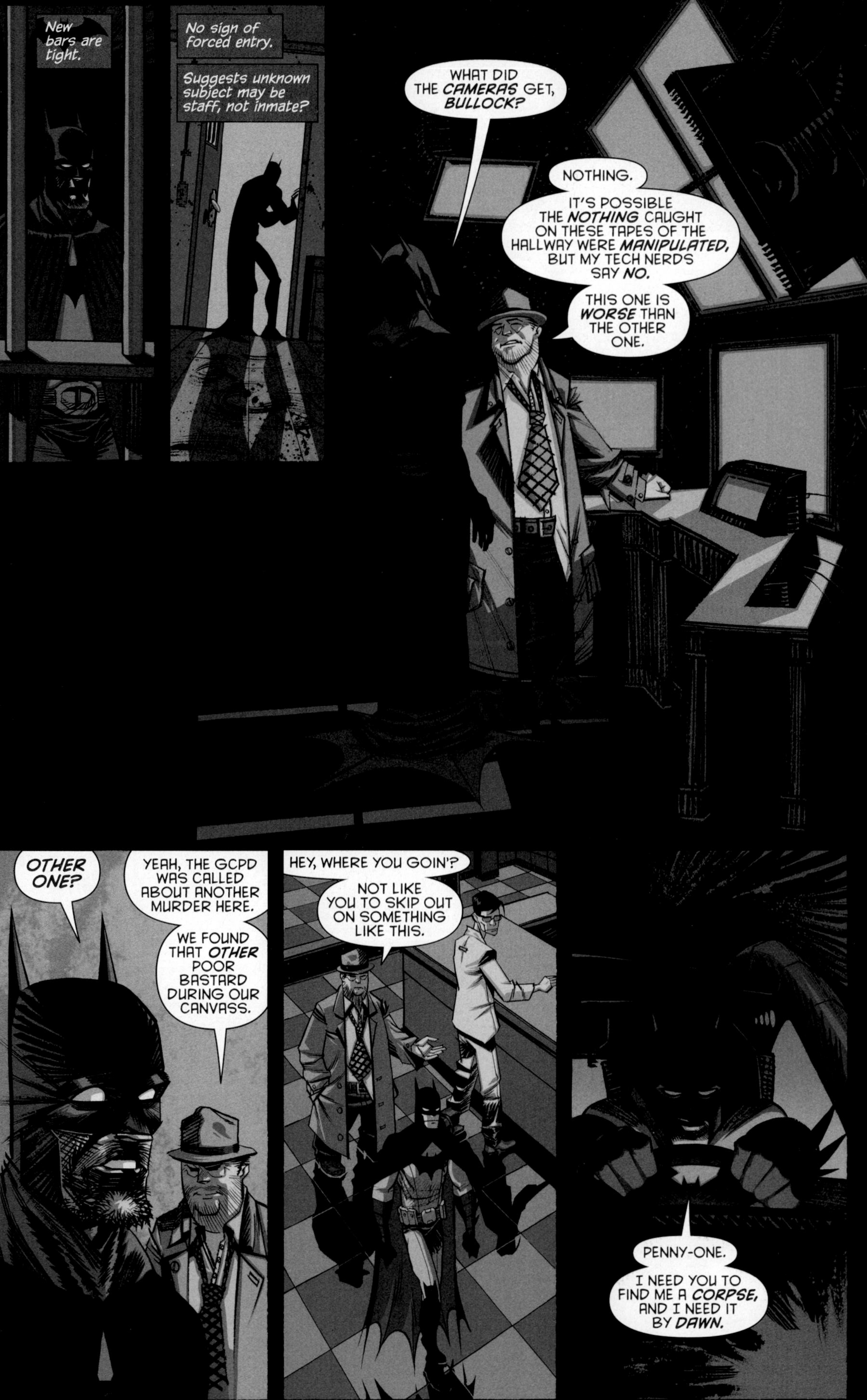
New bars are tight.
No sign of forced entry.
Suggests unknown subject may be staff, not inmate?
WHAT DID THE CAMERAS GET, BULLOCK?
NOTHING.
IT'S POSSIBLE THE NOTHING CAUGHT ON THESE TAPES OF THE HALLWAY WERE MANIPULATED, BUT MY TECH NERDS SAY NO.
THIS ONE IS WORSE THAN THE OTHER ONE.
OTHER ONE?
YEAH, THE GCPD WAS CALLED ABOUT ANOTHER MURDER HERE.
WE FOUND THAT OTHER POOR BASTARD DURING OUR CANVASS.
HEY, WHERE YOU GOIN'?
NOT LIKE YOU TO SKIP OUT ON SOMETHING LIKE THIS.
PENNY-ONE.
I NEED YOU TO FIND ME A CORPSE, AND I NEED IT BY DAWN.

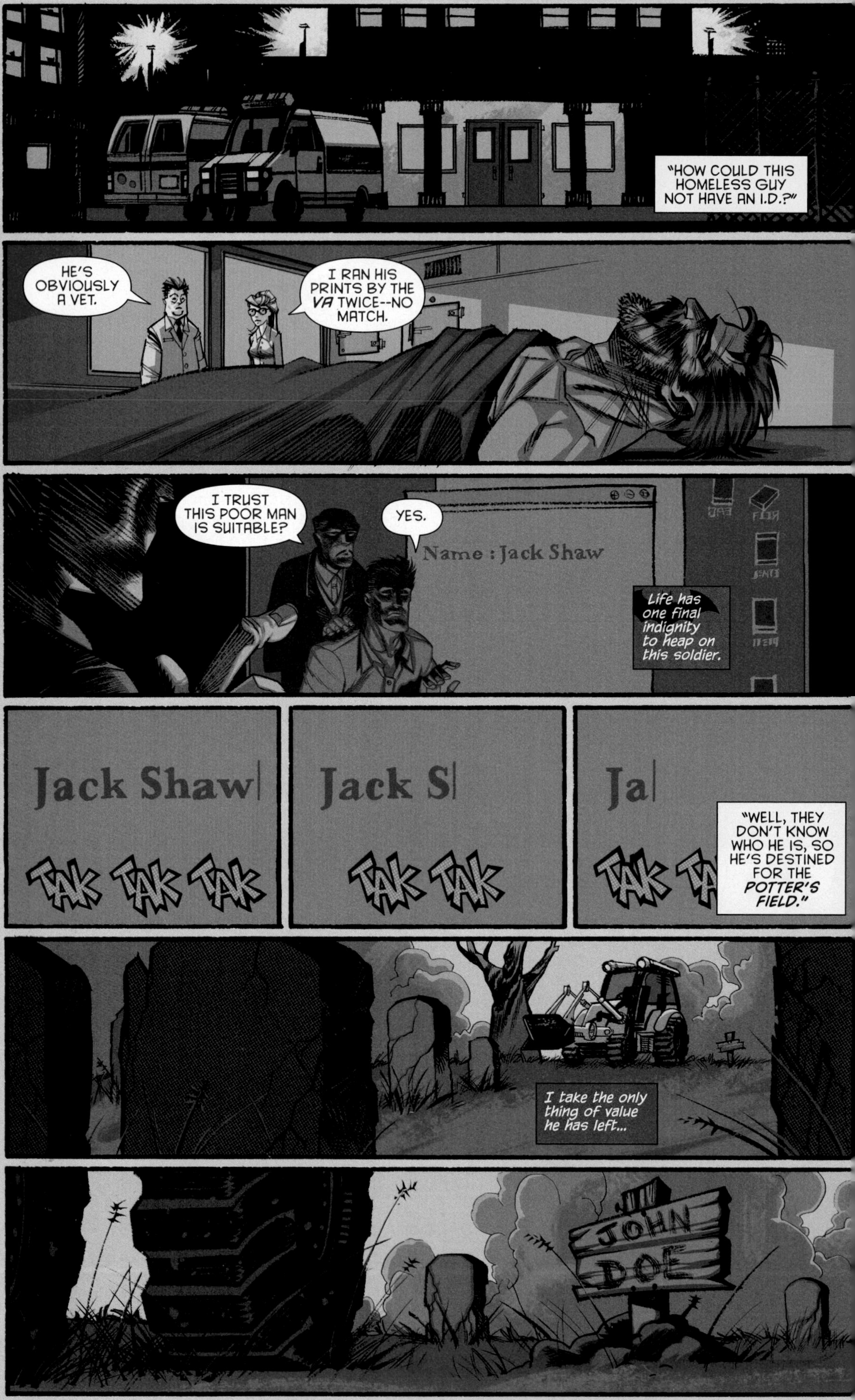
"HOW COULD THIS HOMELESS GUY NOT HAVE AN I.D.?"
HE'S OBVIOUSLY A VET.
I RAN HIS PRINTS BY THE VA TWICE--NO MATCH.
I TRUST THIS POOR MAN IS SUITABLE?
YES.
Name : Jack Shaw
Life has one final indignity to heap on this soldier.
Jack Shaw
TAK TAK TAK
Jack S
TAK TAK
Ja
TAK
"WELL, THEY DON'T KNOW WHO HE IS, SO HE'S DESTINED FOR THE POTTER'S FIELD."
I take the only thing of value he has left...
JOHN DOE

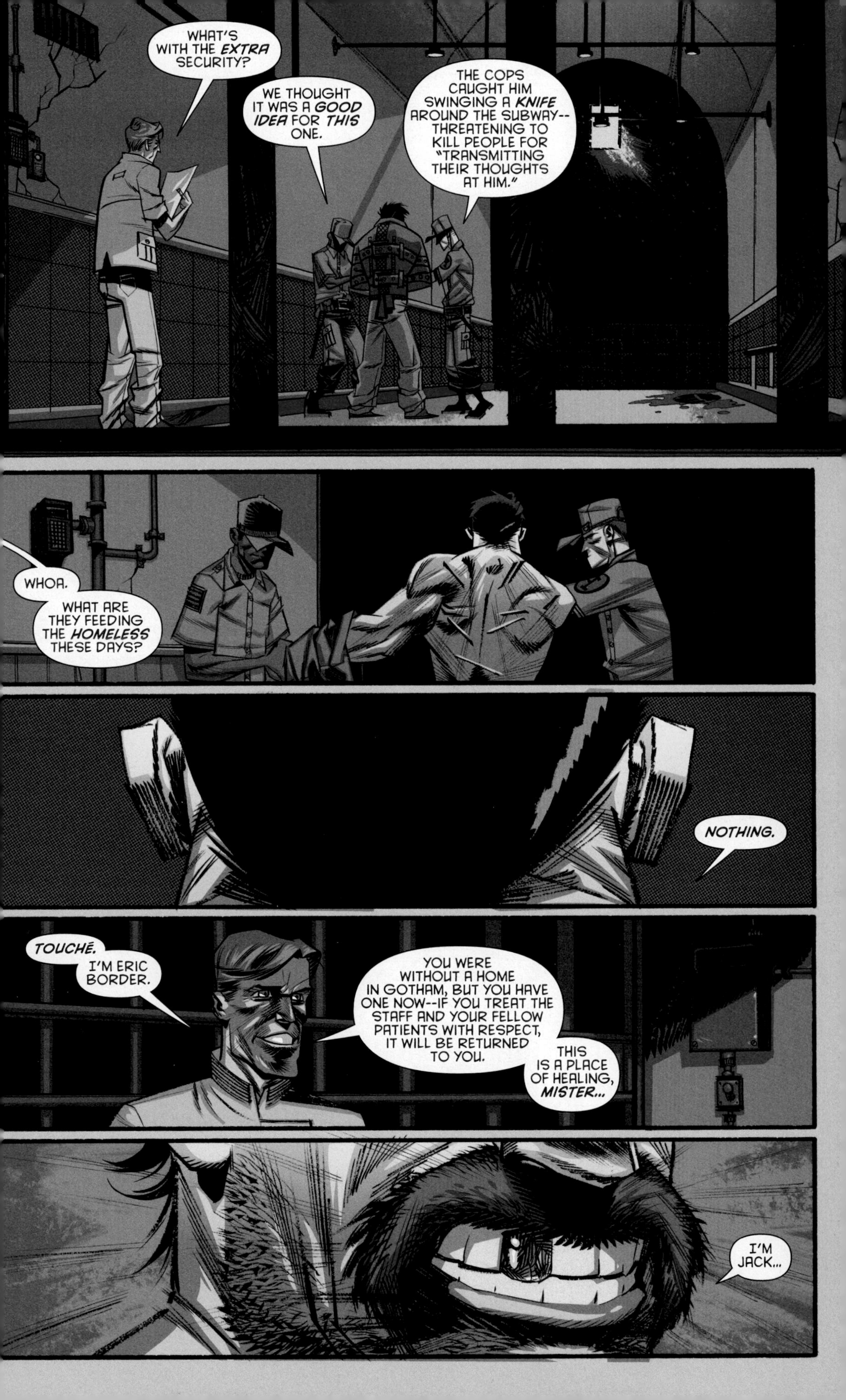
WHAT'S WITH THE EXTRA SECURITY?
WE THOUGHT IT WAS A GOOD IDEA FOR THIS ONE.
THE COPS CAUGHT HIM SWINGING A KNIFE AROUND THE SUBWAY--THREATENING TO KILL PEOPLE FOR "TRANSMITTING THEIR THOUGHTS AT HIM."
WHOA.
WHAT ARE THEY FEEDING THE HOMELESS THESE DAYS?
NOTHING.
TOUCHÉ.
I'M ERIC BORDER.
YOU WERE WITHOUT A HOME IN GOTHAM, BUT YOU HAVE ONE NOW--IF YOU TREAT THE STAFF AND YOUR FELLOW PATIENTS WITH RESPECT, IT WILL BE RETURNED TO YOU.
THIS IS A PLACE OF HEALING, MISTER...
I'M JACK...

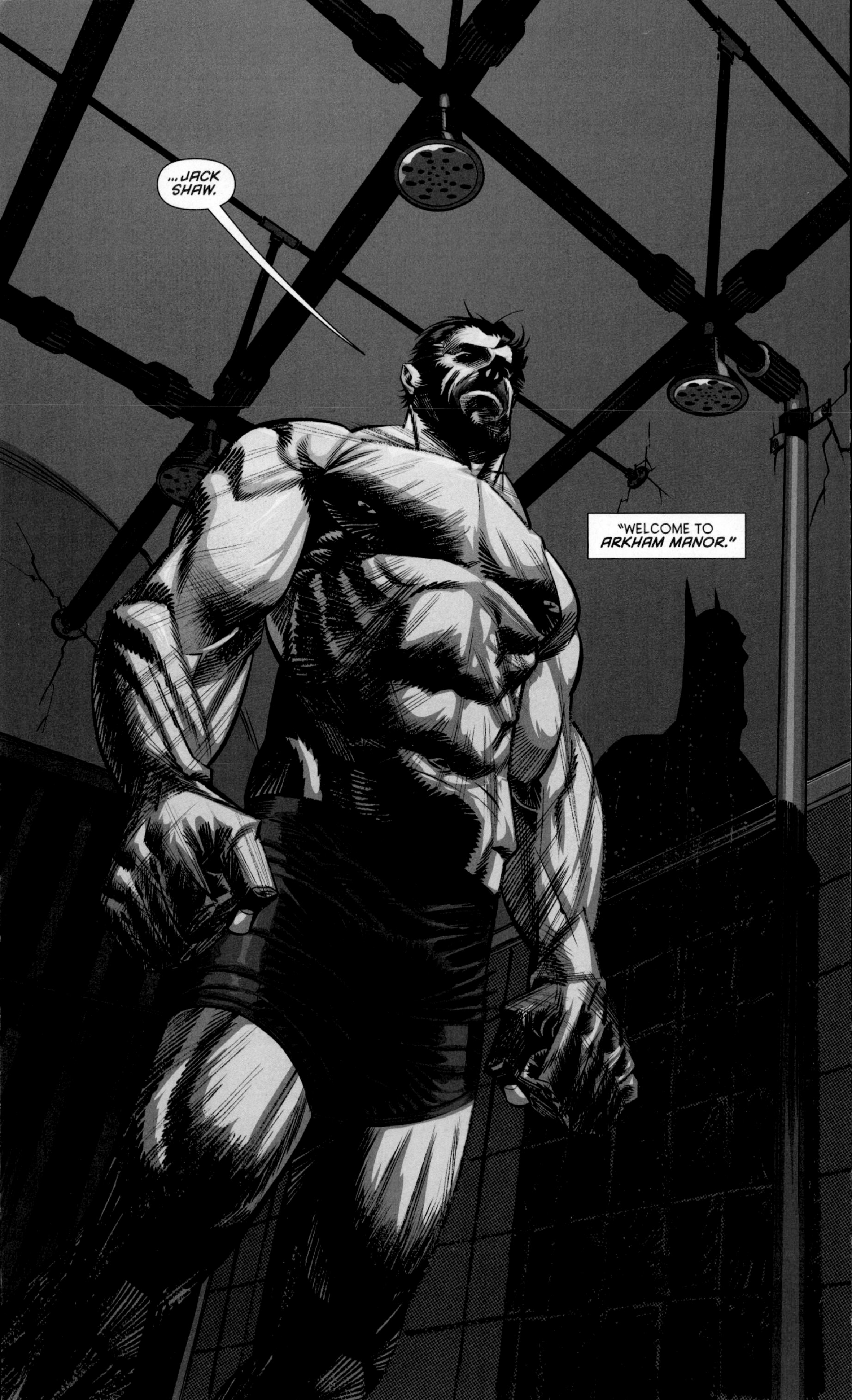
...JACK SHAW.
"WELCOME TO ARKHAM MANOR."

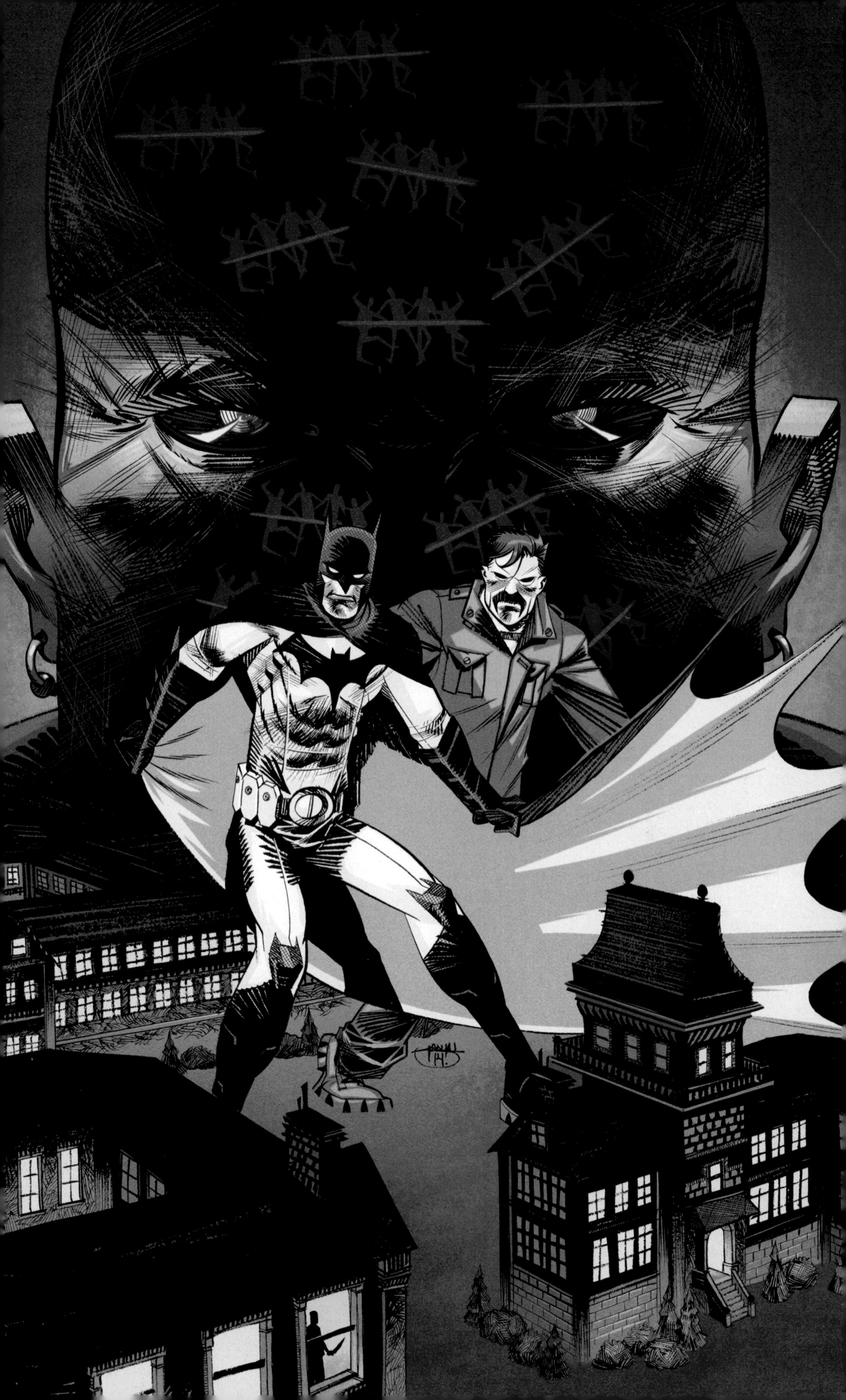

Variant cover art for issue #2 by **CHRIS BRUNNER** and **RICO RENZI**

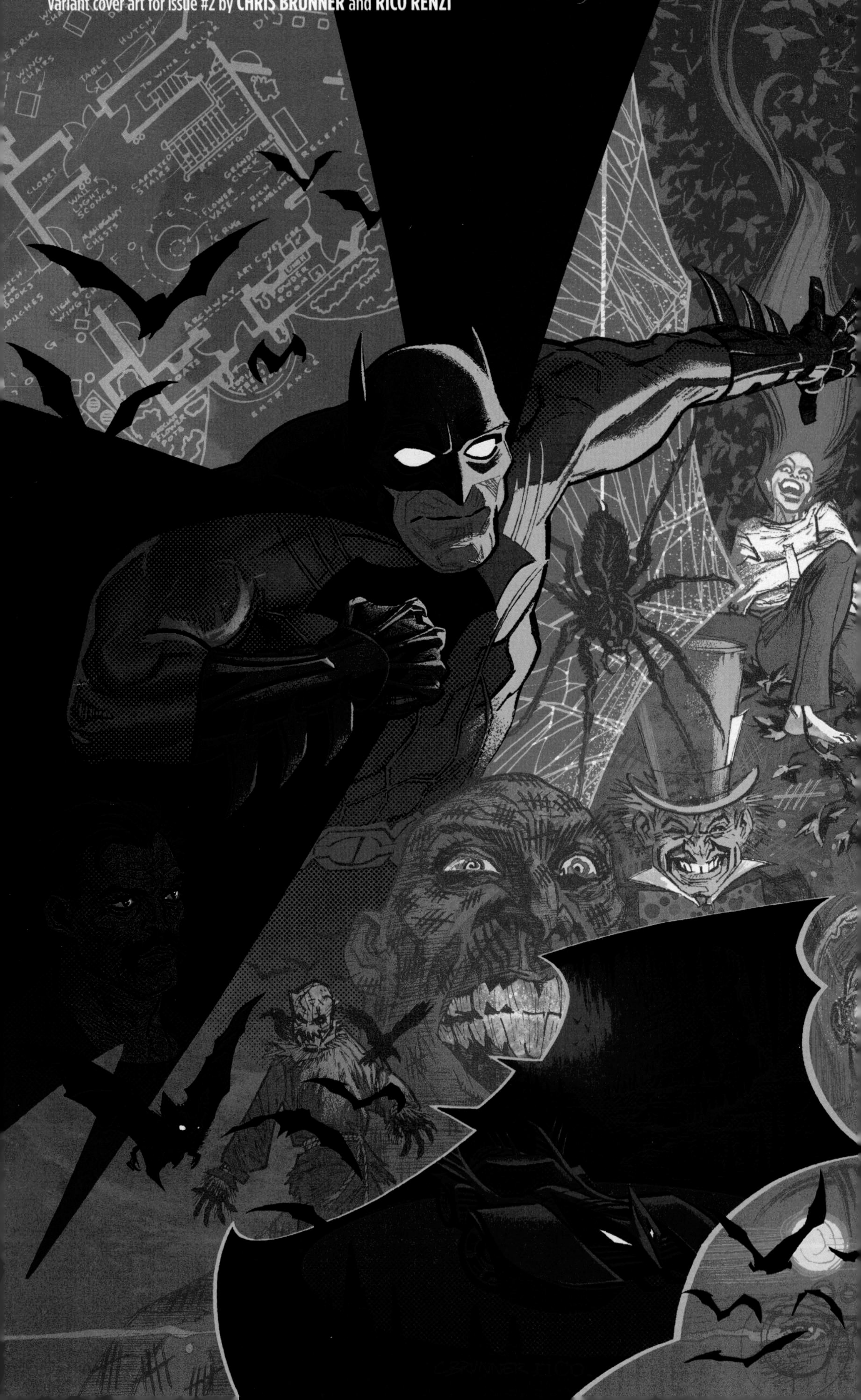

CLOSET
TABLE
HUTCH
WING CHAIRS
CARPETED STAIRS
F O Y E R
ARCHWAY
ENTRANCE

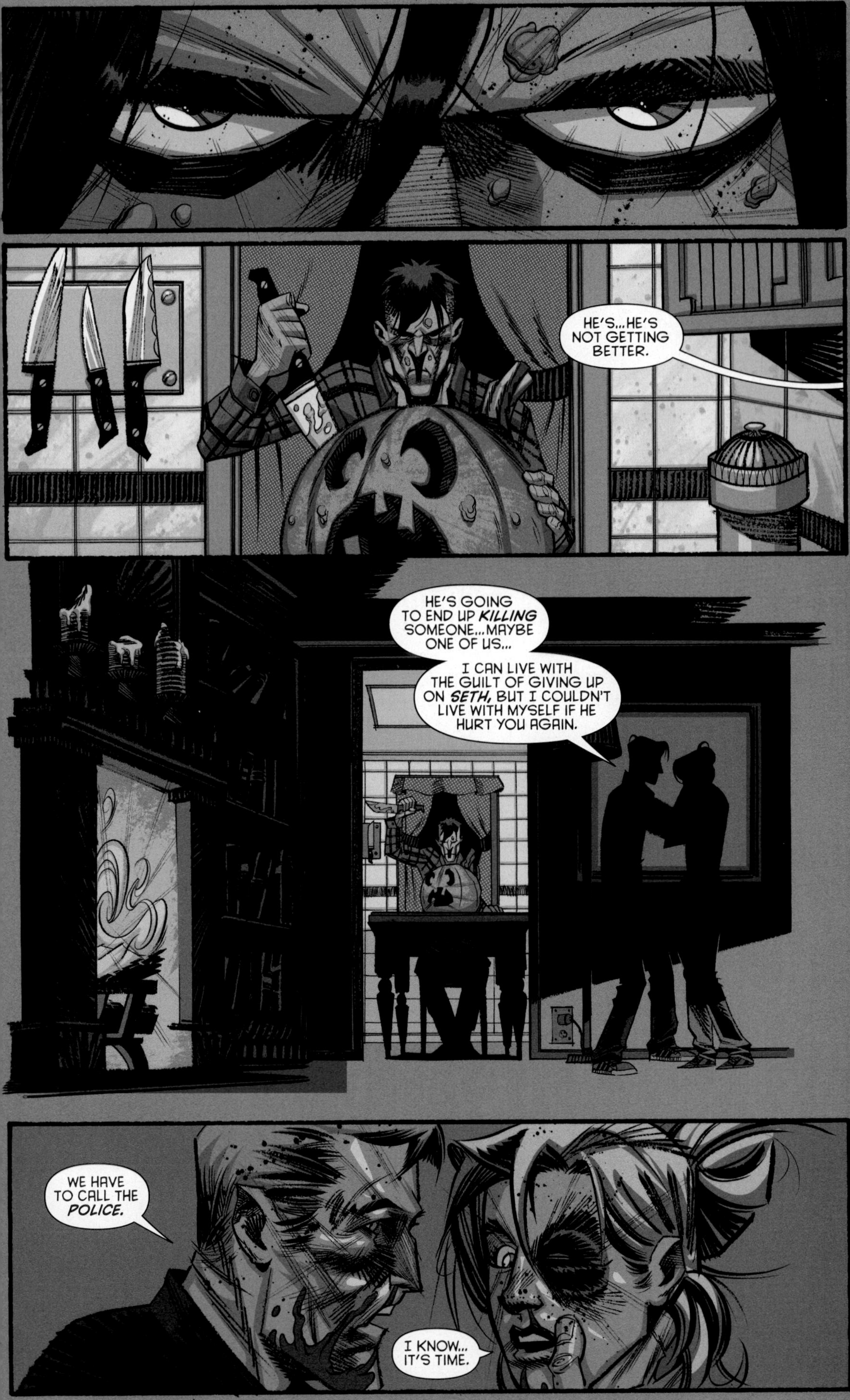

HE'S...HE'S NOT GETTING BETTER.
HE'S GOING TO END UP *KILLING* SOMEONE...MAYBE ONE OF US...
I CAN LIVE WITH THE GUILT OF GIVING UP ON *SETH,* BUT I COULDN'T LIVE WITH MYSELF IF HE HURT YOU AGAIN.
WE HAVE TO CALL THE *POLICE.*
I KNOW... IT'S TIME.

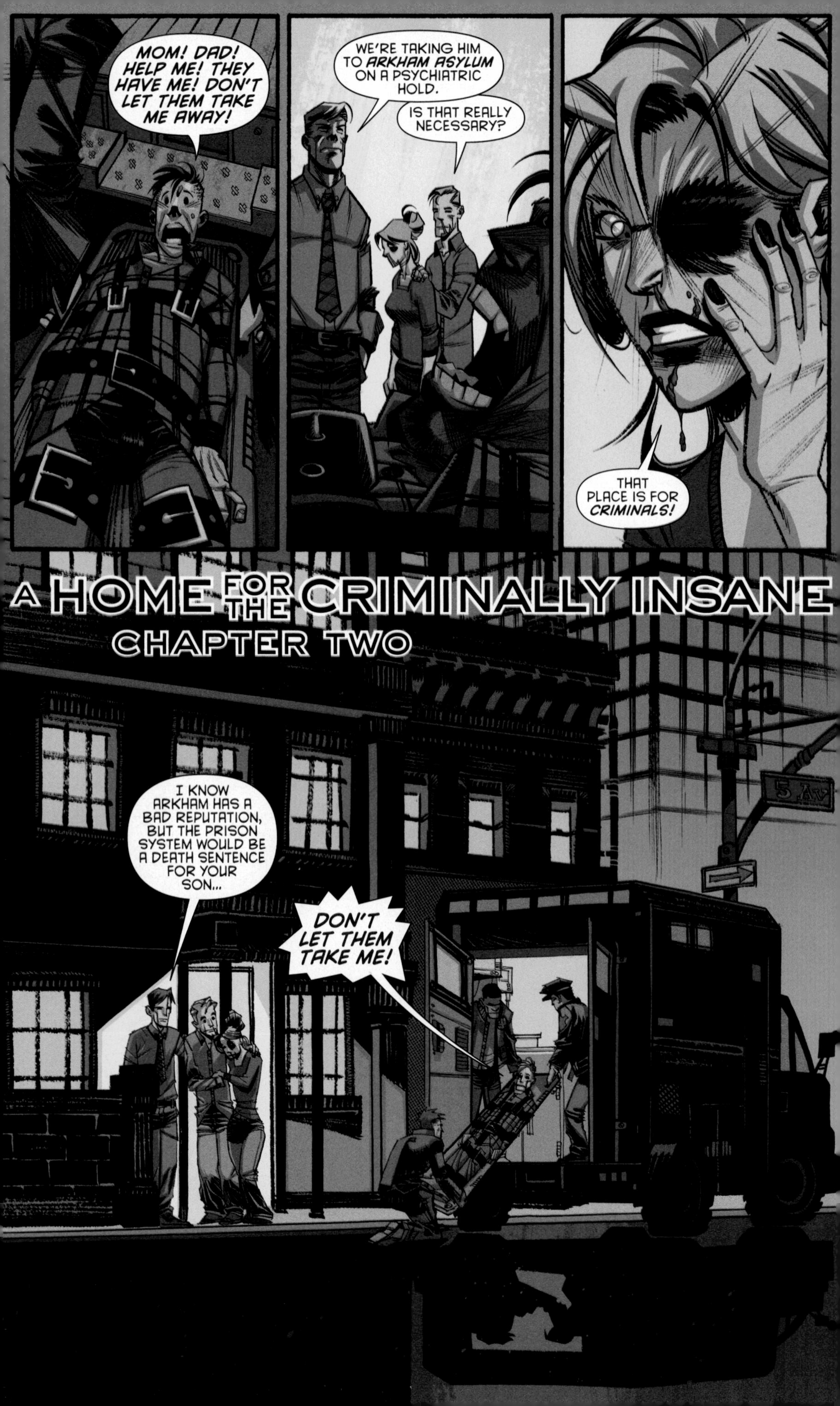
MOM! DAD! HELP ME! THEY HAVE ME! DON'T LET THEM TAKE ME AWAY!
WE'RE TAKING HIM TO ARKHAM ASYLUM ON A PSYCHIATRIC HOLD.
IS THAT REALLY NECESSARY?
THAT PLACE IS FOR CRIMINALS!
A HOME FOR THE CRIMINALLY INSANE
CHAPTER TWO
5 Av
I KNOW ARKHAM HAS A BAD REPUTATION, BUT THE PRISON SYSTEM WOULD BE A DEATH SENTENCE FOR YOUR SON...
DON'T LET THEM TAKE ME!

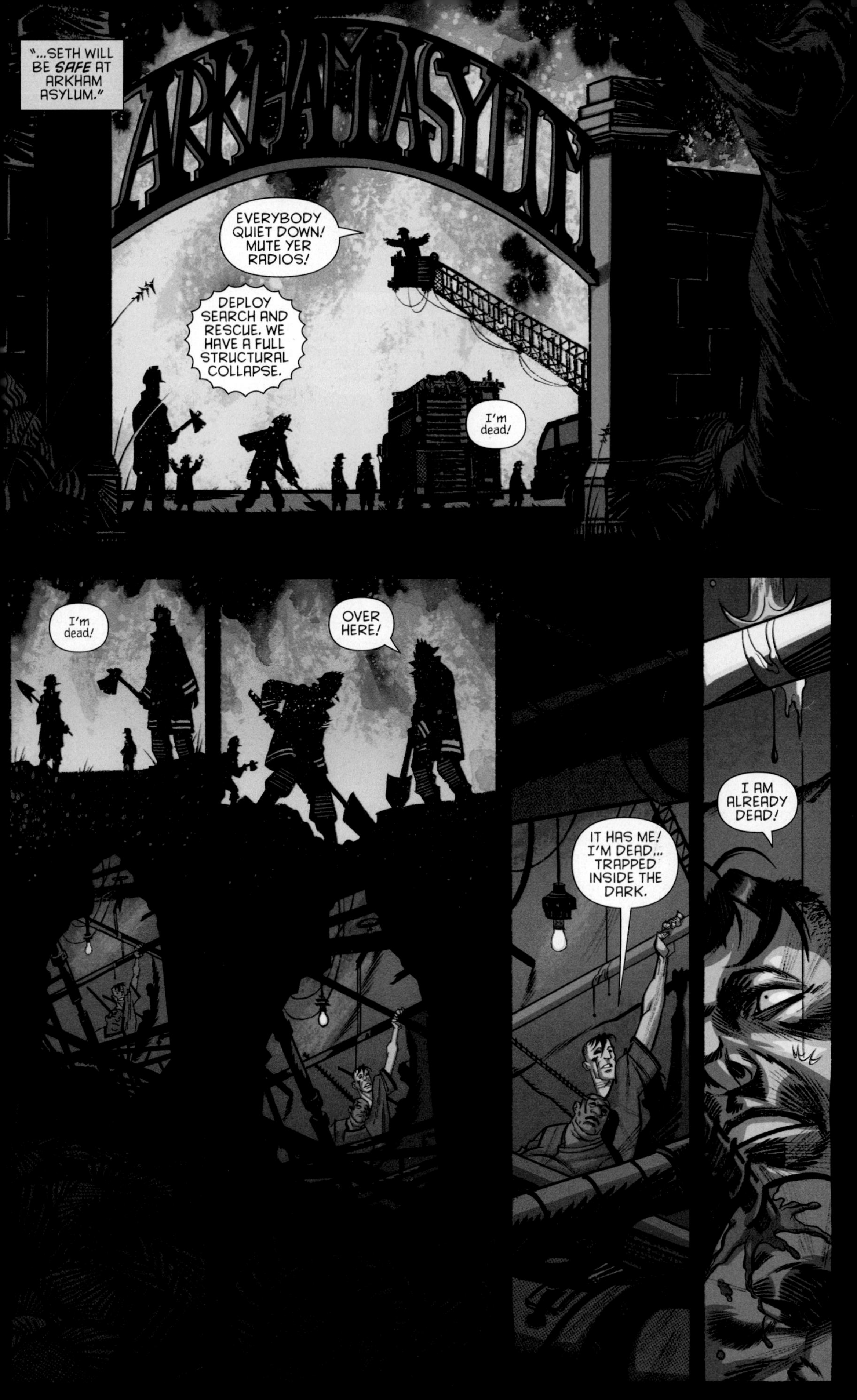

"...SETH WILL BE *SAFE* AT ARKHAM ASYLUM."
ARKHAM ASYLUM
EVERYBODY QUIET DOWN! MUTE YER RADIOS!
DEPLOY SEARCH AND RESCUE. WE HAVE A FULL STRUCTURAL COLLAPSE.
I'm dead!
I'm dead!
OVER HERE!
IT HAS ME! I'M DEAD... TRAPPED INSIDE THE DARK.
I AM ALREADY DEAD!

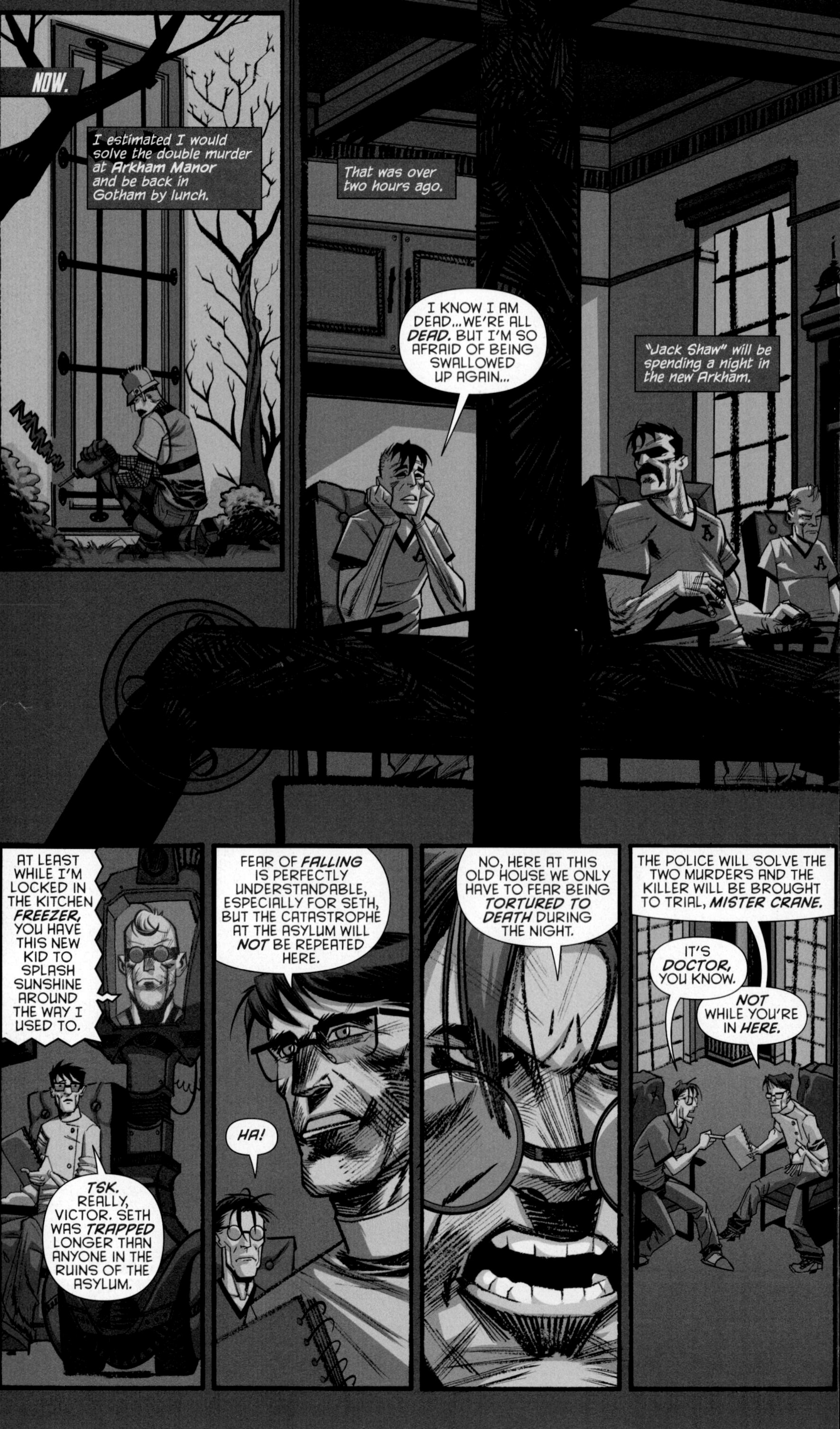

NOW.
I estimated I would solve the double murder at Arkham Manor and be back in Gotham by lunch.
That was over two hours ago.
I KNOW I AM DEAD...WE'RE ALL DEAD. BUT I'M SO AFRAID OF BEING SWALLOWED UP AGAIN...
"Jack Shaw" will be spending a night in the new Arkham.
AT LEAST WHILE I'M LOCKED IN THE KITCHEN FREEZER, YOU HAVE THIS NEW KID TO SPLASH SUNSHINE AROUND THE WAY I USED TO.
TSK. REALLY, VICTOR. SETH WAS TRAPPED LONGER THAN ANYONE IN THE RUINS OF THE ASYLUM.
FEAR OF FALLING IS PERFECTLY UNDERSTANDABLE, ESPECIALLY FOR SETH, BUT THE CATASTROPHE AT THE ASYLUM WILL NOT BE REPEATED HERE.
HA!
NO, HERE AT THIS OLD HOUSE WE ONLY HAVE TO FEAR BEING TORTURED TO DEATH DURING THE NIGHT.
THE POLICE WILL SOLVE THE TWO MURDERS AND THE KILLER WILL BE BROUGHT TO TRIAL, MISTER CRANE.
IT'S DOCTOR, YOU KNOW.
NOT WHILE YOU'RE IN HERE.

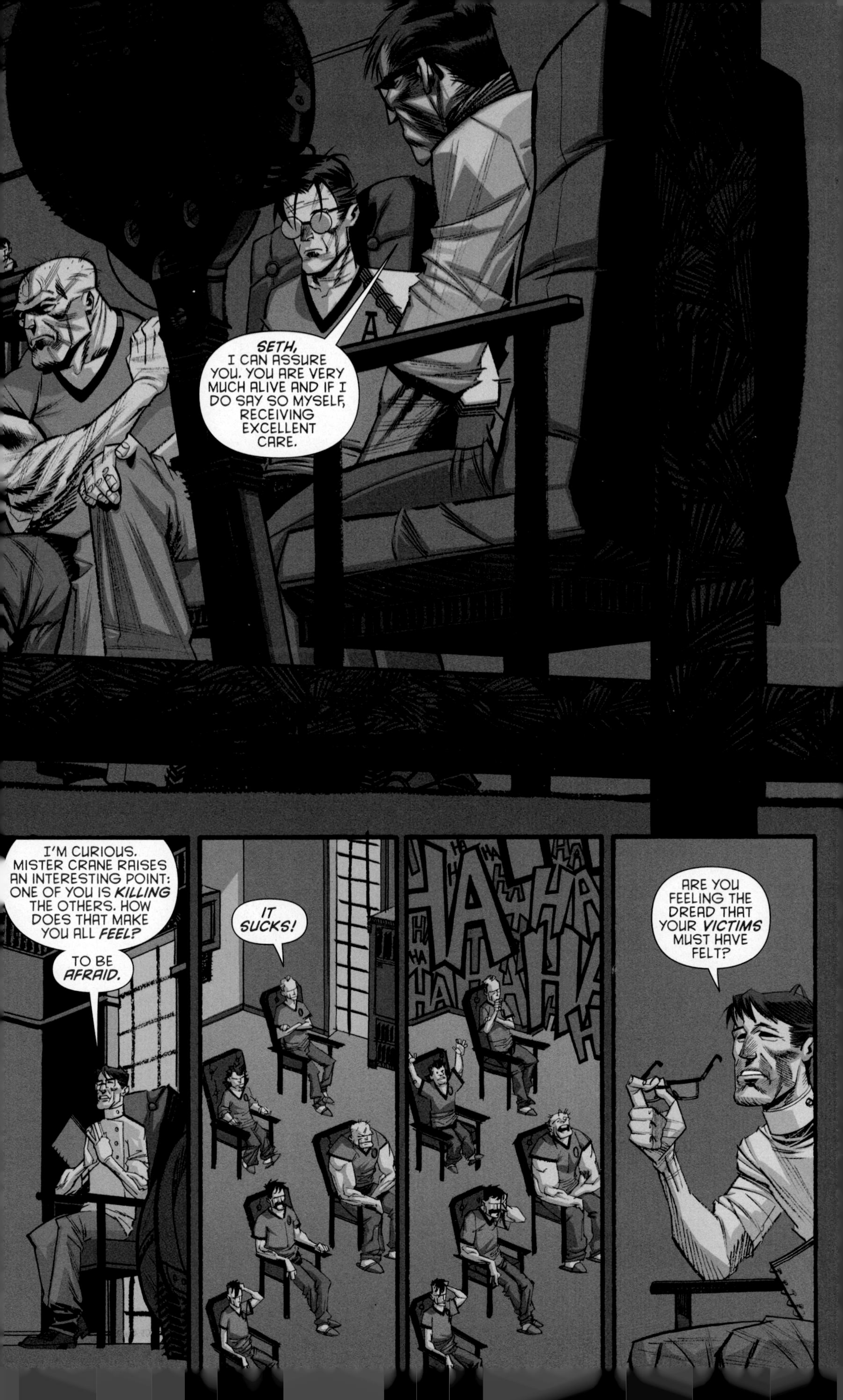
SETH, I CAN ASSURE YOU. YOU ARE VERY MUCH ALIVE AND IF I DO SAY SO MYSELF, RECEIVING EXCELLENT CARE.
I'M CURIOUS. MISTER CRANE RAISES AN INTERESTING POINT: ONE OF YOU IS KILLING THE OTHERS. HOW DOES THAT MAKE YOU ALL FEEL?
TO BE AFRAID.
IT SUCKS!
HA HA HA HA HA
ARE YOU FEELING THE DREAD THAT YOUR VICTIMS MUST HAVE FELT?

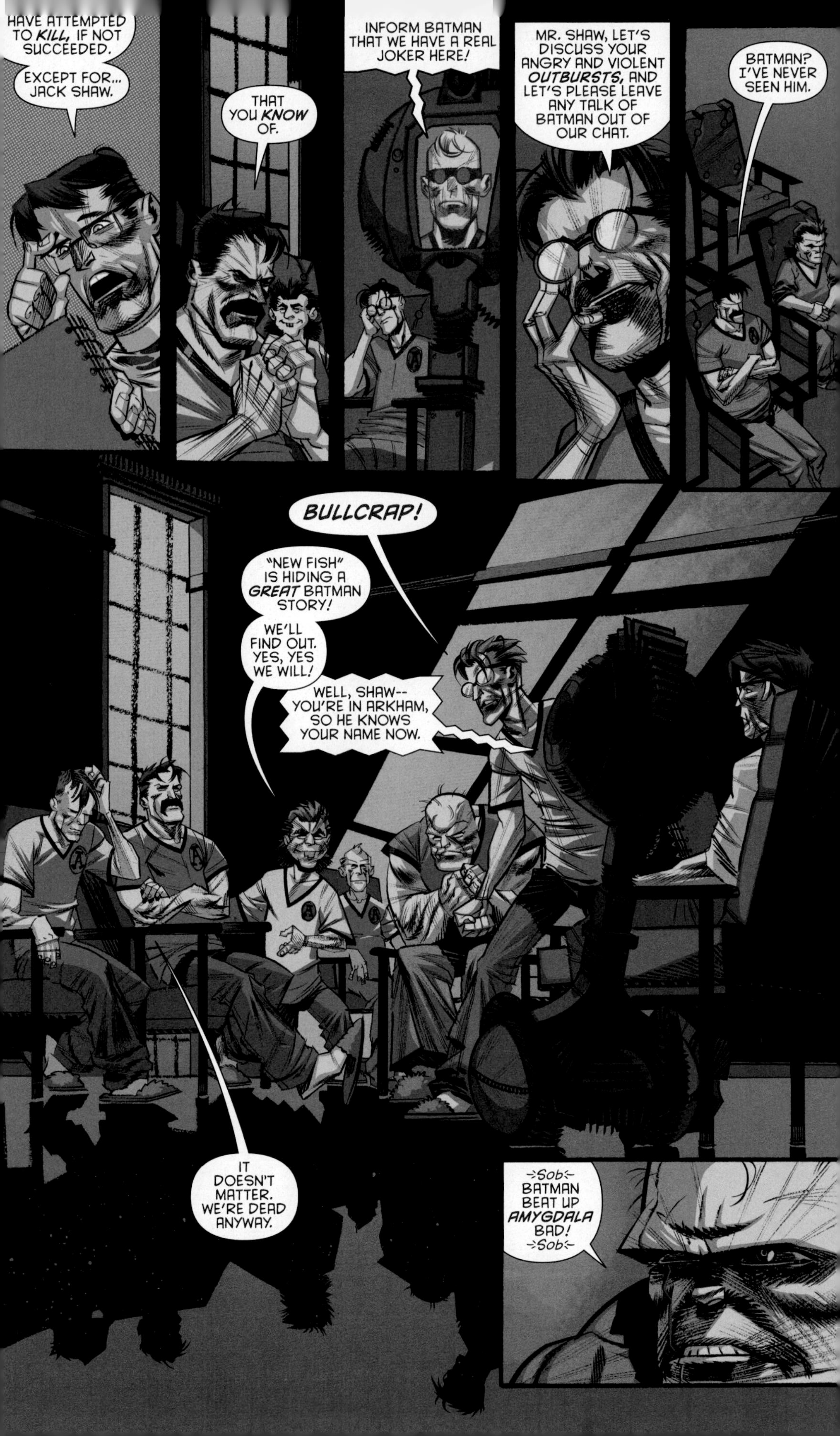

HAVE ATTEMPTED TO KILL, IF NOT SUCCEEDED.
EXCEPT FOR... JACK SHAW.
THAT YOU KNOW OF.
INFORM BATMAN THAT WE HAVE A REAL JOKER HERE!
MR. SHAW, LET'S DISCUSS YOUR ANGRY AND VIOLENT OUTBURSTS, AND LET'S PLEASE LEAVE ANY TALK OF BATMAN OUT OF OUR CHAT.
BATMAN? I'VE NEVER SEEN HIM.
BULLCRAP!
"NEW FISH" IS HIDING A GREAT BATMAN STORY!
WE'LL FIND OUT. YES, YES WE WILL!
WELL, SHAW-- YOU'RE IN ARKHAM, SO HE KNOWS YOUR NAME NOW.
IT DOESN'T MATTER. WE'RE DEAD ANYWAY.
-Sob- BATMAN BEAT UP AMYGDALA BAD! -Sob-

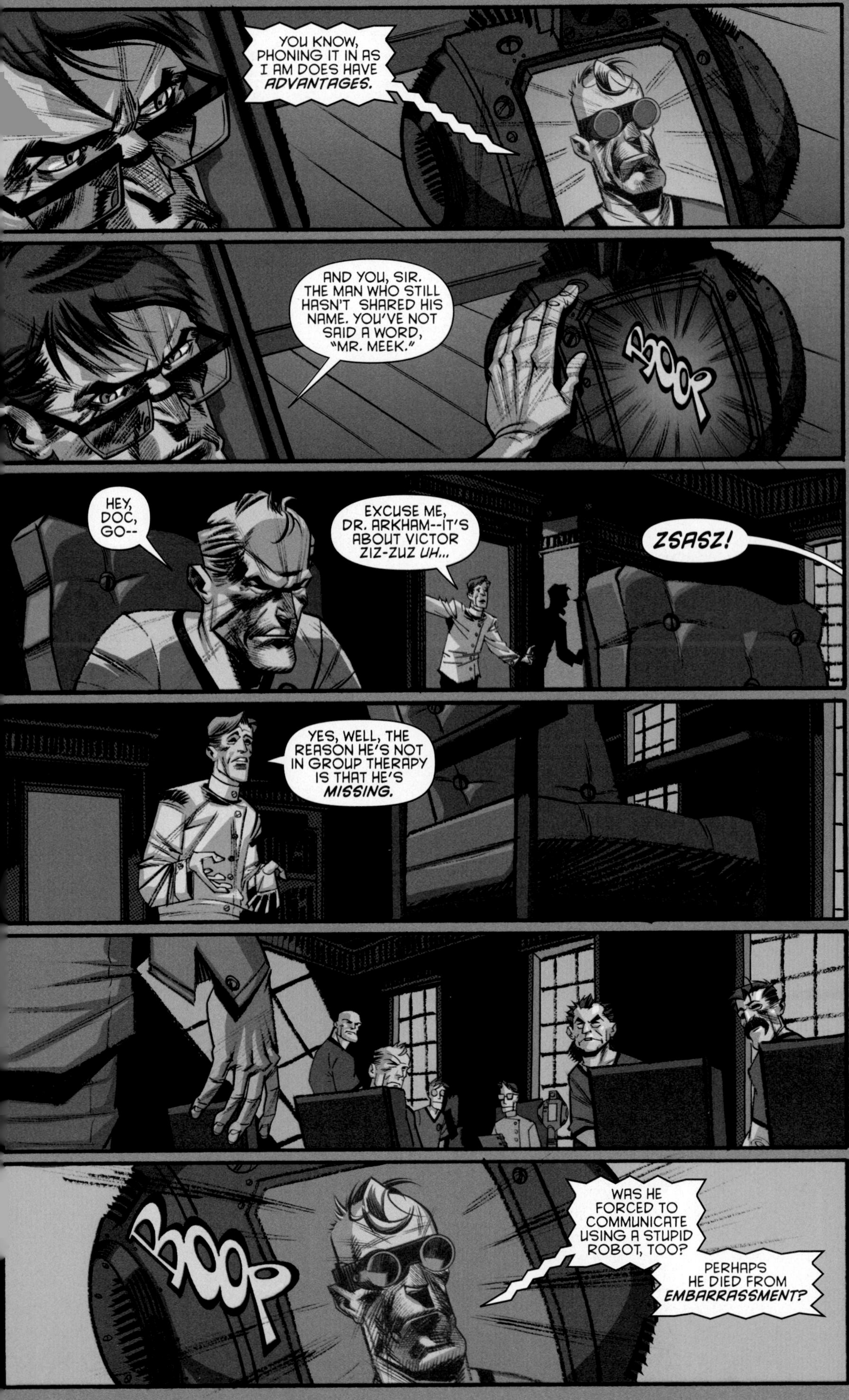
YOU KNOW, PHONING IT IN AS I AM DOES HAVE *ADVANTAGES.*
AND YOU, SIR. THE MAN WHO STILL HASN'T SHARED HIS NAME. YOU'VE NOT SAID A WORD, "MR. MEEK."
BADOOP
HEY, DOC, GO--
EXCUSE ME, DR. ARKHAM--IT'S ABOUT VICTOR ZIZ-ZUZ *UH...*
ZSASZ!
YES, WELL, THE REASON HE'S NOT IN GROUP THERAPY IS THAT HE'S *MISSING.*
BADOOP
WAS HE FORCED TO COMMUNICATE USING A STUPID ROBOT, TOO?
PERHAPS HE DIED FROM *EMBARRASSMENT?*

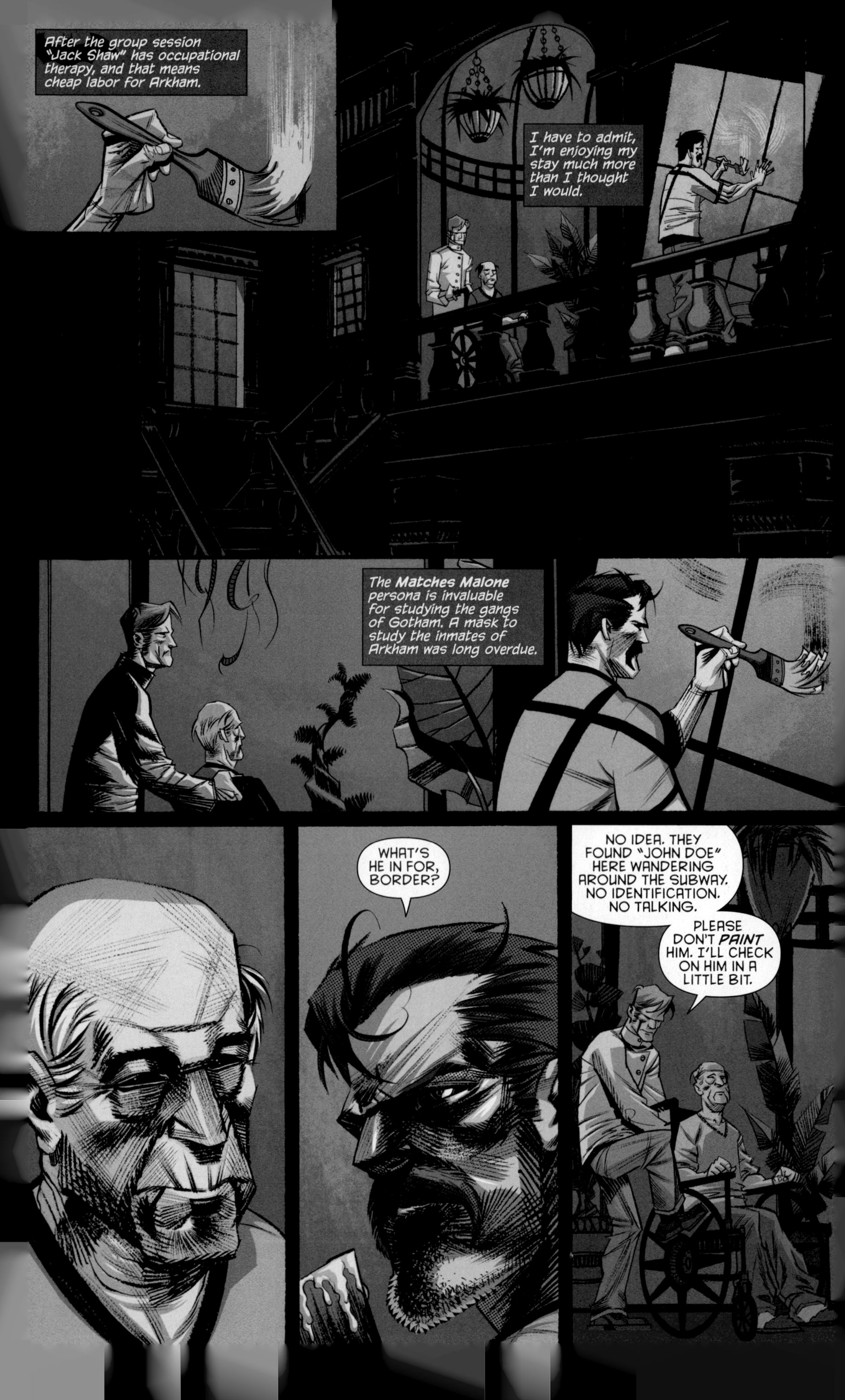

After the group session "Jack Shaw" has occupational therapy, and that means cheap labor for Arkham.
I have to admit, I'm enjoying my stay much more than I thought I would.
The **Matches Malone** persona is invaluable for studying the gangs of Gotham. A mask to study the inmates of Arkham was long overdue.
WHAT'S HE IN FOR, BORDER?
NO IDEA. THEY FOUND "JOHN DOE" HERE WANDERING AROUND THE SUBWAY. NO IDENTIFICATION. NO TALKING.
PLEASE DON'T ***PAINT*** HIM. I'LL CHECK ON HIM IN A LITTLE BIT.

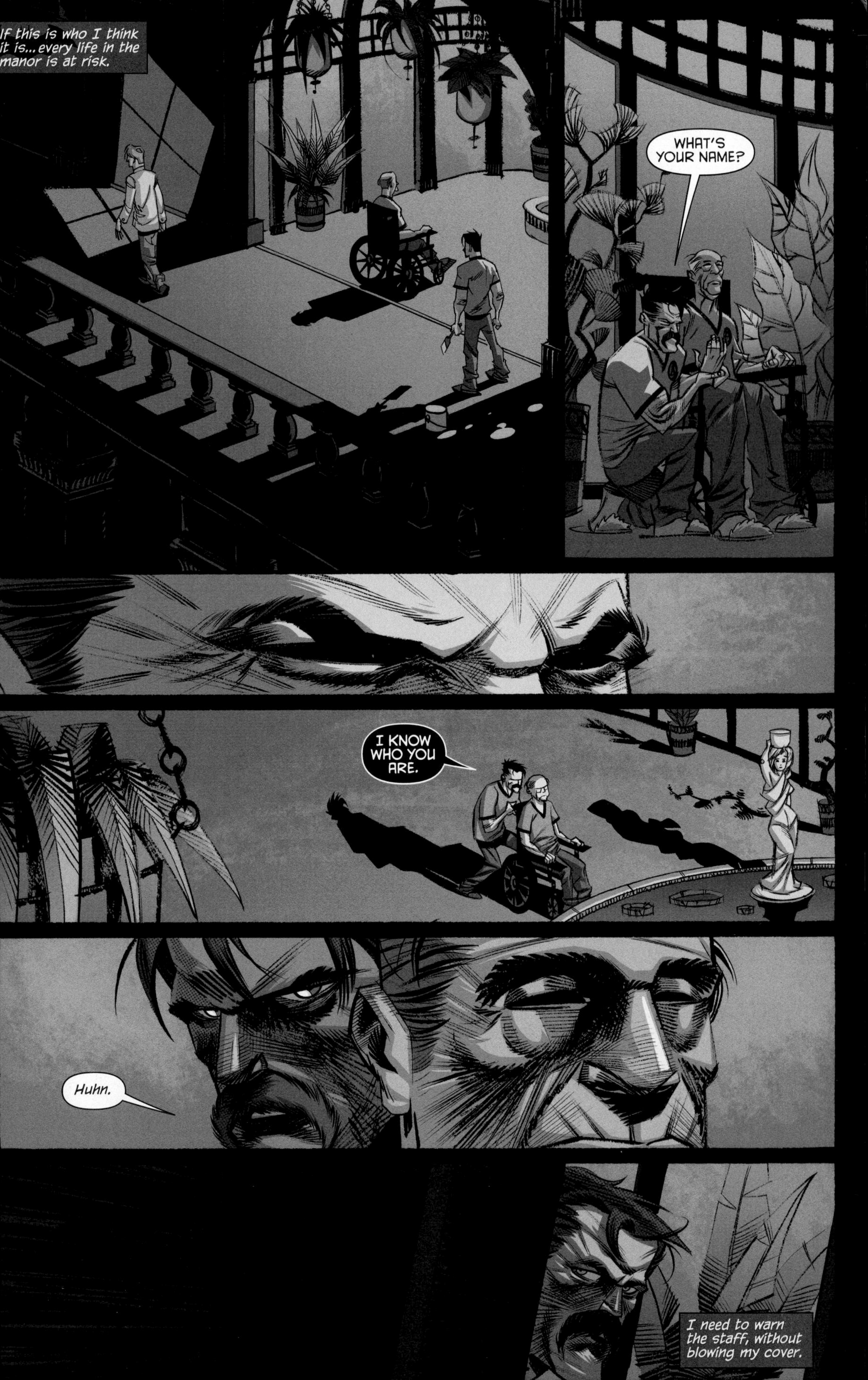
If this is who I think it is... every life in the manor is at risk.
WHAT'S YOUR NAME?
I KNOW WHO YOU ARE.
Huhn.
I need to warn the staff, without blowing my cover.

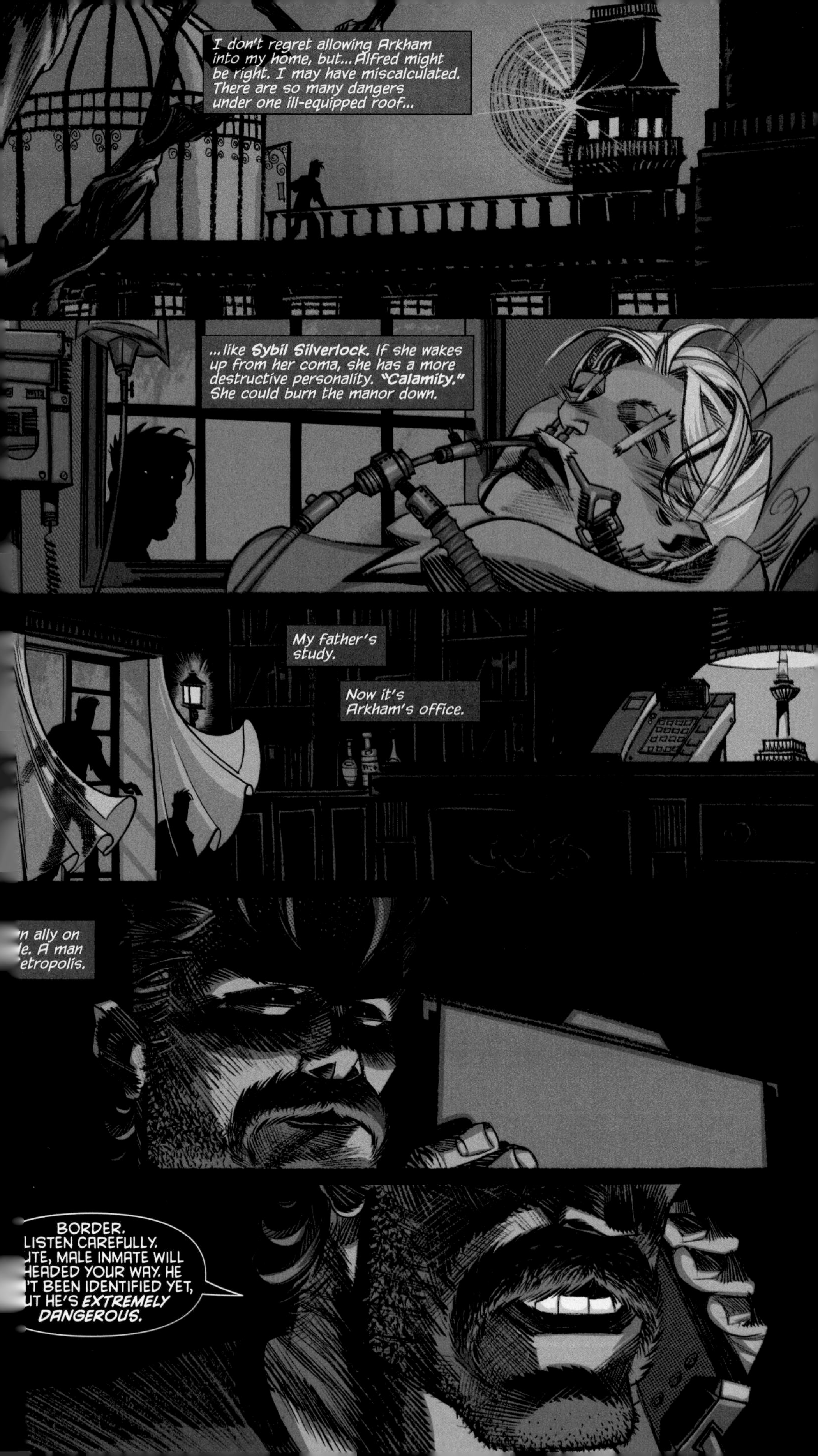
I don't regret allowing Arkham into my home, but... Alfred might be right. I may have miscalculated. There are so many dangers under one ill-equipped roof...
...like Sybil Silverlock. If she wakes up from her coma, she has a more destructive personality. "Calamity." She could burn the manor down.
My father's study.
Now it's Arkham's office.
n ally on
le. A man
etropolis.
BORDER.
LISTEN CAREFULLY.
UTE, MALE INMATE WILL
HEADED YOUR WAY. HE
'T BEEN IDENTIFIED YET,
UT HE'S EXTREMELY
DANGEROUS.

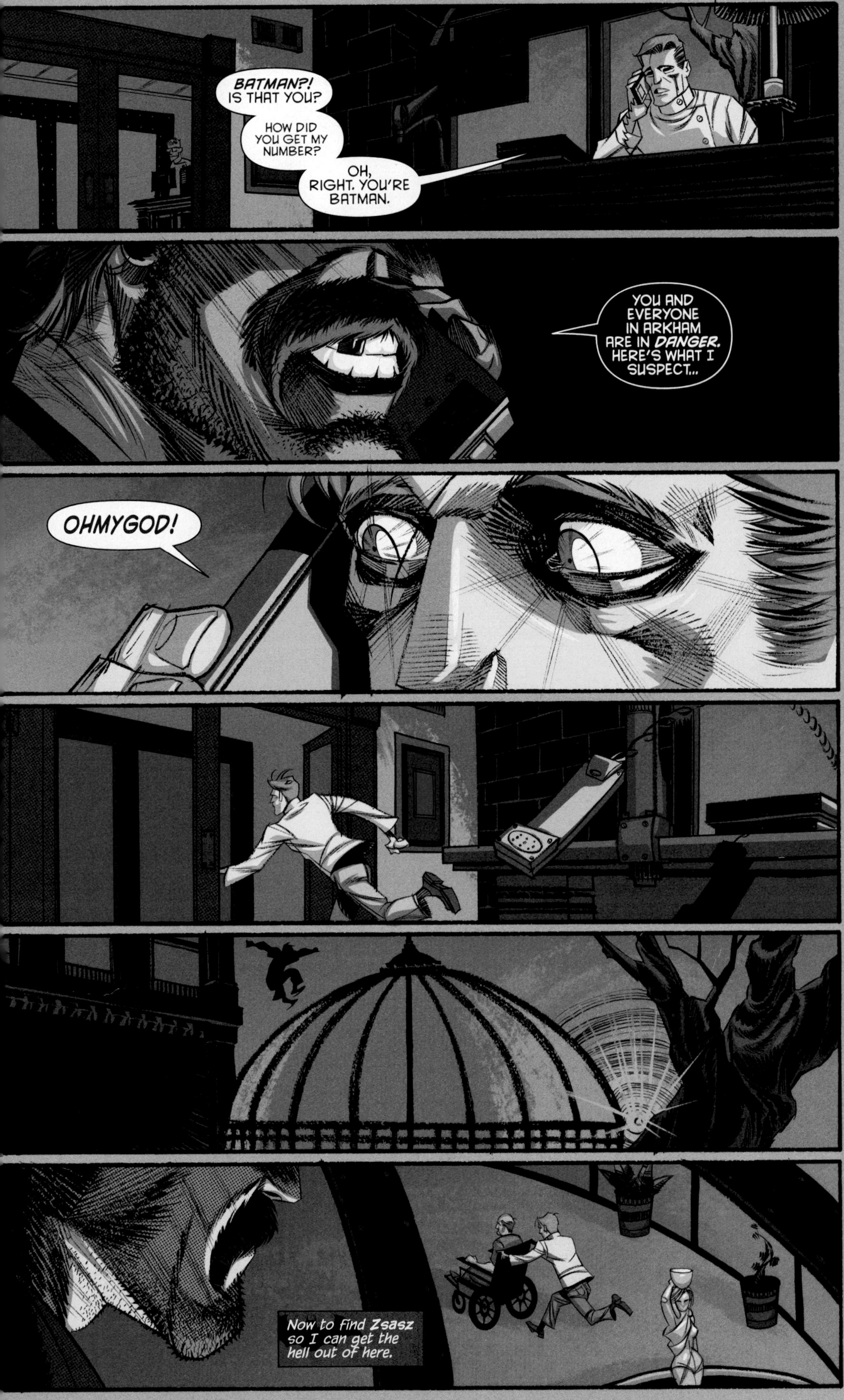
BATMAN?! IS THAT YOU?
HOW DID YOU GET MY NUMBER?
OH, RIGHT. YOU'RE BATMAN.
YOU AND EVERYONE IN ARKHAM ARE IN DANGER. HERE'S WHAT I SUSPECT...
OHMYGOD!
Now to find Zsasz so I can get the hell out of here.

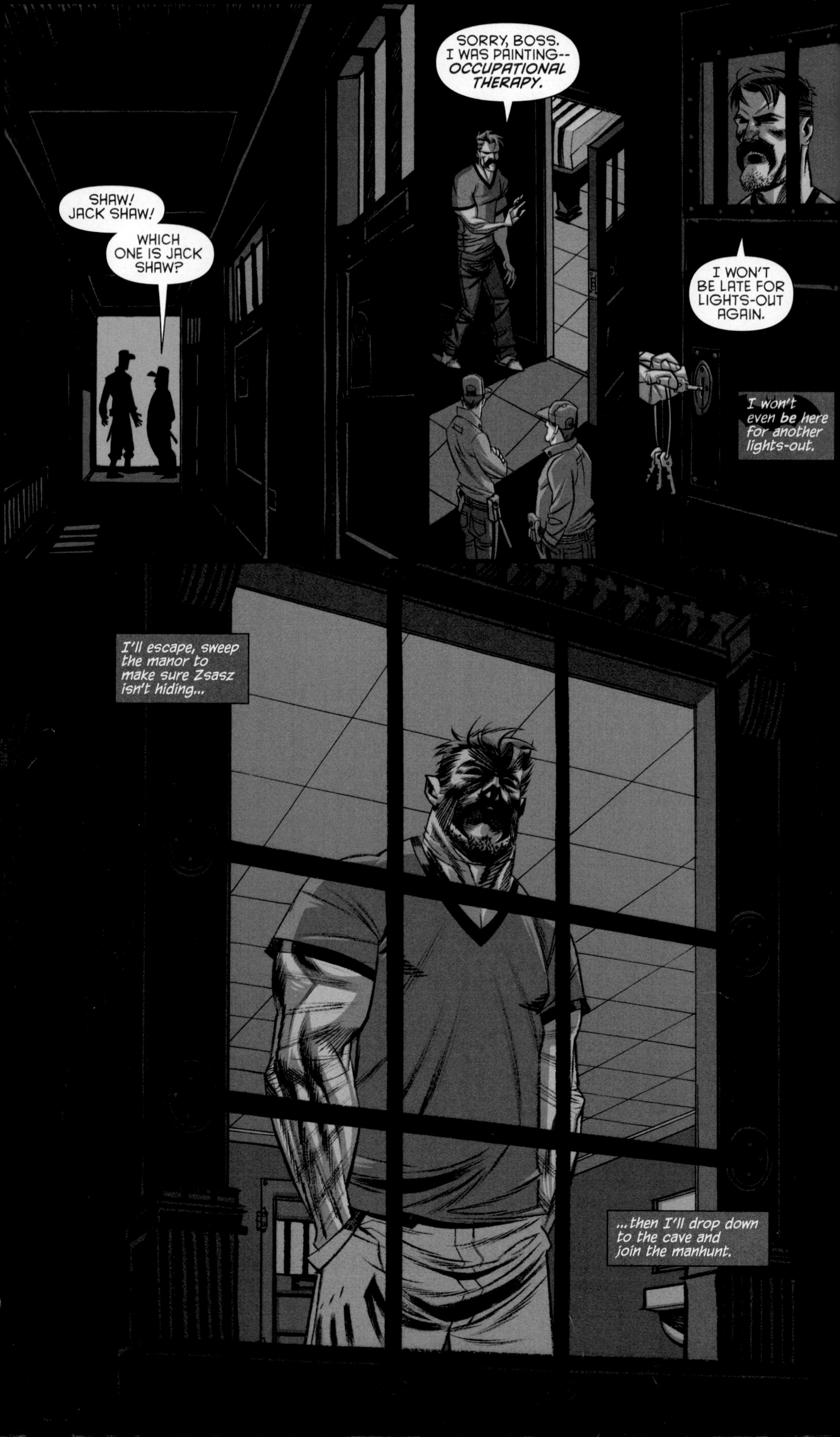
SHAW! JACK SHAW!
WHICH ONE IS JACK SHAW?
SORRY, BOSS. I WAS PAINTING-- OCCUPATIONAL THERAPY.
I WON'T BE LATE FOR LIGHTS-OUT AGAIN.
I won't even be here for another lights-out.
I'll escape, sweep the manor to make sure Zsasz isn't hiding...
...then I'll drop down to the cave and join the manhunt.

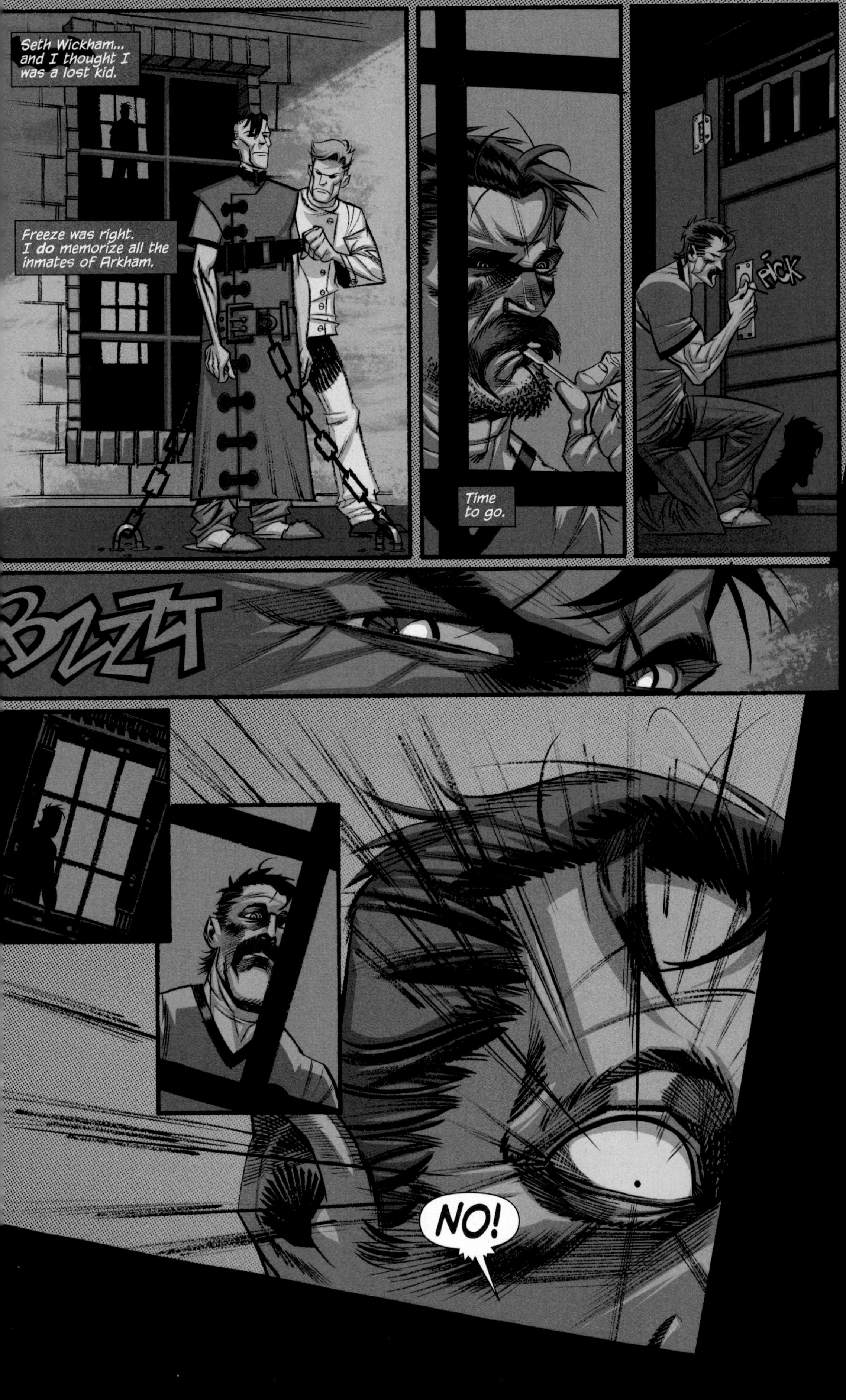
Seth Wickham... and I thought I was a lost kid.
Freeze was right. I do memorize all the inmates of Arkham.
Time to go.
PICK
BZZZT
NO!

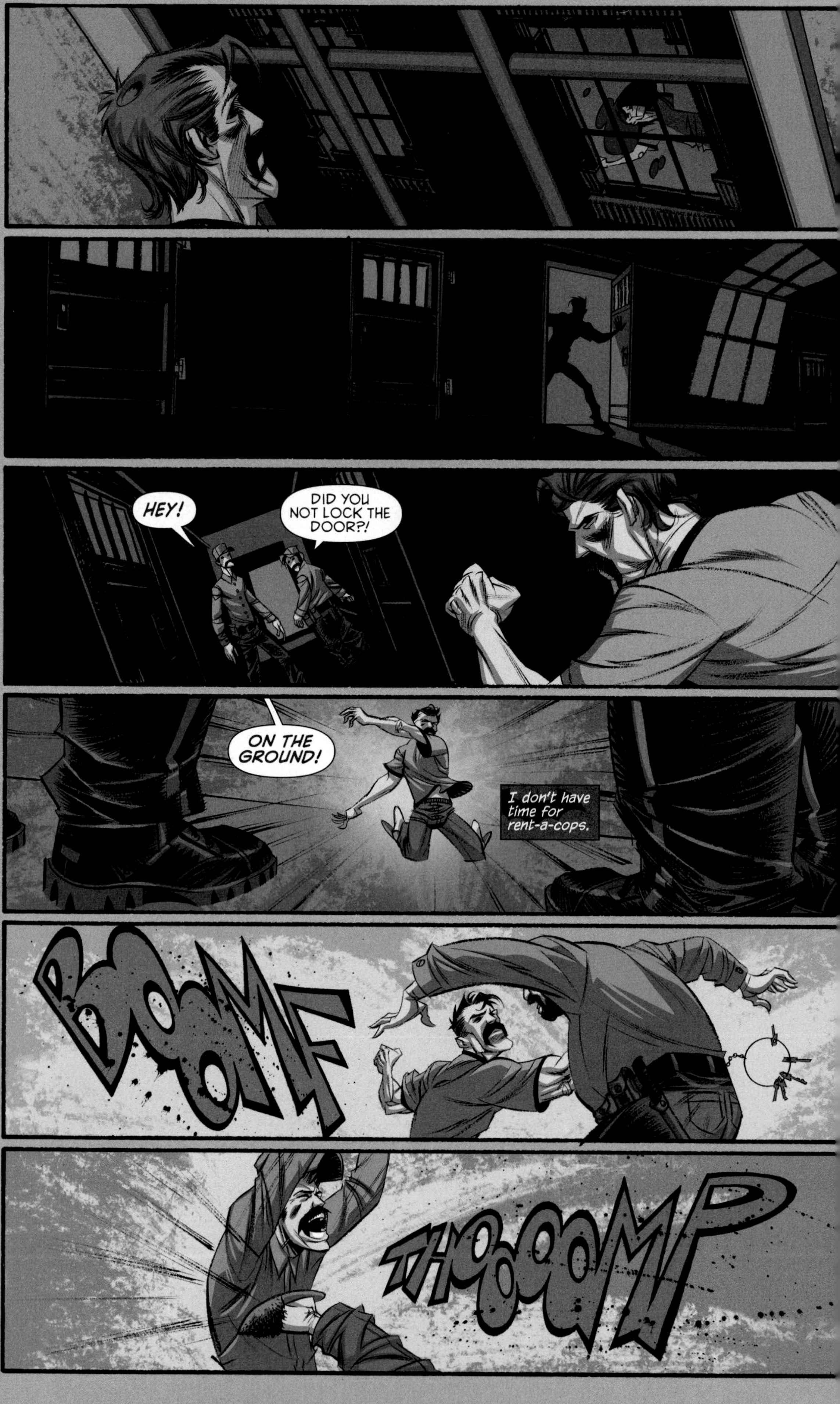
HEY!
DID YOU NOT LOCK THE DOOR?!
ON THE GROUND!
I don't have time for rent-a-cops.
BOOMF
THOOOOMP

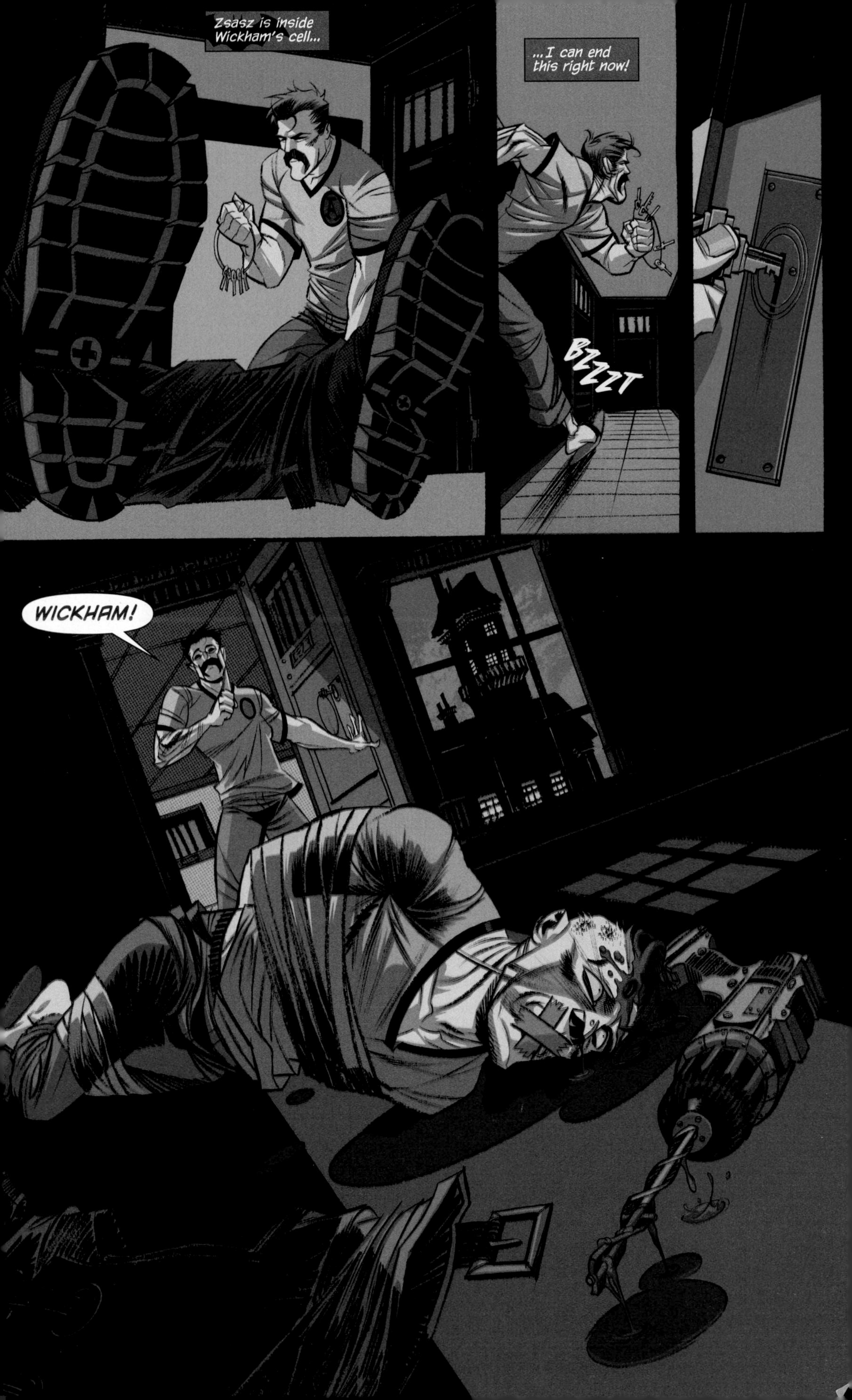
Zsasz is inside Wickham's cell...
...I can end this right now!
BZZZT
WICKHAM!

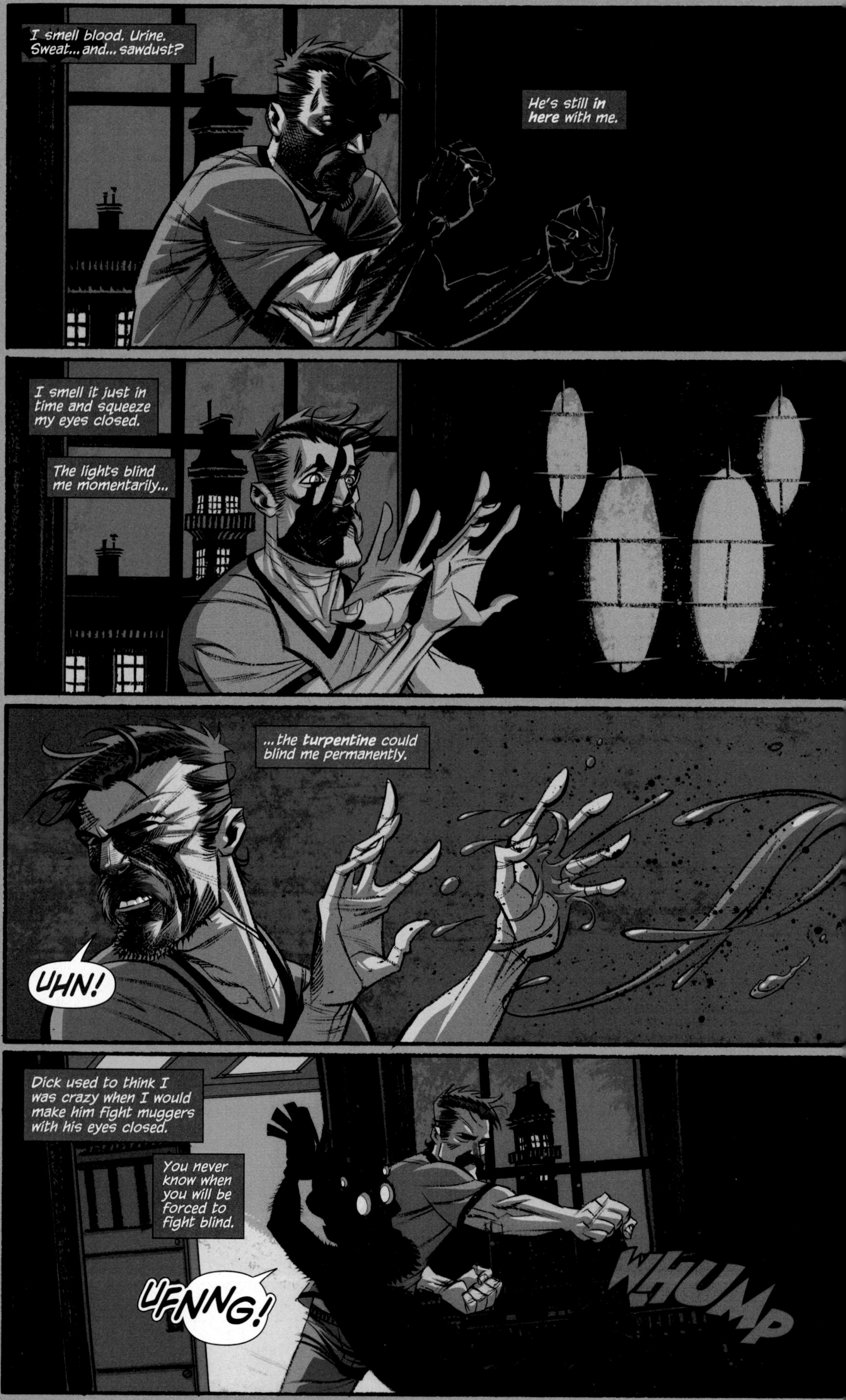
I smell blood. Urine. Sweat... and... sawdust?
He's still **in here** with me.
I smell it just in time and squeeze my eyes closed.
The lights blind me momentarily...
...the **turpentine** could blind me permanently.
UHN!
Dick used to think I was crazy when I would make him fight muggers with his eyes closed.
You never know when you will be forced to fight blind.
UFNNG!
WHUMP

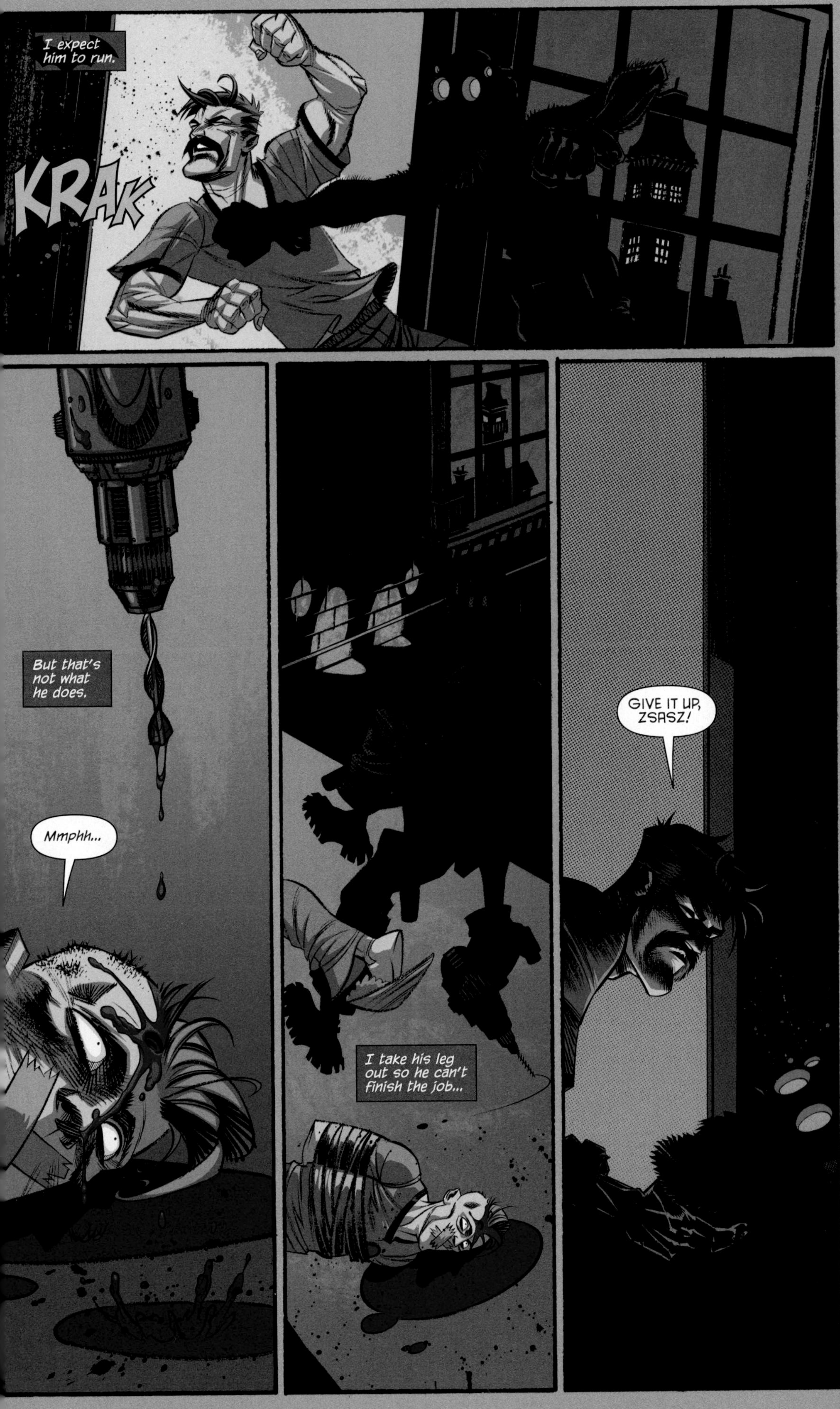
I expect him to run.
KRAK
But that's not what he does.
Mmphh...
I take his leg out so he can't finish the job...
GIVE IT UP, ZSASZ!

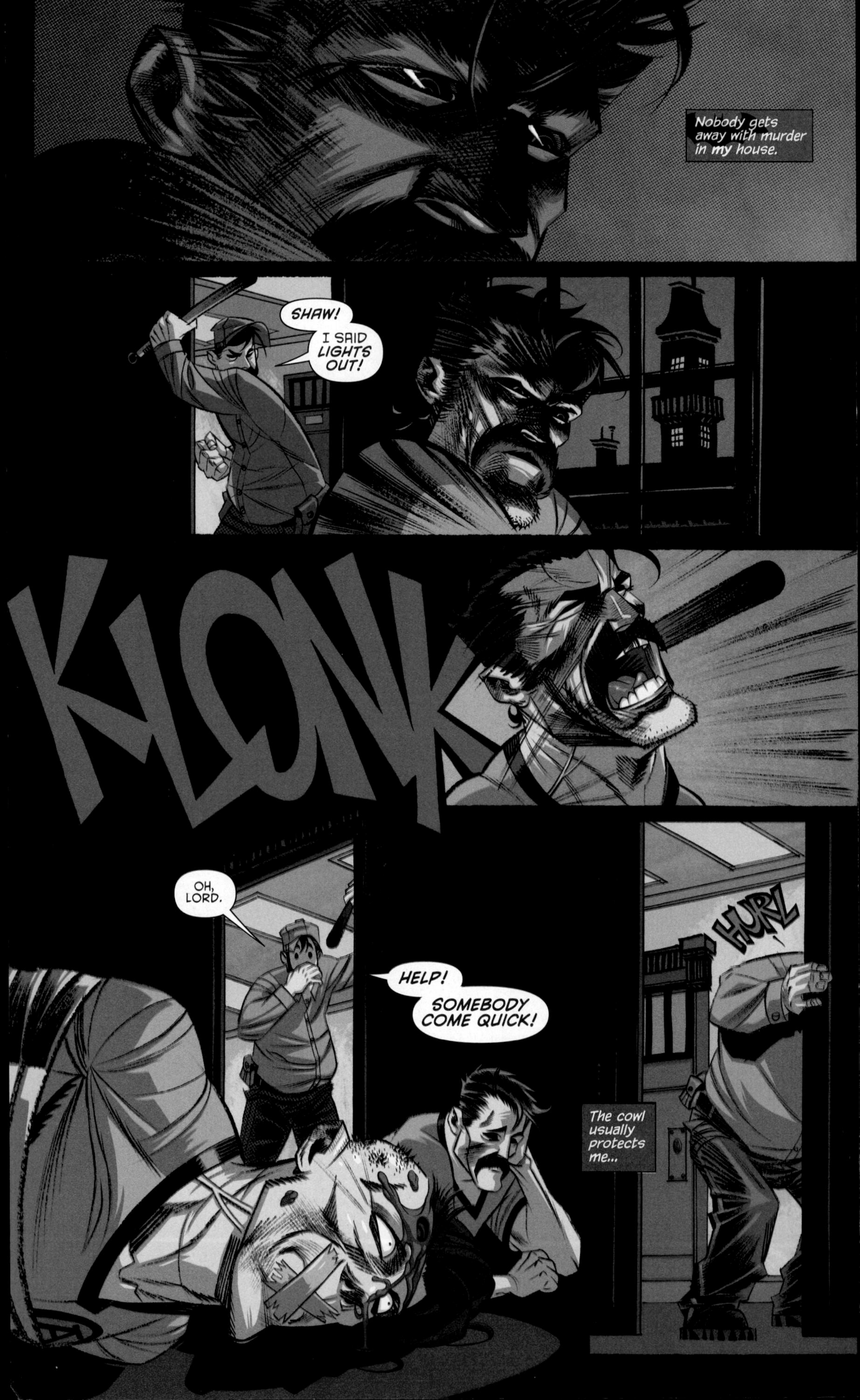

Nobody gets away with murder in my house.
SHAW! I SAID LIGHTS OUT!
KLONK
OH, LORD.
HELP! SOMEBODY COME QUICK!
HURL
The cowl usually protects me...

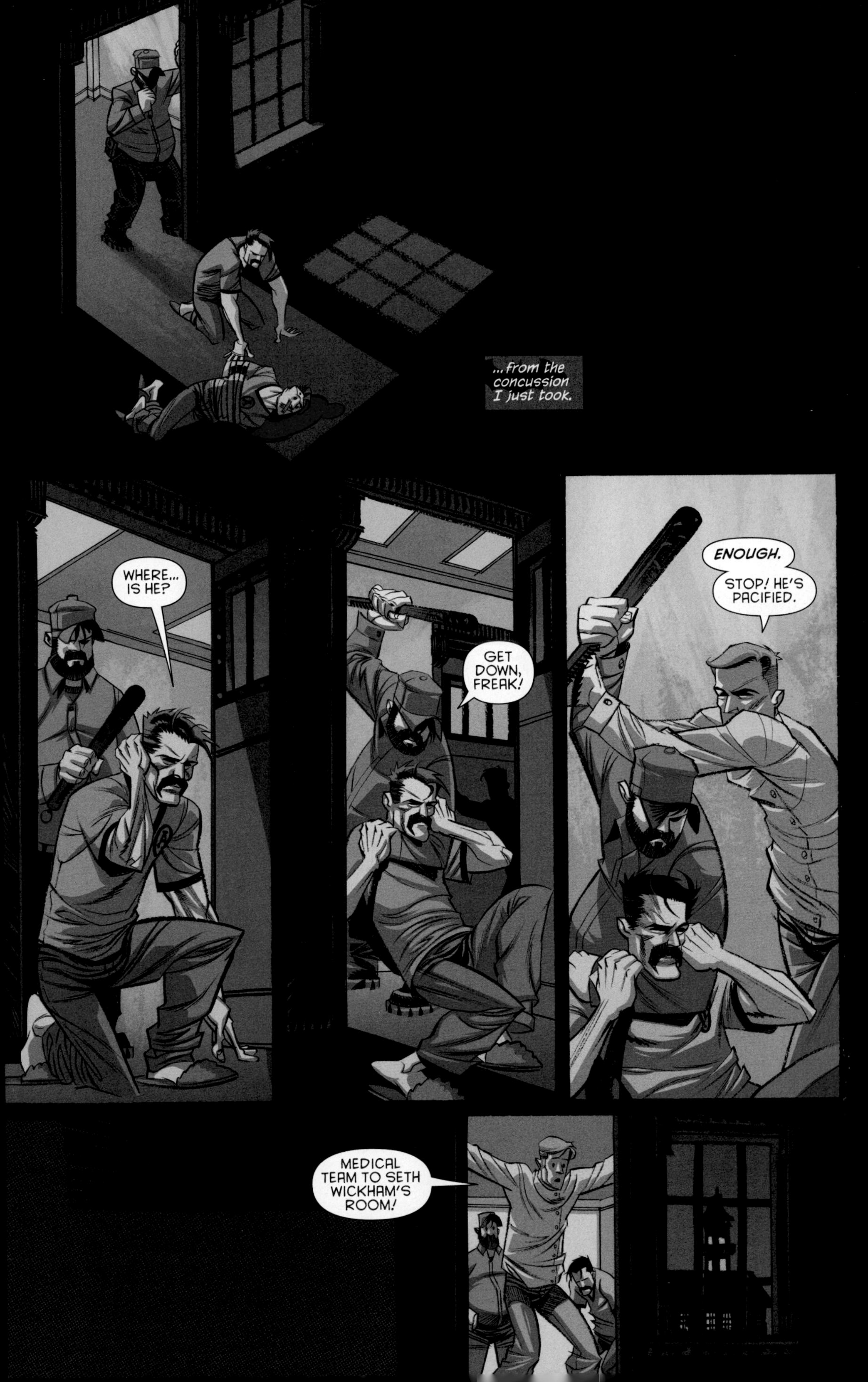
...from the concussion I just took.
WHERE... IS HE?
GET DOWN, FREAK!
ENOUGH.
STOP! HE'S PACIFIED.
MEDICAL TEAM TO SETH WICKHAM'S ROOM!

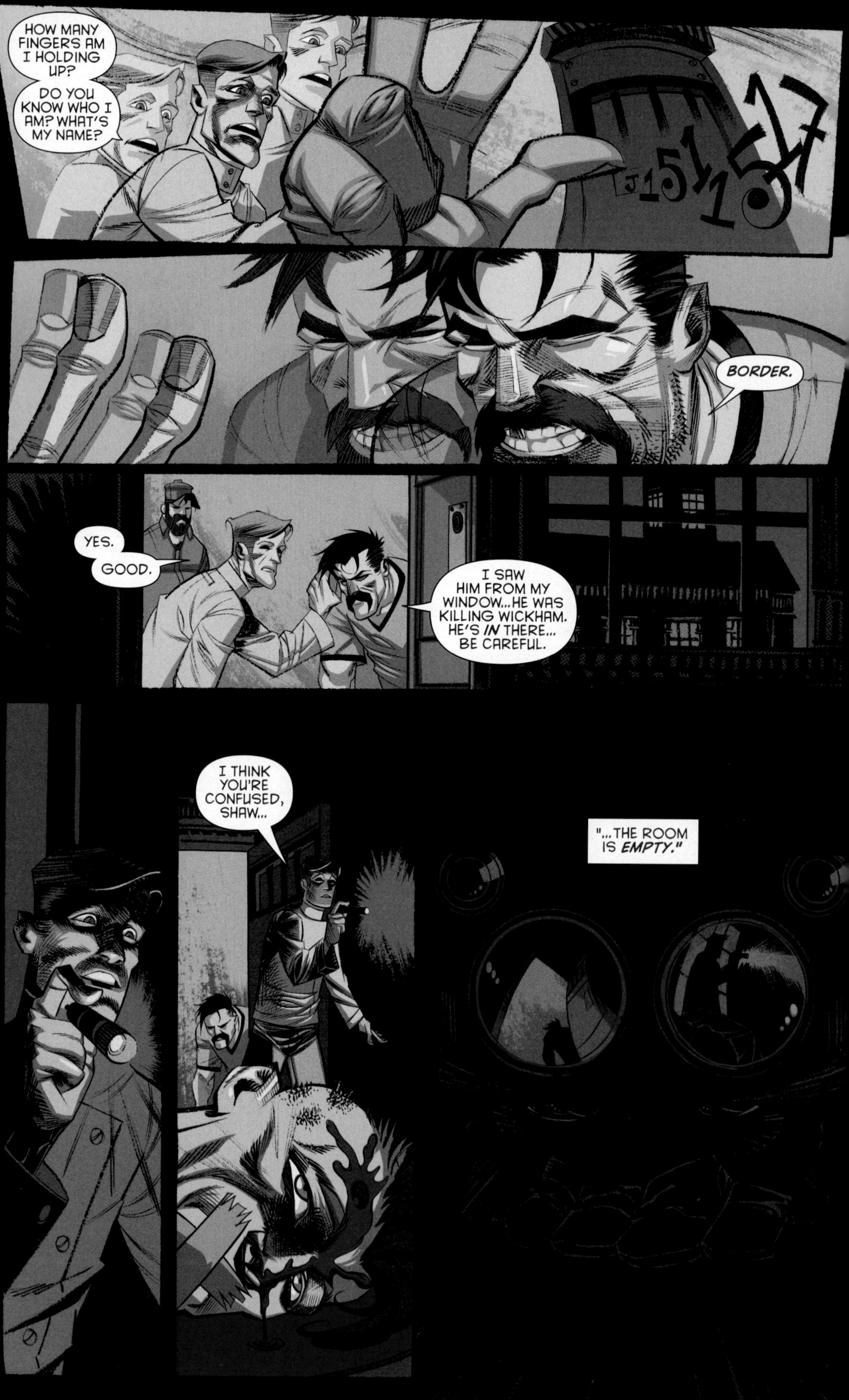
HOW MANY FINGERS AM I HOLDING UP?
DO YOU KNOW WHO I AM? WHAT'S MY NAME?
J15115347
BORDER.
YES.
GOOD.
I SAW HIM FROM MY WINDOW...HE WAS KILLING WICKHAM. HE'S IN THERE... BE CAREFUL.
I THINK YOU'RE CONFUSED, SHAW...
"...THE ROOM IS EMPTY."

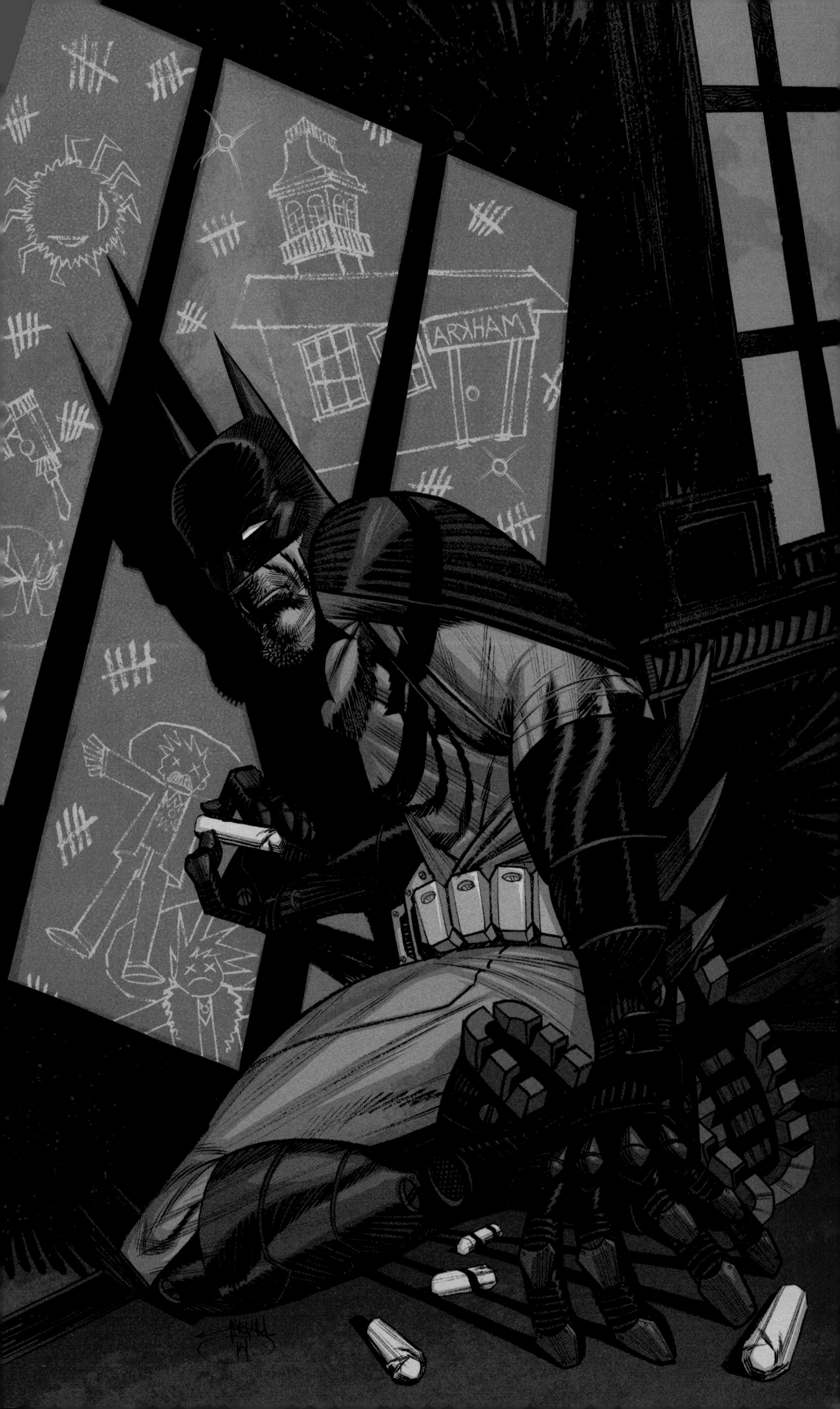
ARKHAM

Variant cover art for issue #3 by **NATHAN FOX** and **RICO RENZI**

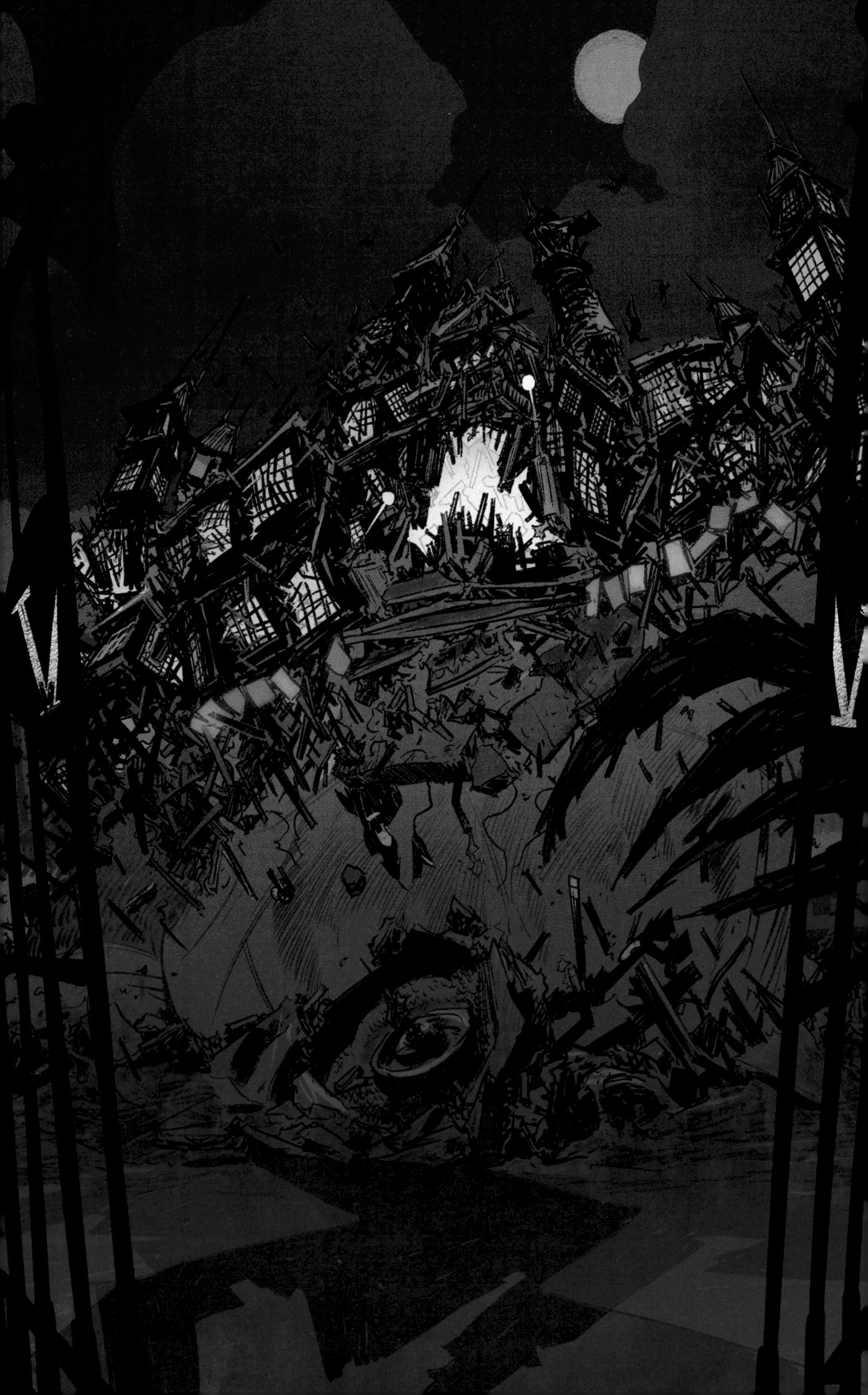

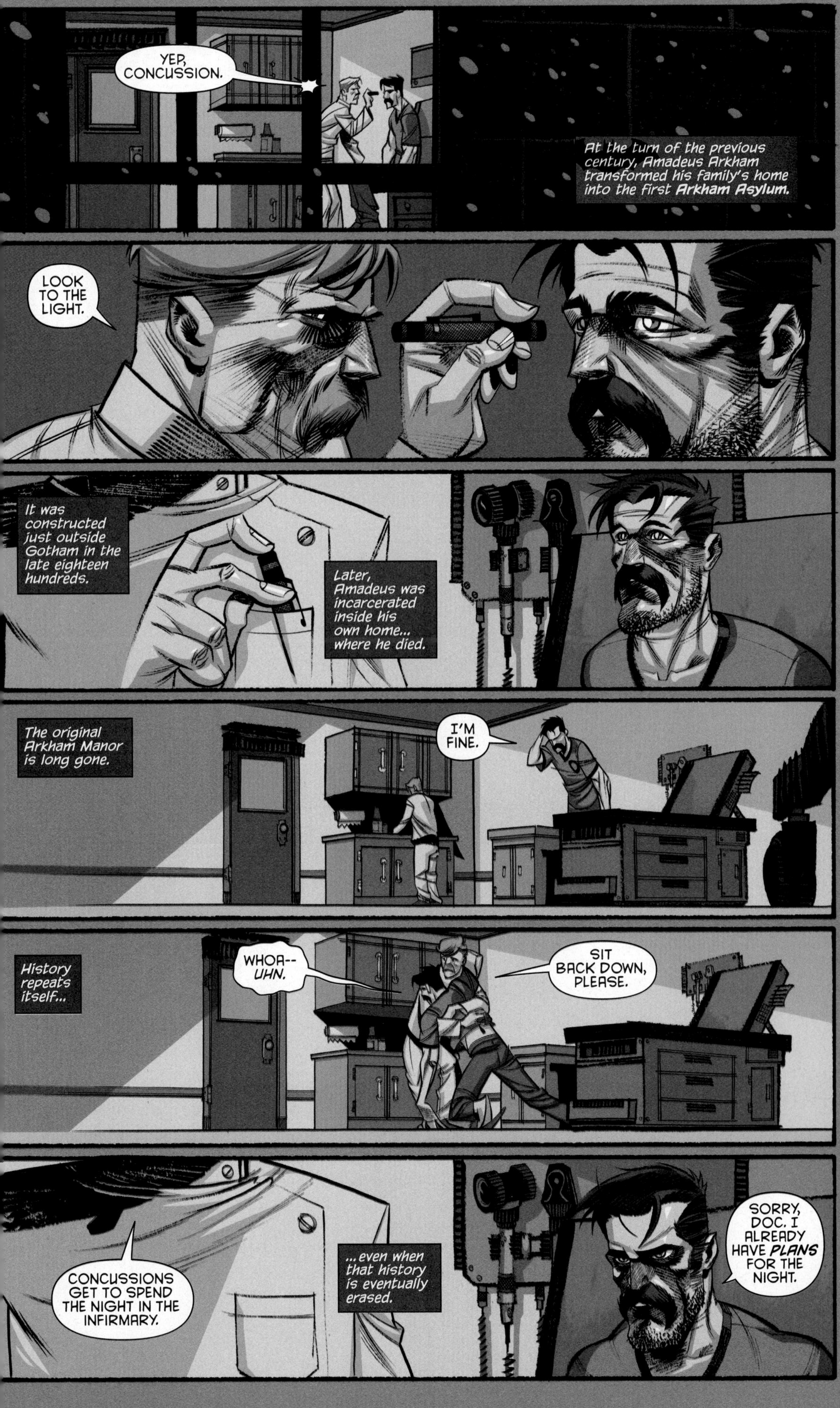
YEP, CONCUSSION.
At the turn of the previous century, Amadeus Arkham transformed his family's home into the first Arkham Asylum.
LOOK TO THE LIGHT.
It was constructed just outside Gotham in the late eighteen hundreds.
Later, Amadeus was incarcerated inside his own home... where he died.
The original Arkham Manor is long gone.
I'M FINE.
History repeats itself...
WHOA-- UHN.
SIT BACK DOWN, PLEASE.
CONCUSSIONS GET TO SPEND THE NIGHT IN THE INFIRMARY.
...even when that history is eventually erased.
SORRY, DOC. I ALREADY HAVE PLANS FOR THE NIGHT.

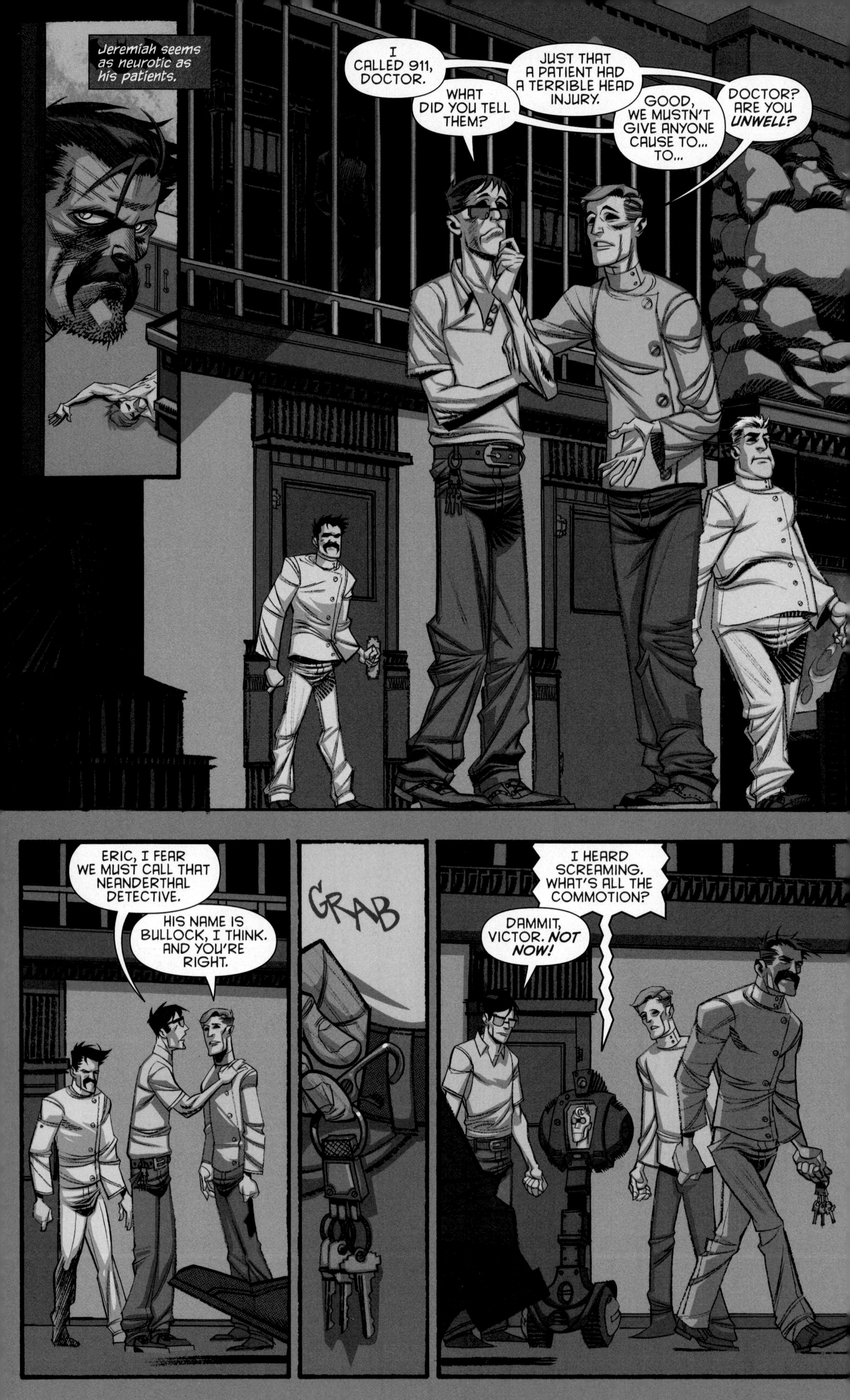
Jeremiah seems as neurotic as his patients.
I CALLED 911, DOCTOR.
WHAT DID YOU TELL THEM?
JUST THAT A PATIENT HAD A TERRIBLE HEAD INJURY.
GOOD, WE MUSTN'T GIVE ANYONE CAUSE TO... TO...
DOCTOR? ARE YOU *UNWELL?*
ERIC, I FEAR WE MUST CALL THAT NEANDERTHAL DETECTIVE.
HIS NAME IS BULLOCK, I THINK. AND YOU'RE RIGHT.
GRAB
I HEARD SCREAMING. WHAT'S ALL THE COMMOTION?
DAMMIT, VICTOR. ***NOT NOW!***

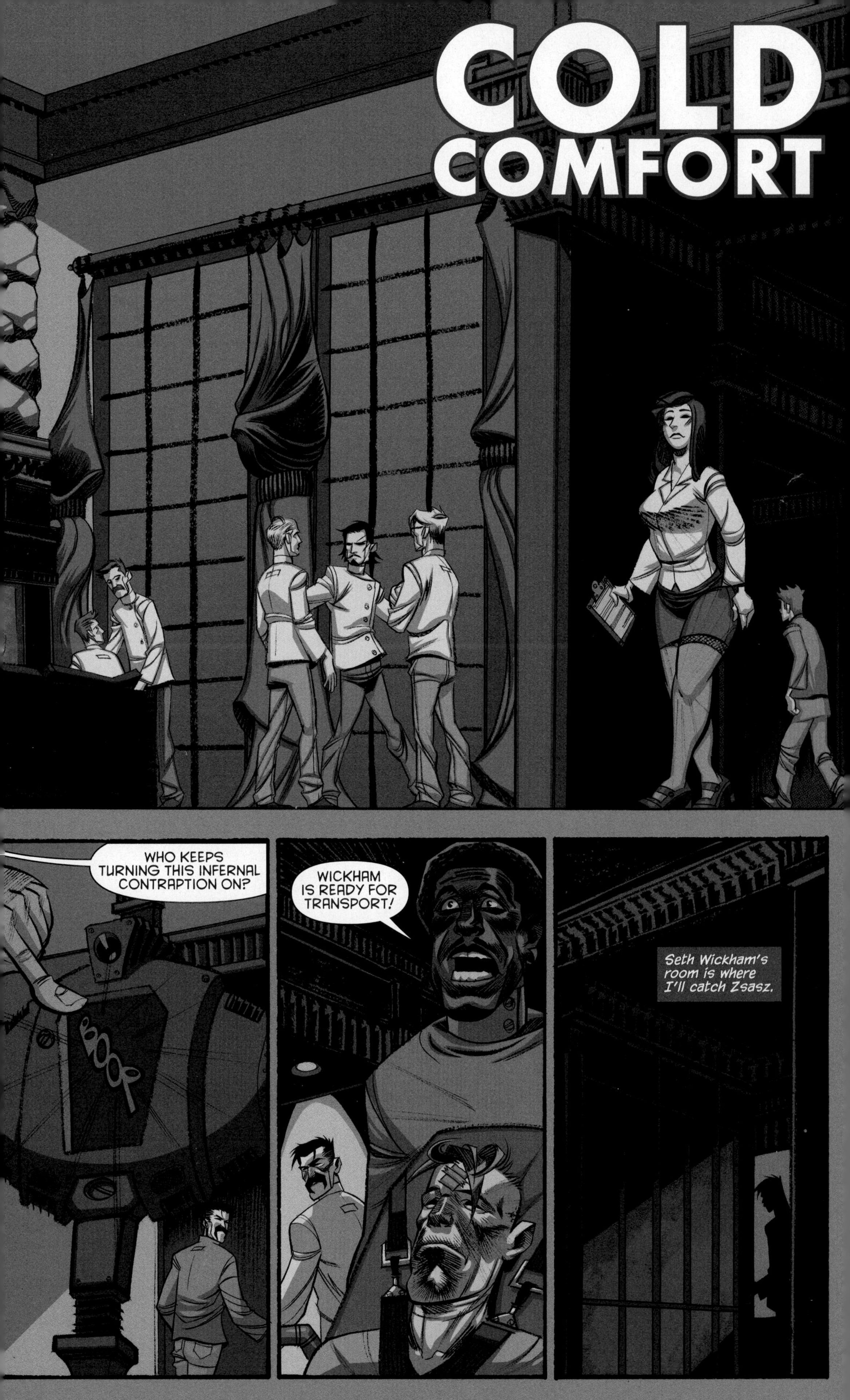
COLD
COMFORT
WHO KEEPS TURNING THIS INFERNAL CONTRAPTION ON?
BOOP
WICKHAM IS READY FOR TRANSPORT!
Seth Wickham's room is where I'll catch Zsasz.

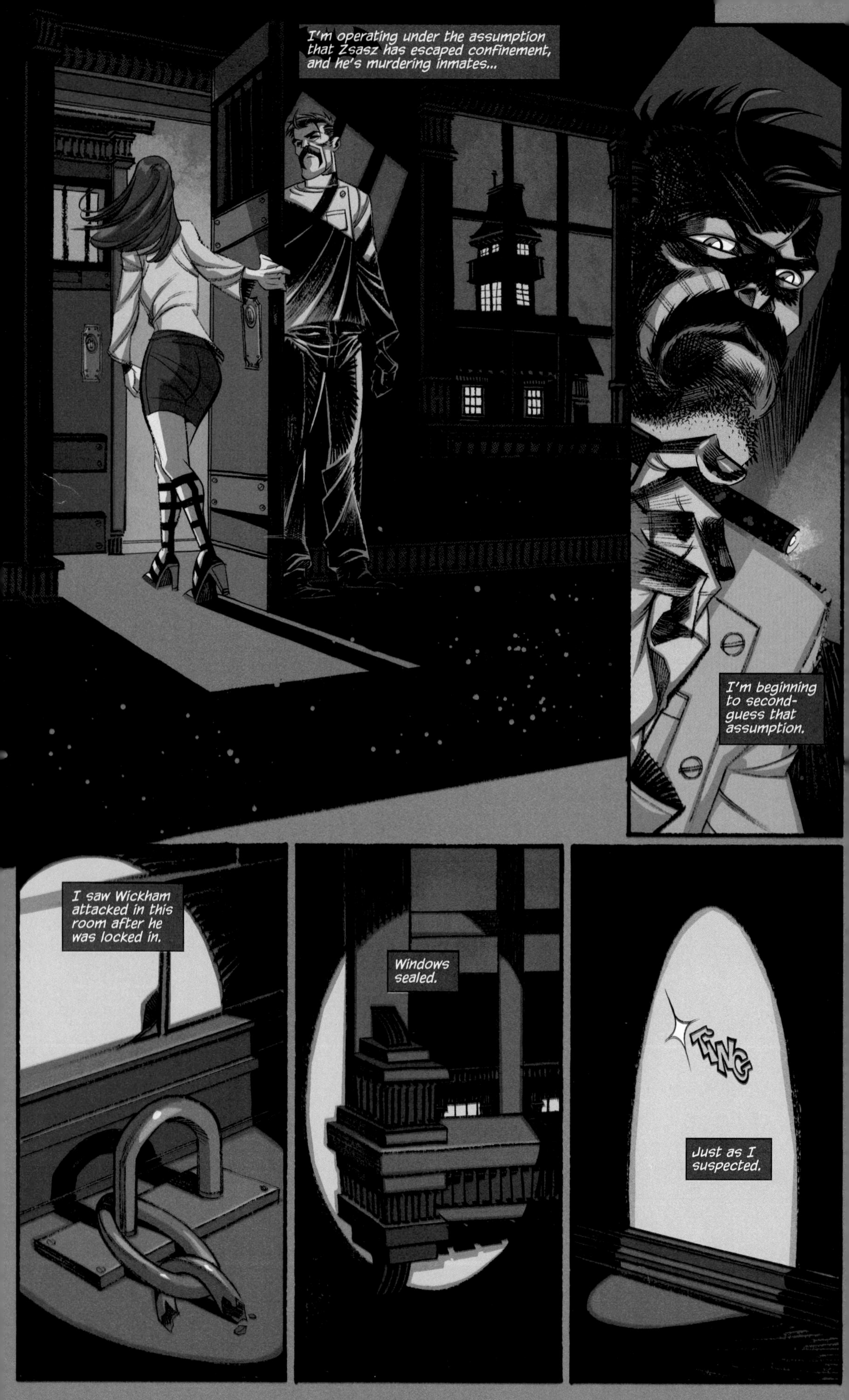

I'm operating under the assumption that Zsasz has escaped confinement, and he's murdering inmates...
I'm beginning to second-guess that assumption.
I saw Wickham attacked in this room after he was locked in.
Windows sealed.
TING
Just as I suspected.

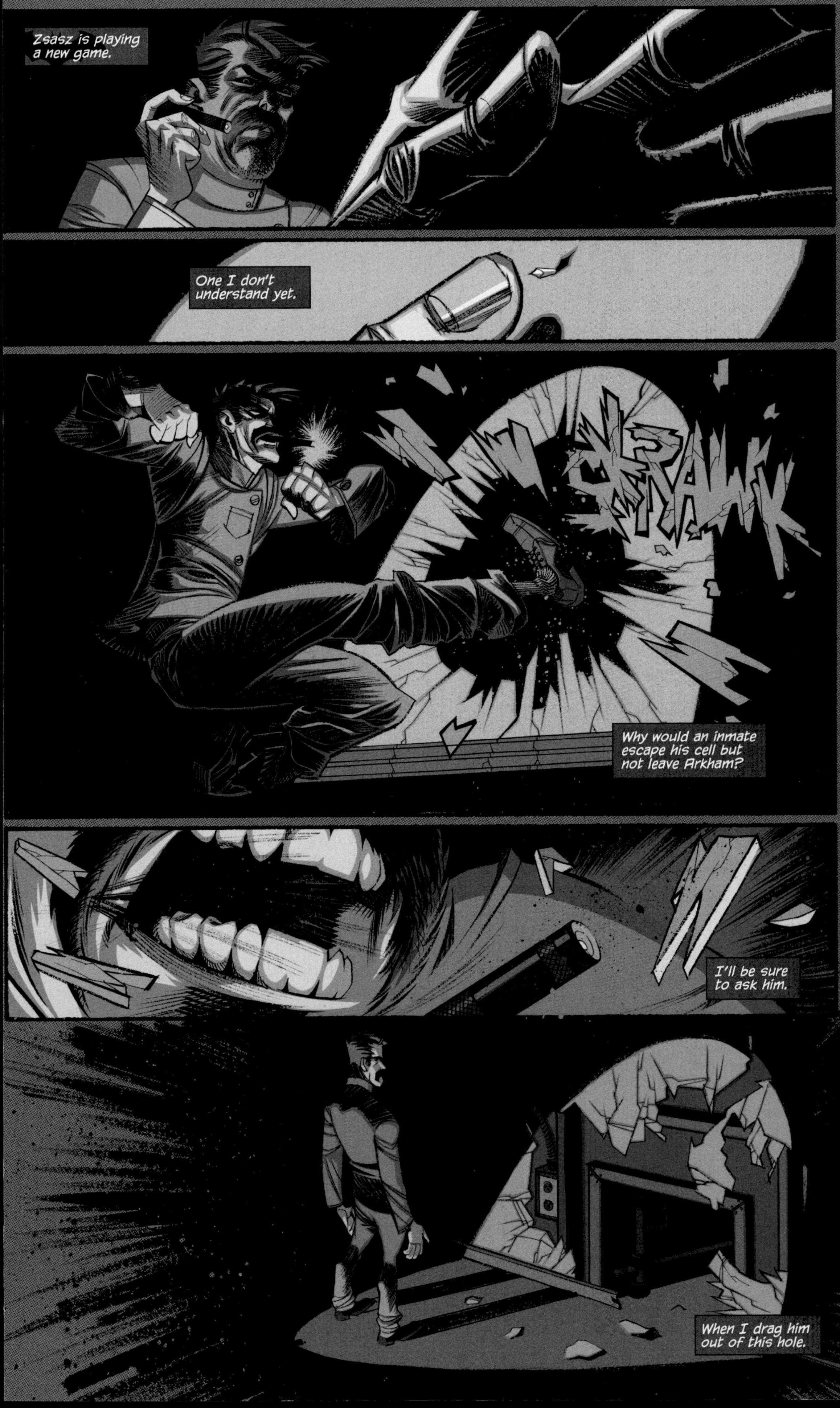
Zsasz is playing a new game.
One I don't understand yet.
KRAWK
Why would an inmate escape his cell but not leave Arkham?
I'll be sure to ask him.
When I drag him out of this hole.

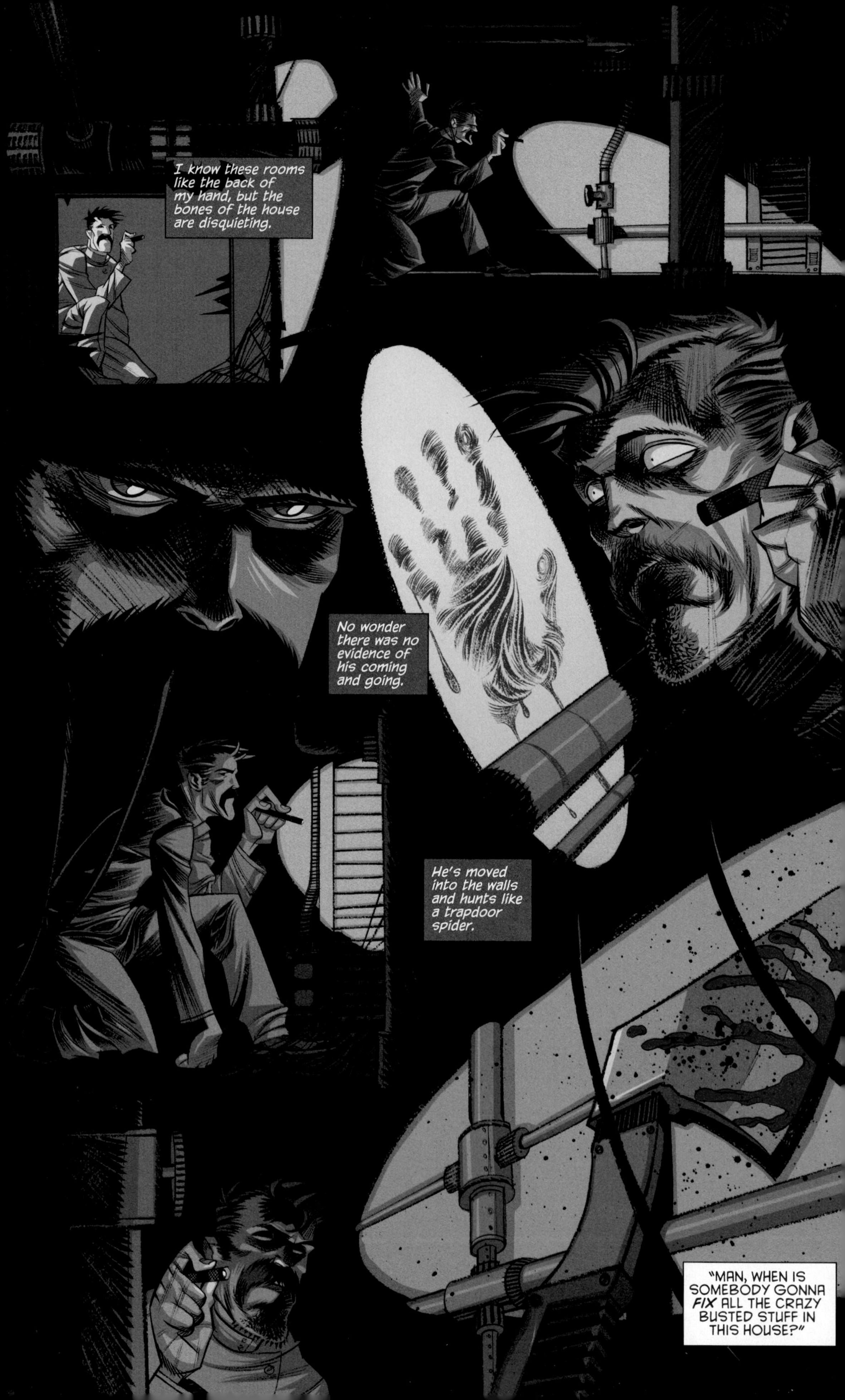
I know these rooms like the back of my hand, but the bones of the house are disquieting.
No wonder there was no evidence of his coming and going.
He's moved into the walls and hunts like a trapdoor spider.
"MAN, WHEN IS SOMEBODY GONNA *FIX* ALL THE CRAZY BUSTED STUFF IN THIS HOUSE?"

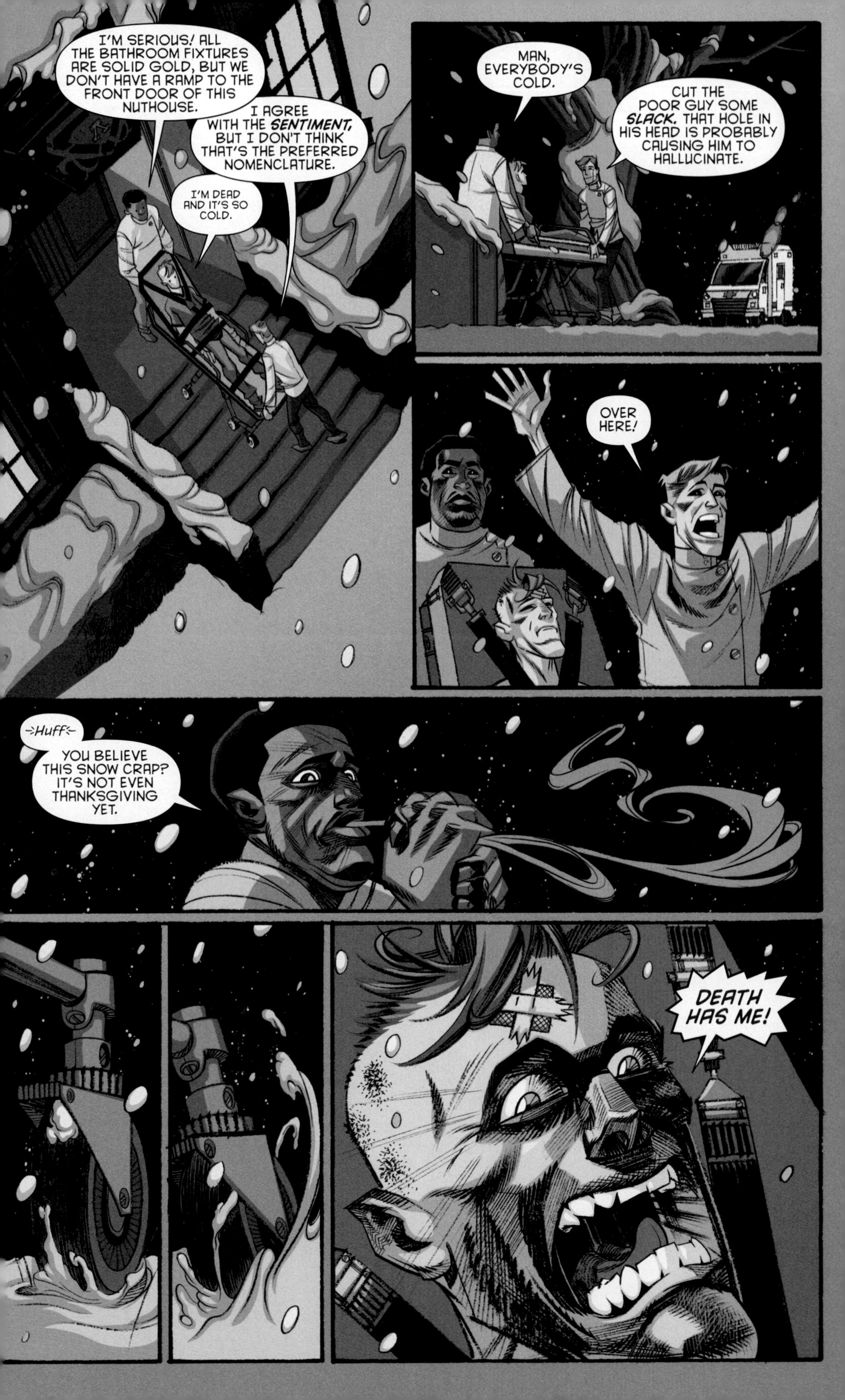
I'M SERIOUS! ALL THE BATHROOM FIXTURES ARE SOLID GOLD, BUT WE DON'T HAVE A RAMP TO THE FRONT DOOR OF THIS NUTHOUSE.
I AGREE WITH THE SENTIMENT, BUT I DON'T THINK THAT'S THE PREFERRED NOMENCLATURE.
I'M DEAD AND IT'S SO COLD.
MAN, EVERYBODY'S COLD.
CUT THE POOR GUY SOME SLACK. THAT HOLE IN HIS HEAD IS PROBABLY CAUSING HIM TO HALLUCINATE.
OVER HERE!
-Huff-
YOU BELIEVE THIS SNOW CRAP? IT'S NOT EVEN THANKSGIVING YET.
DEATH HAS ME!

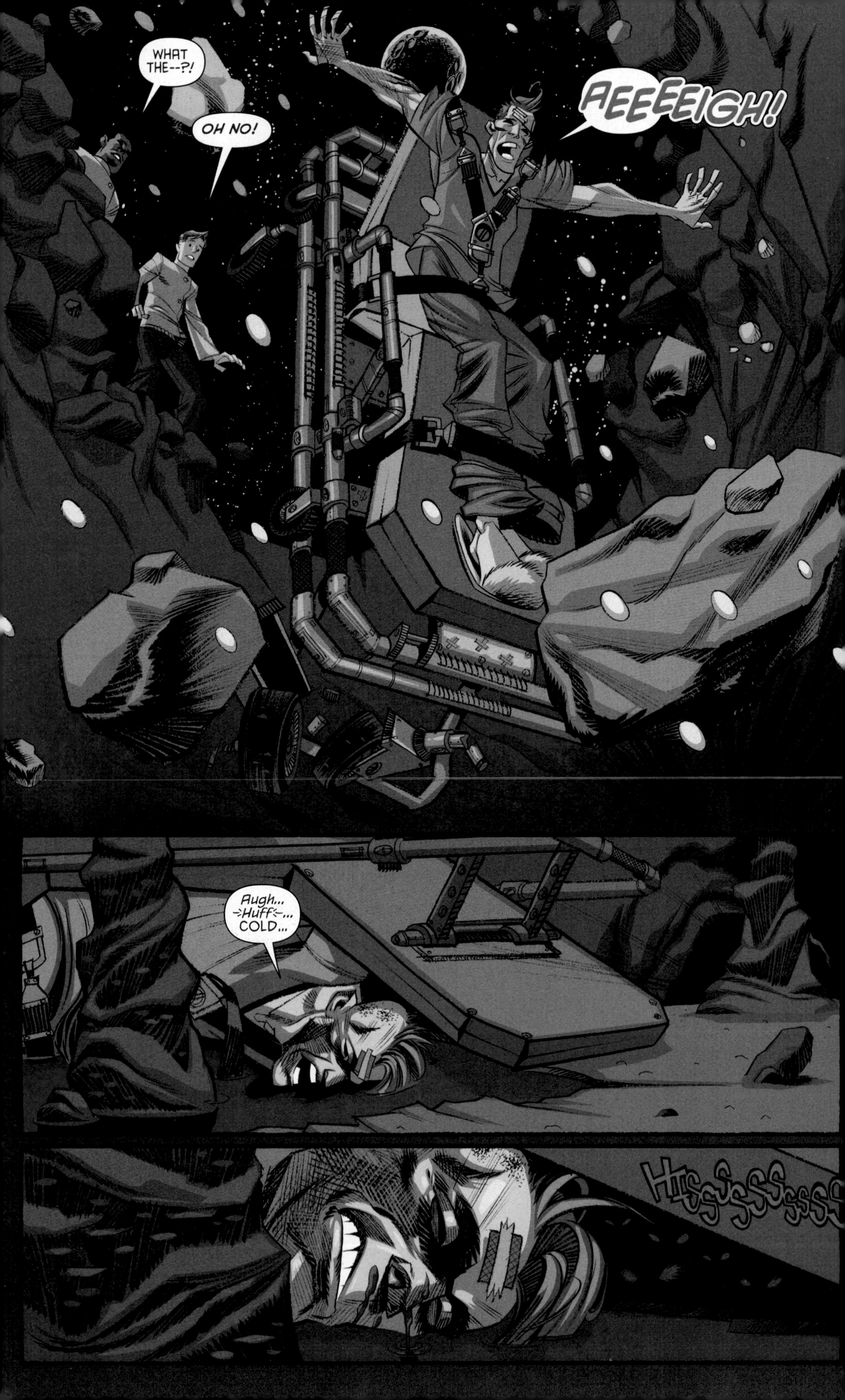
WHAT THE--?!
OH NO!
AEEEEEIGH!
Augh... -Huff-... COLD...
HISSSSSSSSS

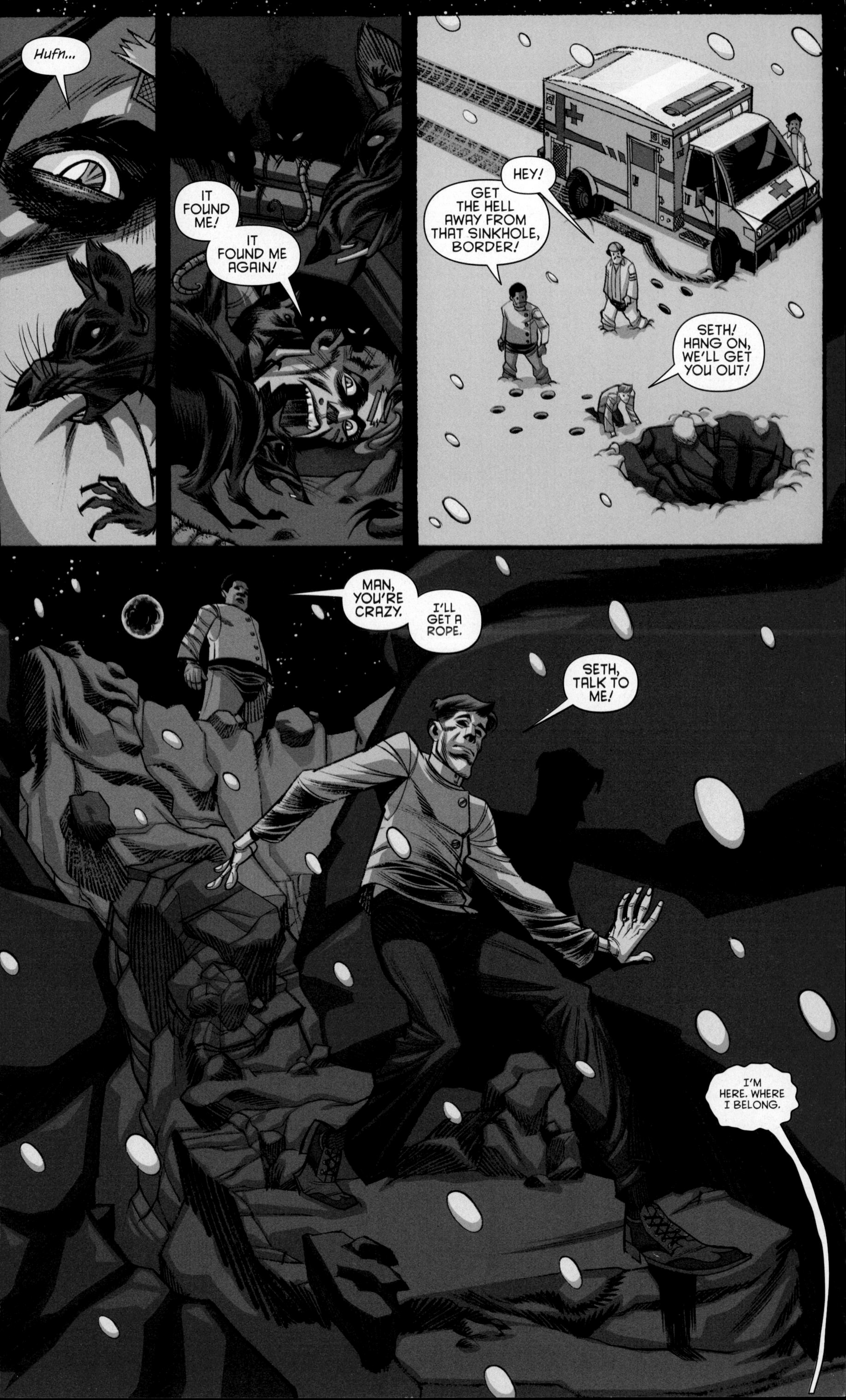

Hufn...
IT FOUND ME!
IT FOUND ME AGAIN!
HEY!
GET THE HELL AWAY FROM THAT SINKHOLE, BORDER!
SETH! HANG ON, WE'LL GET YOU OUT!
MAN, YOU'RE CRAZY.
I'LL GET A ROPE.
SETH, TALK TO ME!
I'M HERE. WHERE I BELONG.

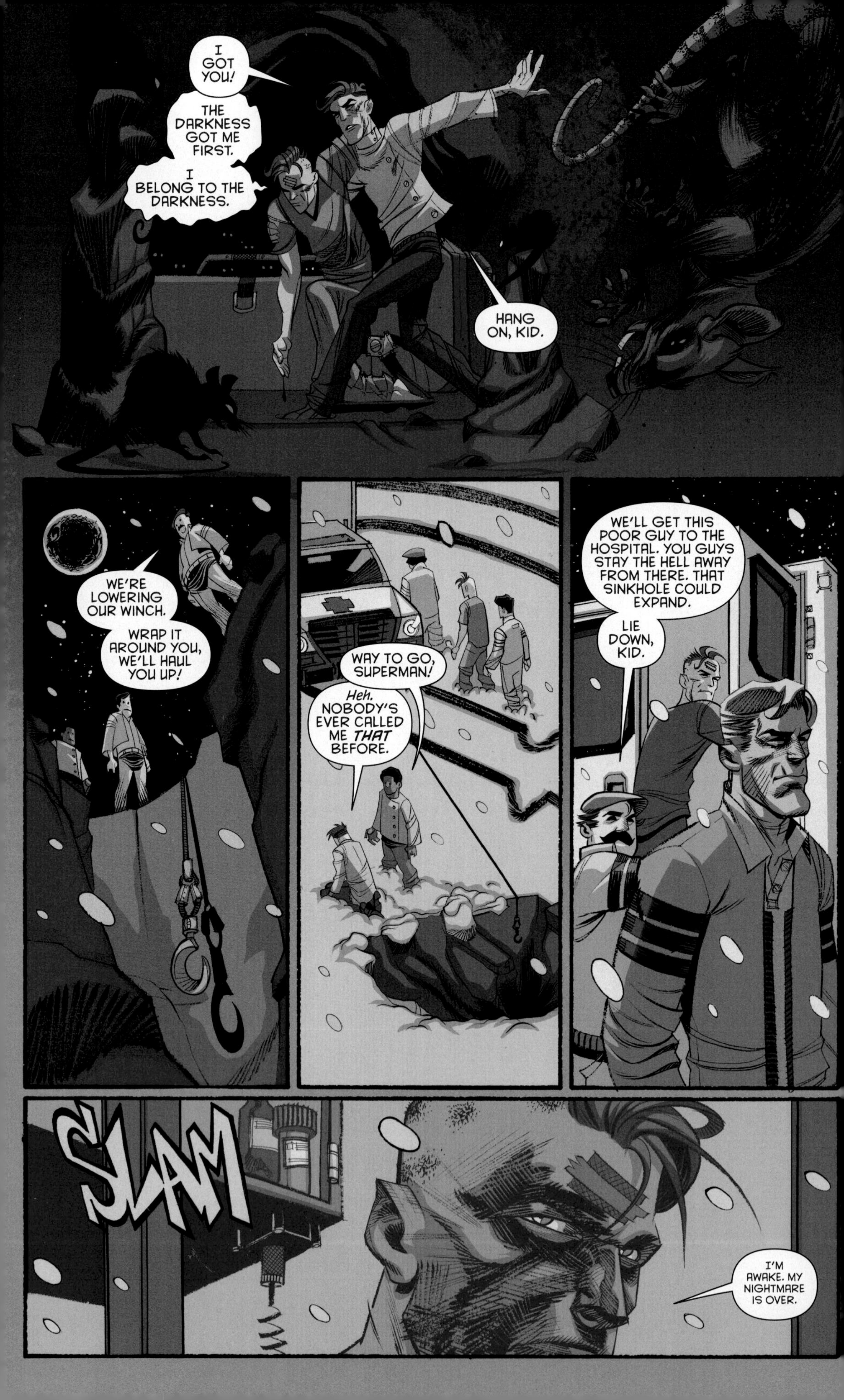
I GOT YOU!
THE DARKNESS GOT ME FIRST.
I BELONG TO THE DARKNESS.
HANG ON, KID.
WE'RE LOWERING OUR WINCH.
WRAP IT AROUND YOU, WE'LL HAUL YOU UP!
WAY TO GO, SUPERMAN!
Heh. NOBODY'S EVER CALLED ME THAT BEFORE.
WE'LL GET THIS POOR GUY TO THE HOSPITAL. YOU GUYS STAY THE HELL AWAY FROM THERE. THAT SINKHOLE COULD EXPAND.
LIE DOWN, KID.
SLAM
I'M AWAKE. MY NIGHTMARE IS OVER.

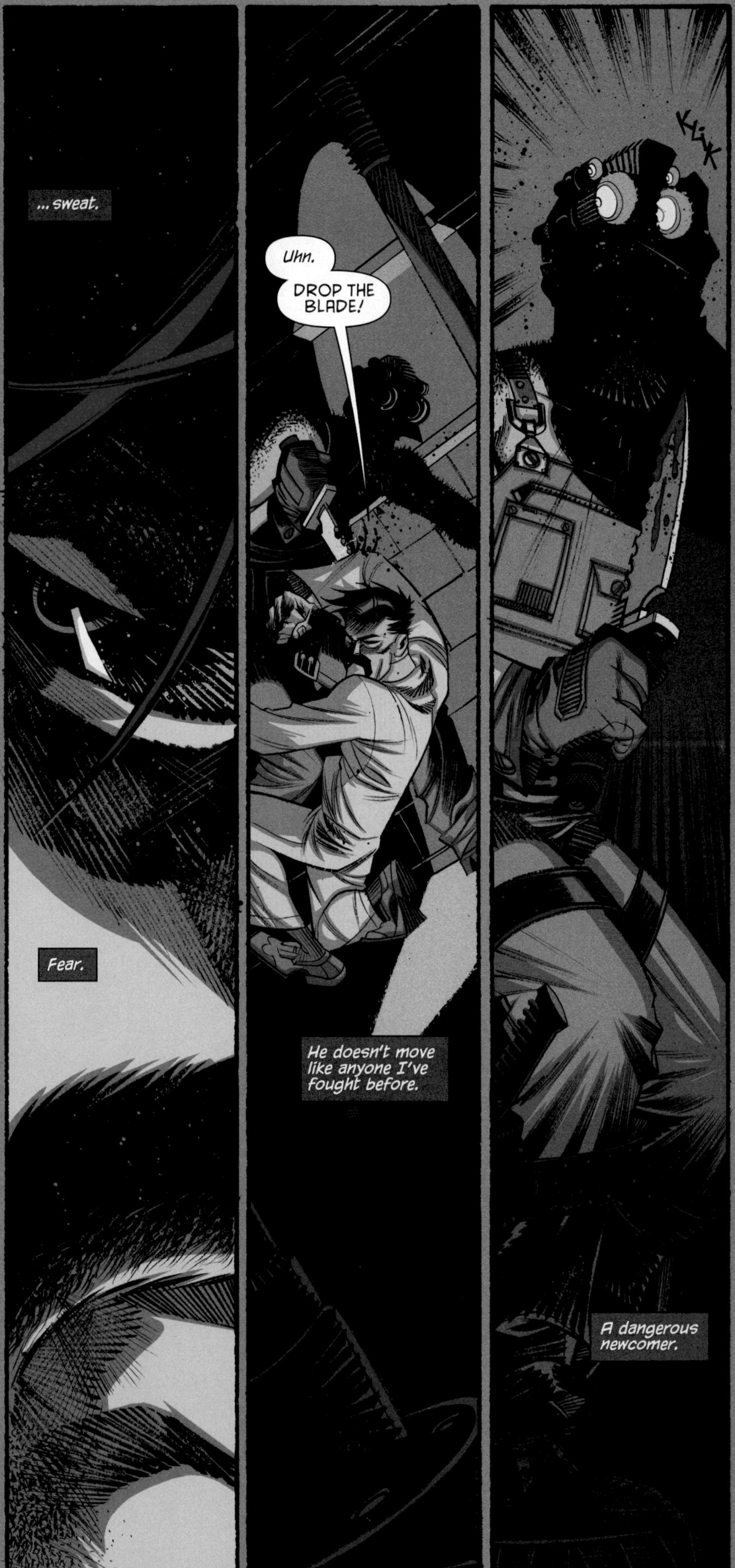
...sweat.
Fear.
Uhn.
DROP THE BLADE!
He doesn't move like anyone I've fought before.
KLIK
A dangerous newcomer.

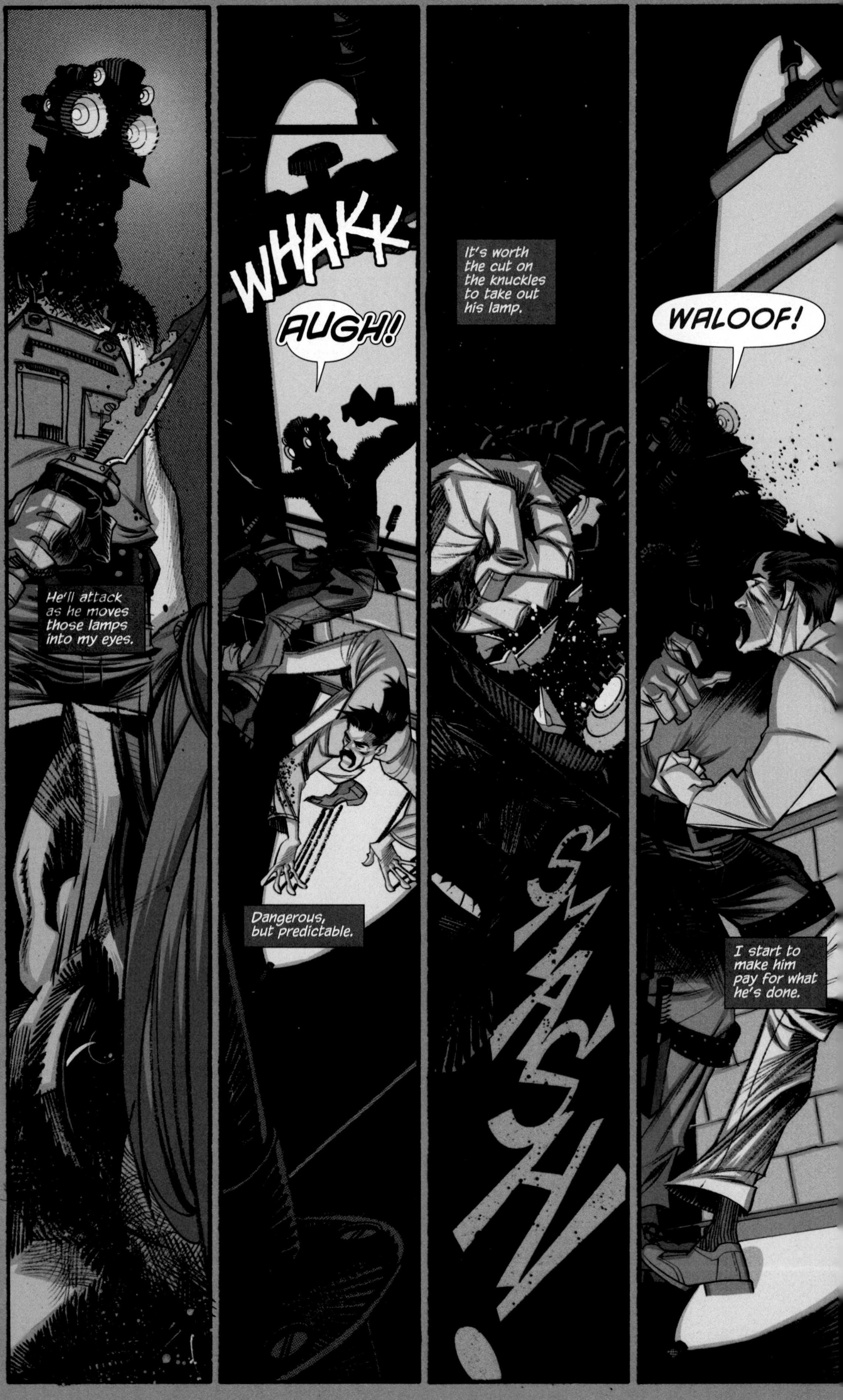
He'll attack as he moves those lamps into my eyes.
WHAKK
AUGH!
Dangerous, but predictable.
It's worth the cut on the knuckles to take out his lamp.
SMASH!
WALOOF!
I start to make him pay for what he's done.

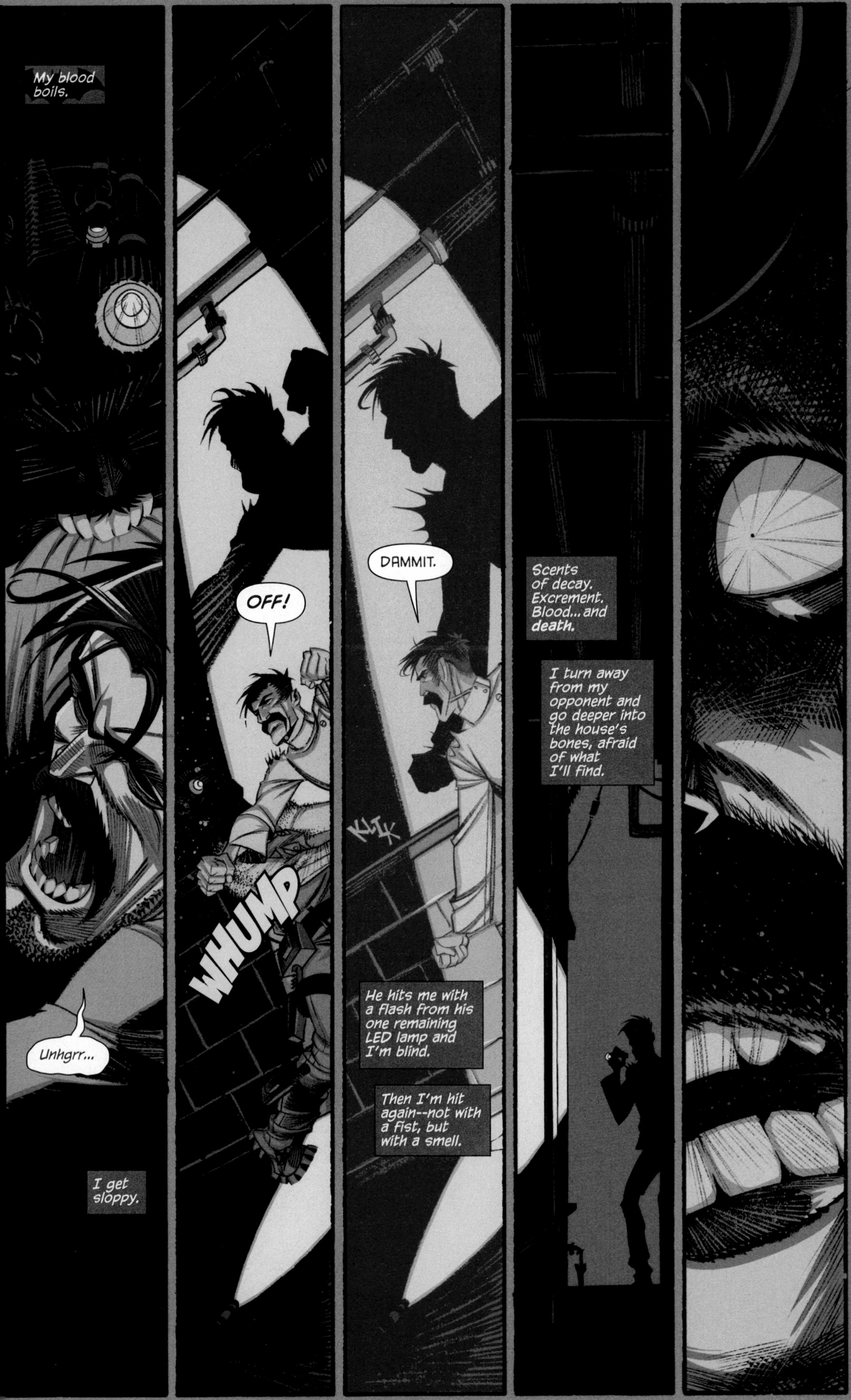

My blood boils.
Unhgrr...
I get sloppy.
OFF!
WHUMP
DAMMIT.
KLIK
He hits me with a flash from his one remaining LED lamp and I'm blind.
Then I'm hit again--not with a fist, but with a smell.
Scents of decay. Excrement. Blood...and death.
I turn away from my opponent and go deeper into the house's bones, afraid of what I'll find.

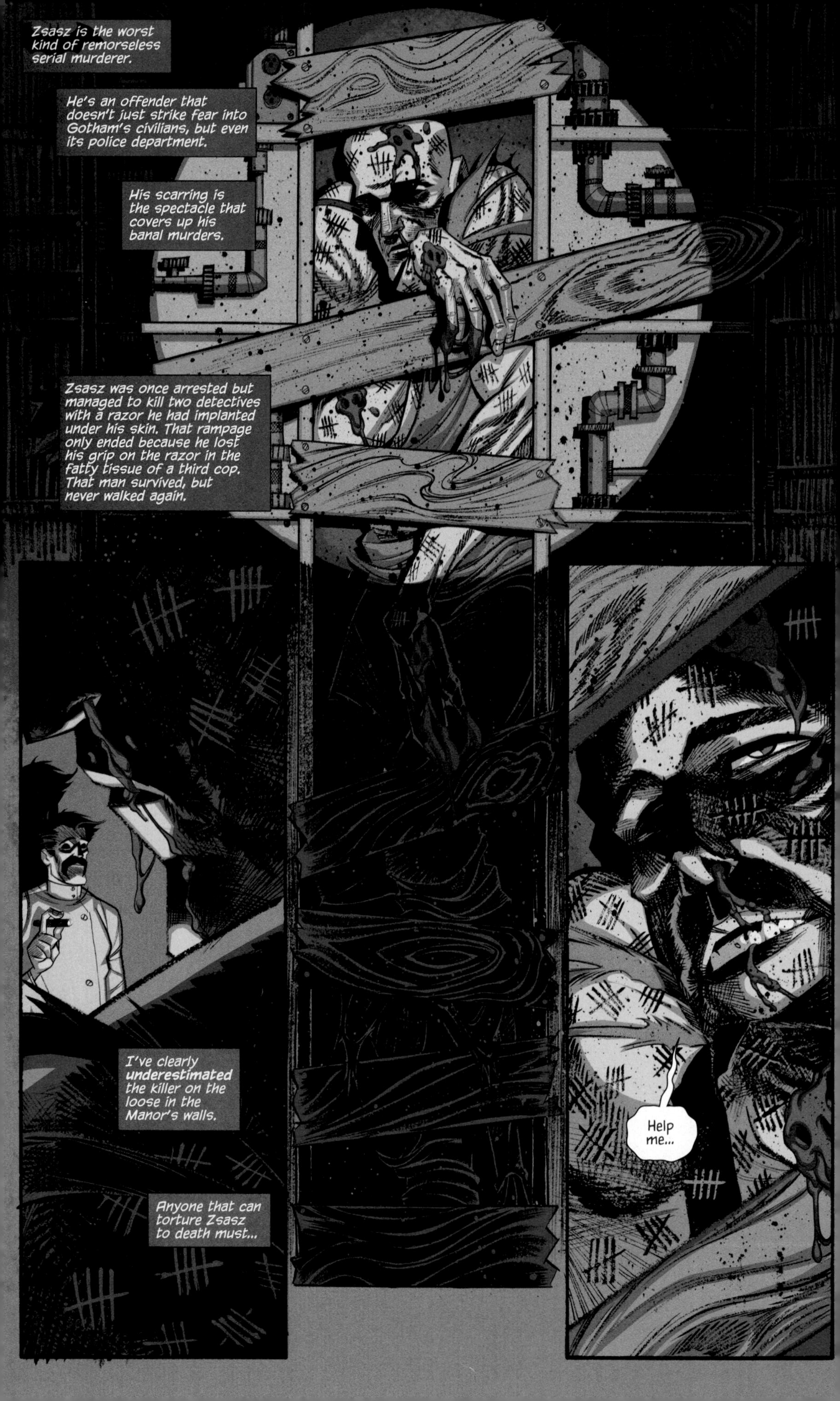
Zsasz is the worst kind of remorseless serial murderer.
He's an offender that doesn't just strike fear into Gotham's civilians, but even its police department.
His scarring is the spectacle that covers up his banal murders.
Zsasz was once arrested but managed to kill two detectives with a razor he had implanted under his skin. That rampage only ended because he lost his grip on the razor in the fatty tissue of a third cop. That man survived, but never walked again.
I've clearly **underestimated** the killer on the loose in the Manor's walls.
Help me...
Anyone that can torture Zsasz to death must...

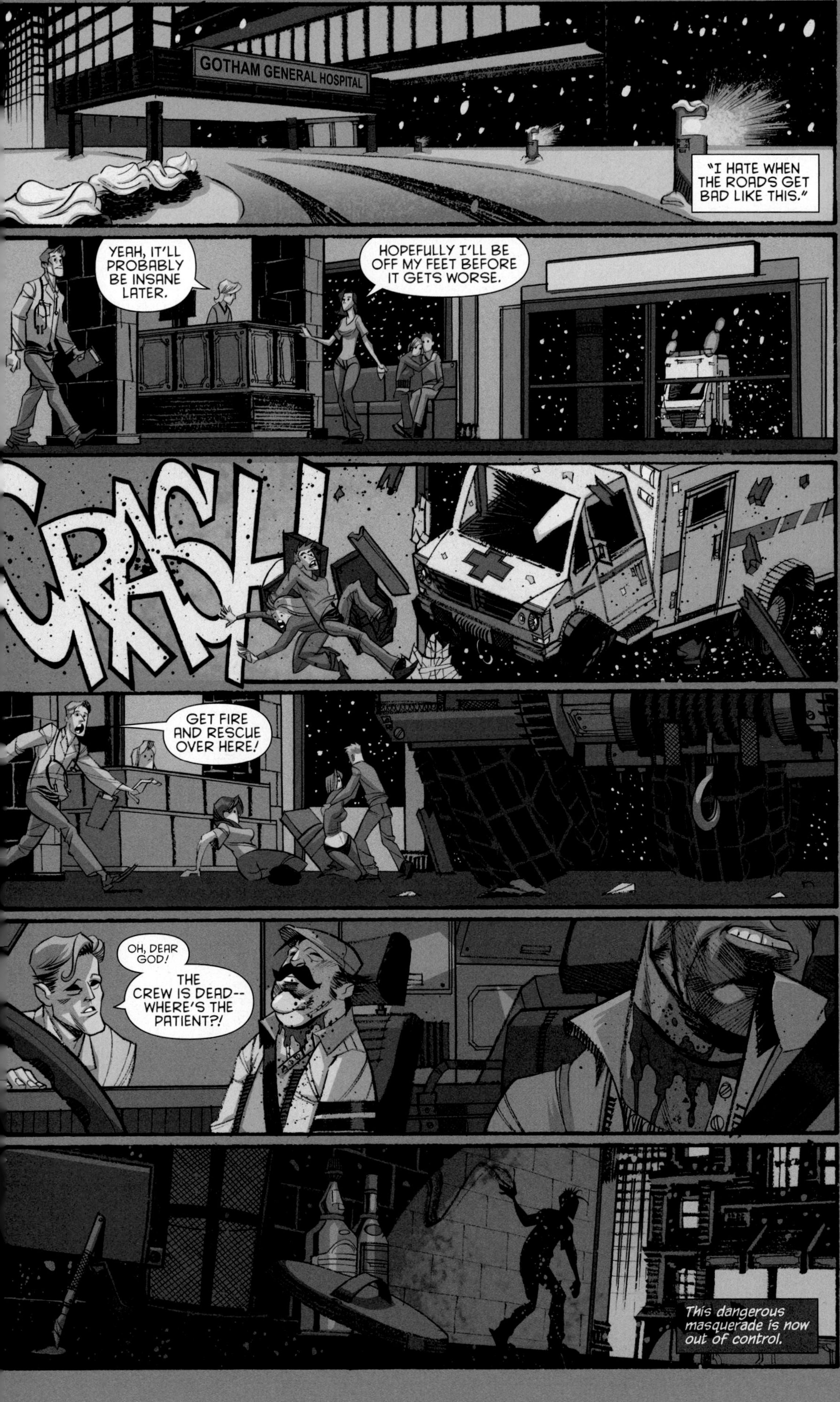
GOTHAM GENERAL HOSPITAL
"I HATE WHEN THE ROADS GET BAD LIKE THIS."
YEAH, IT'LL PROBABLY BE INSANE LATER.
HOPEFULLY I'LL BE OFF MY FEET BEFORE IT GETS WORSE.
CRASH!
GET FIRE AND RESCUE OVER HERE!
OH, DEAR GOD!
THE CREW IS DEAD-- WHERE'S THE PATIENT?!
This dangerous masquerade is now out of control.

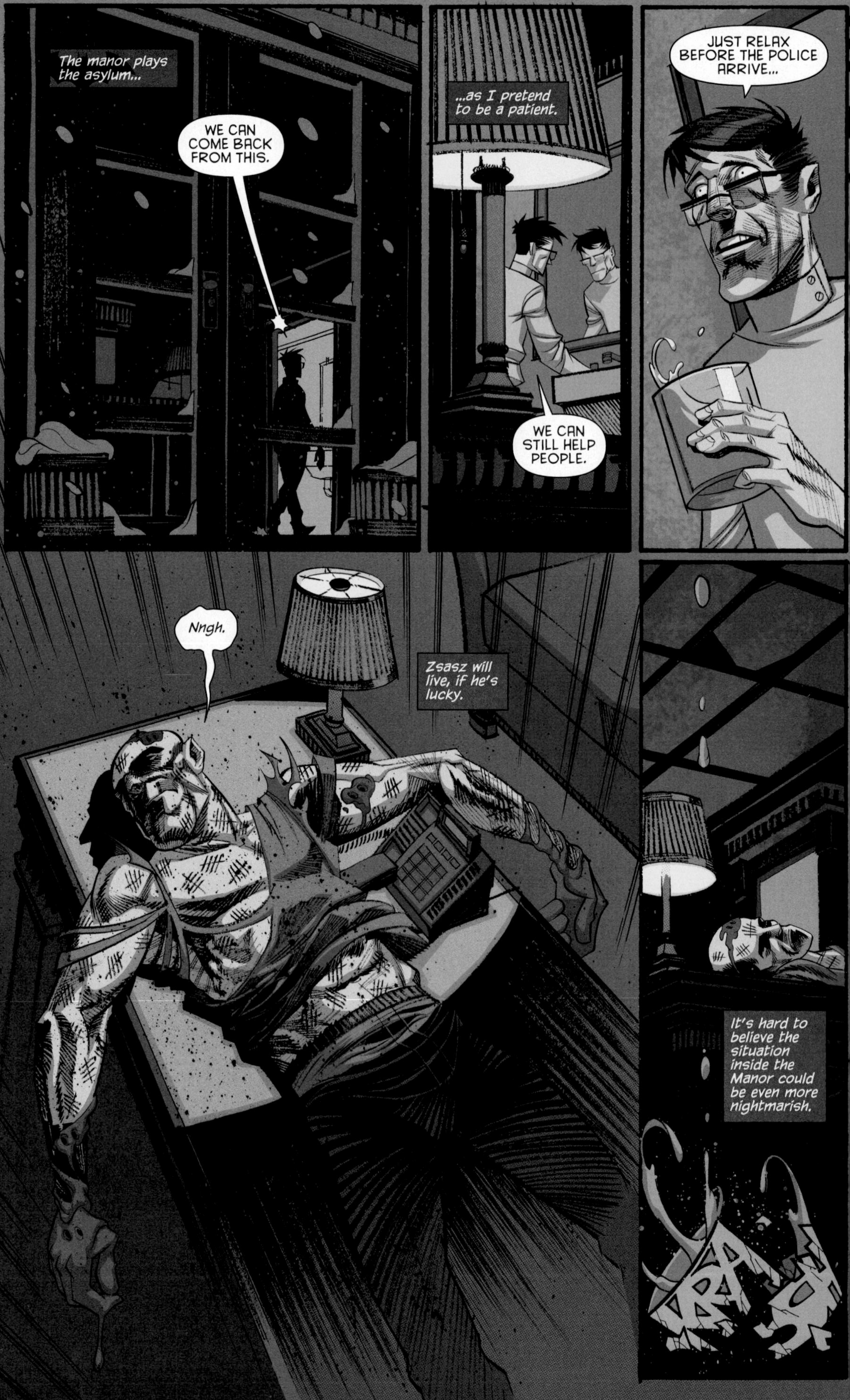
The manor plays the asylum...
WE CAN COME BACK FROM THIS.
...as I pretend to be a patient.
WE CAN STILL HELP PEOPLE.
JUST RELAX BEFORE THE POLICE ARRIVE...
Nngh.
Zsasz will live, if he's lucky.
It's hard to believe the situation inside the Manor could be even more nightmarish.
CRASH

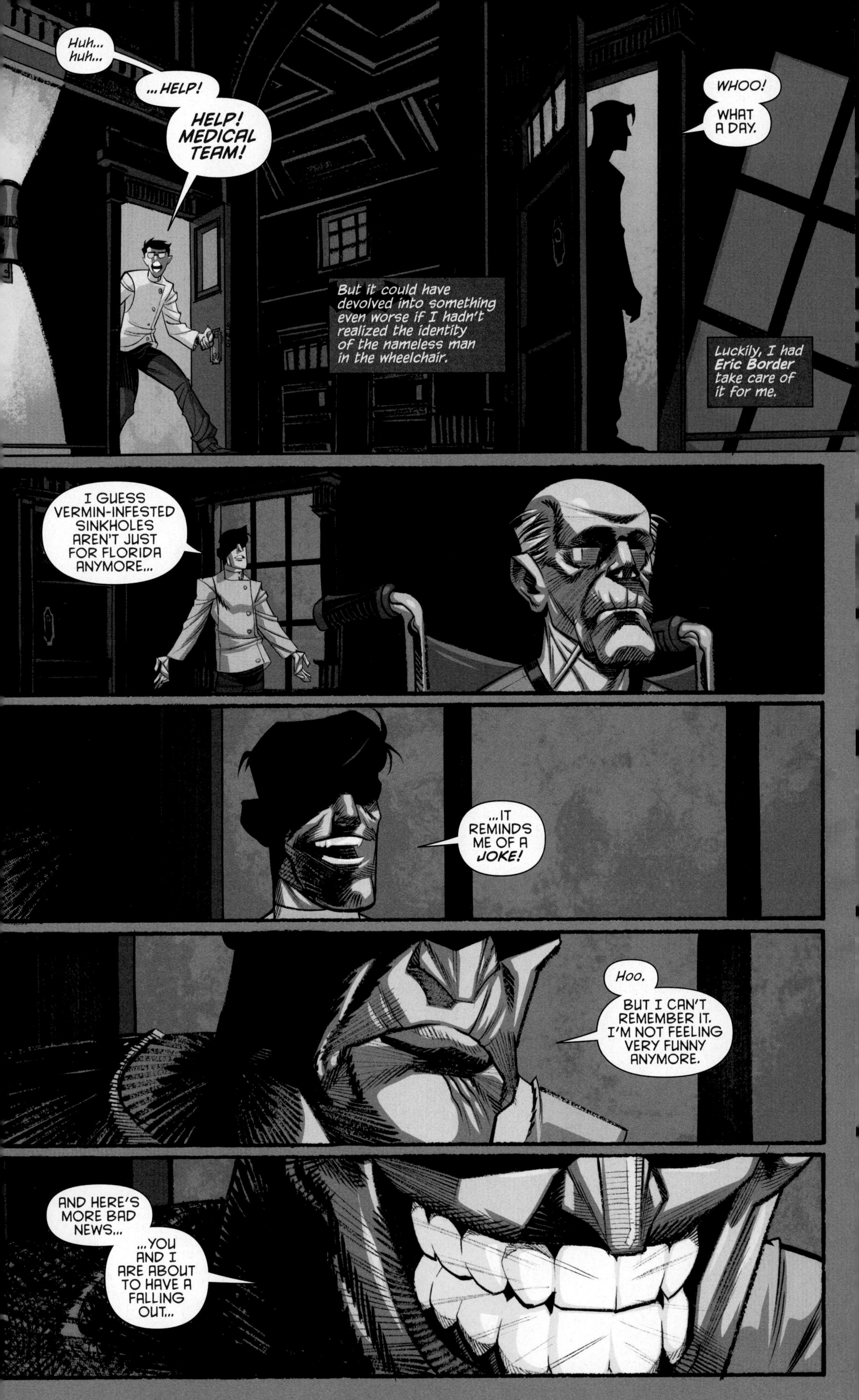

Huh... huh...
...HELP!
HELP! MEDICAL TEAM!
But it could have devolved into something even worse if I hadn't realized the identity of the nameless man in the wheelchair.
WHOO!
WHAT A DAY.
Luckily, I had Eric Border take care of it for me.
I GUESS VERMIN-INFESTED SINKHOLES AREN'T JUST FOR FLORIDA ANYMORE...
...IT REMINDS ME OF A JOKE!
Hoo.
BUT I CAN'T REMEMBER IT. I'M NOT FEELING VERY FUNNY ANYMORE.
AND HERE'S MORE BAD NEWS...
...YOU AND I ARE ABOUT TO HAVE A FALLING OUT...

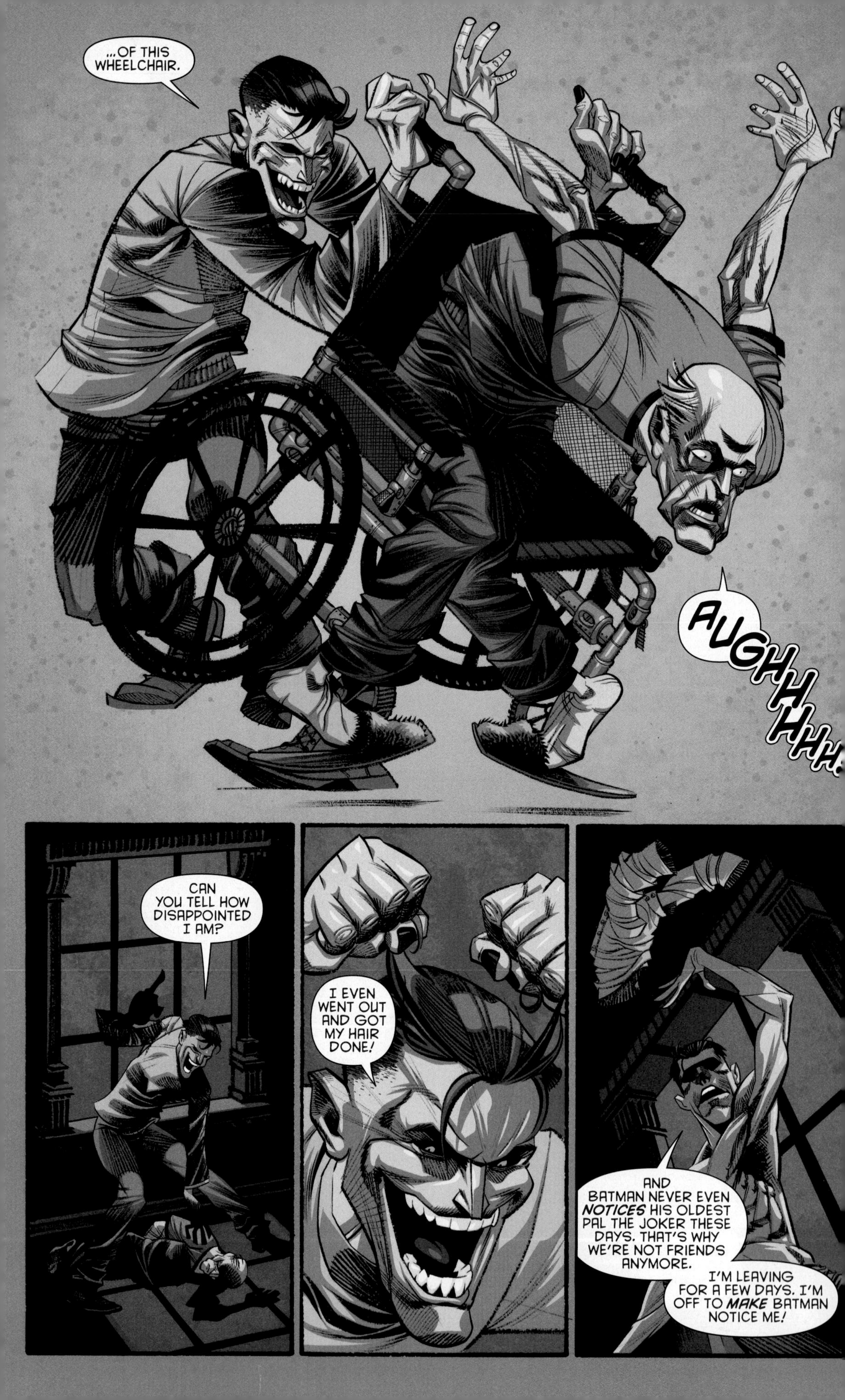
...OF THIS WHEELCHAIR.
AUGHHHHHH!
CAN YOU TELL HOW DISAPPOINTED I AM?
I EVEN WENT OUT AND GOT MY HAIR DONE!
AND BATMAN NEVER EVEN *NOTICES* HIS OLDEST PAL THE JOKER THESE DAYS. THAT'S WHY WE'RE NOT FRIENDS ANYMORE.
I'M LEAVING FOR A FEW DAYS. I'M OFF TO *MAKE* BATMAN NOTICE ME!

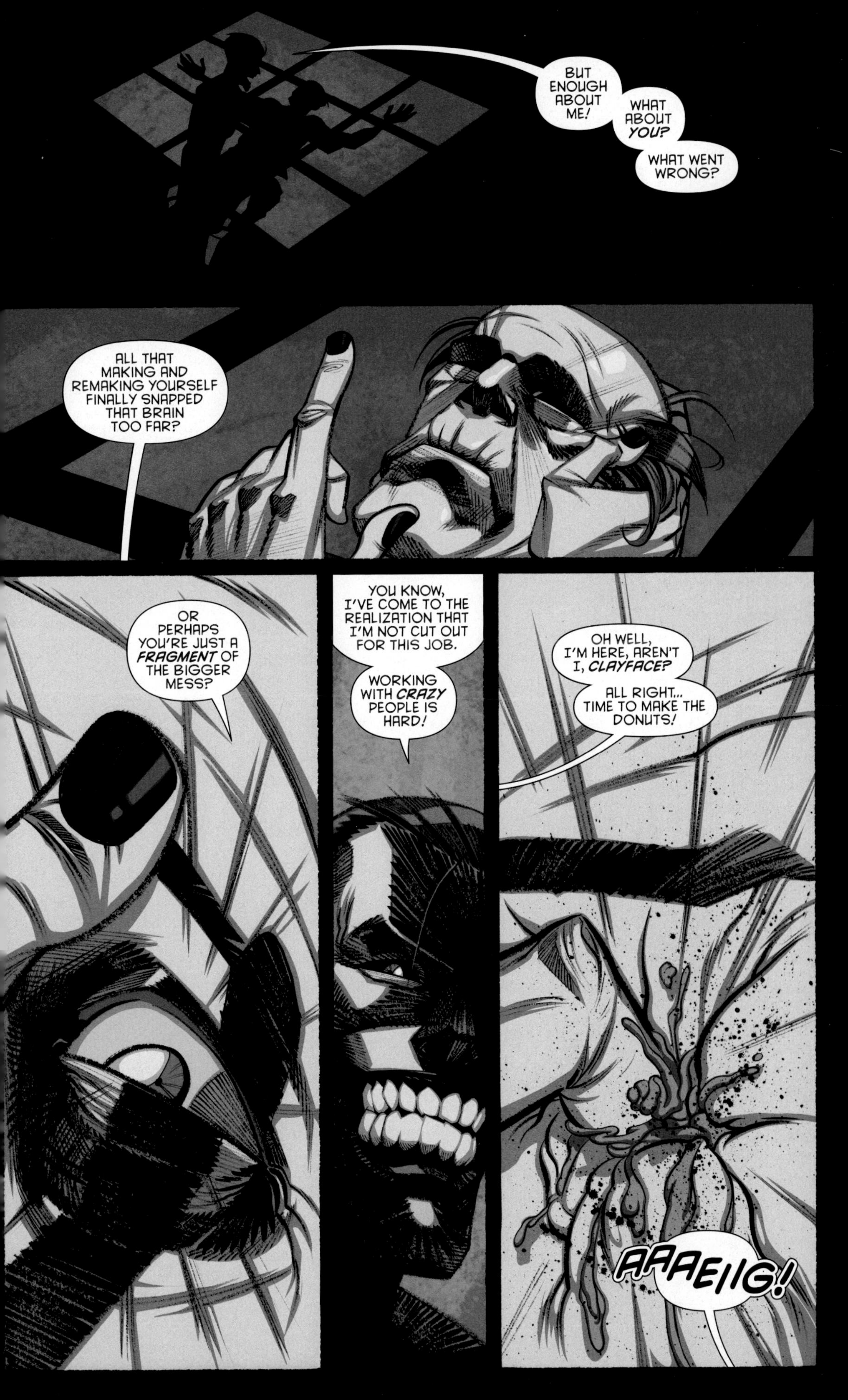
BUT ENOUGH ABOUT ME!
WHAT ABOUT *YOU?*
WHAT WENT WRONG?
ALL THAT MAKING AND REMAKING YOURSELF FINALLY SNAPPED THAT BRAIN TOO FAR?
OR PERHAPS YOU'RE JUST A *FRAGMENT* OF THE BIGGER MESS?
YOU KNOW, I'VE COME TO THE REALIZATION THAT I'M NOT CUT OUT FOR THIS JOB.
WORKING WITH *CRAZY* PEOPLE IS HARD!
OH WELL, I'M HERE, AREN'T I, *CLAYFACE?*
ALL RIGHT... TIME TO MAKE THE DONUTS!
AAAEIIG!

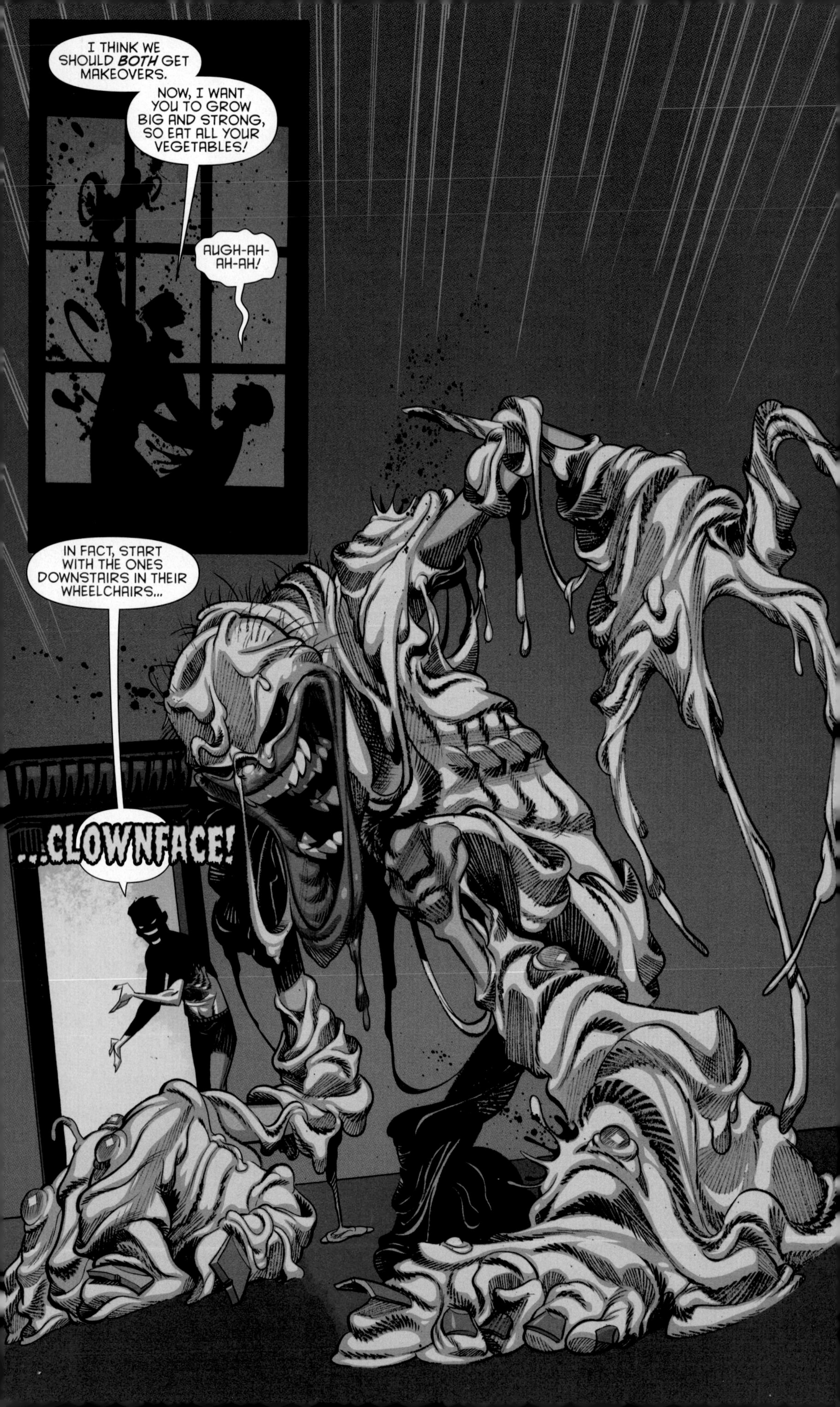
I THINK WE SHOULD BOTH GET MAKEOVERS.
NOW, I WANT YOU TO GROW BIG AND STRONG, SO EAT ALL YOUR VEGETABLES!
AUGH-AH-AH-AH!
IN FACT, START WITH THE ONES DOWNSTAIRS IN THEIR WHEELCHAIRS...
...CLOWNFACE!

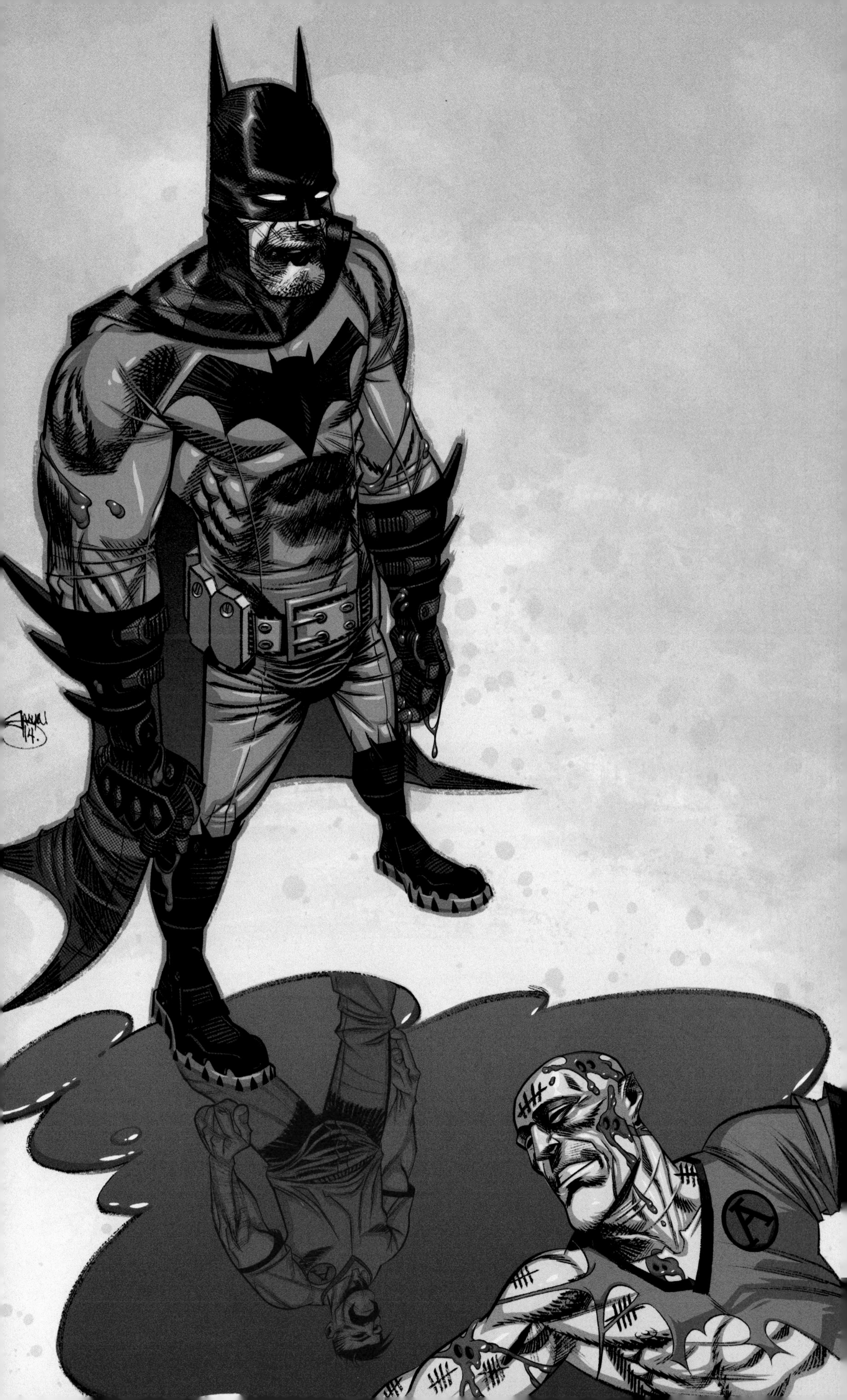

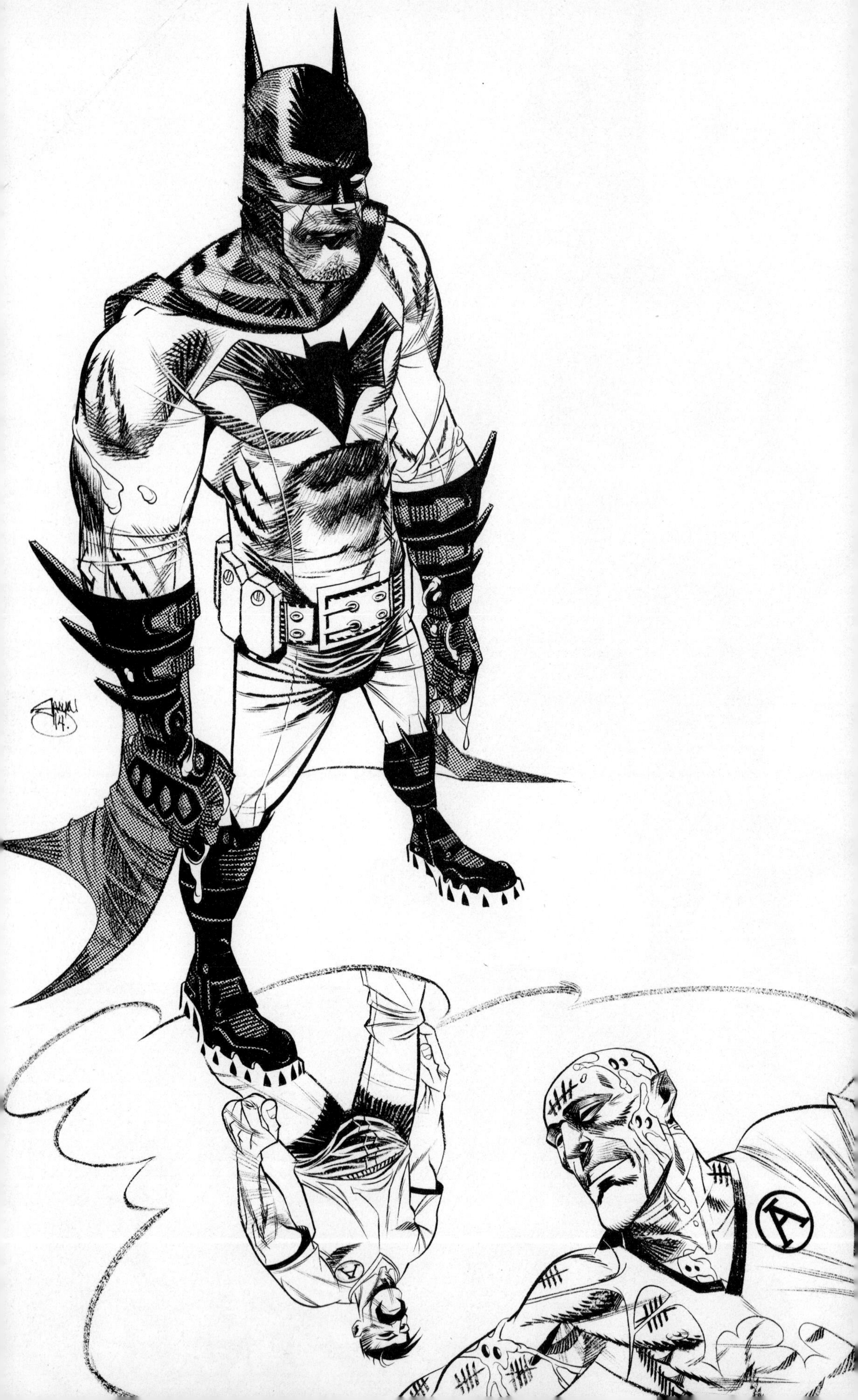

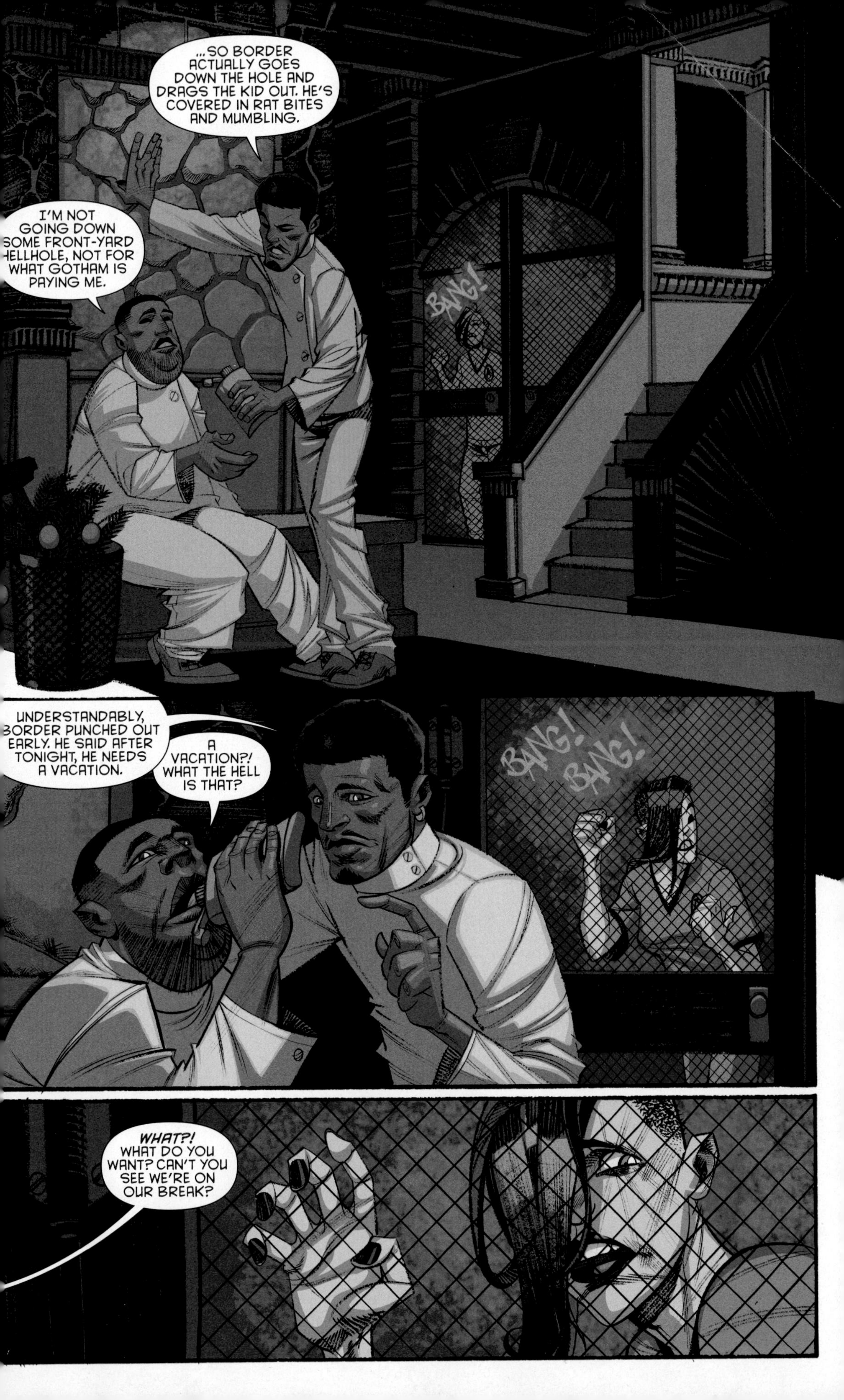
...SO BORDER ACTUALLY GOES DOWN THE HOLE AND DRAGS THE KID OUT. HE'S COVERED IN RAT BITES AND MUMBLING.
I'M NOT GOING DOWN SOME FRONT-YARD HELLHOLE, NOT FOR WHAT GOTHAM IS PAYING ME.
BANG!
UNDERSTANDABLY, BORDER PUNCHED OUT EARLY. HE SAID AFTER TONIGHT, HE NEEDS A VACATION.
A VACATION?! WHAT THE HELL IS THAT?
BANG! BANG!
WHAT?! WHAT DO YOU WANT? CAN'T YOU SEE WE'RE ON OUR BREAK?

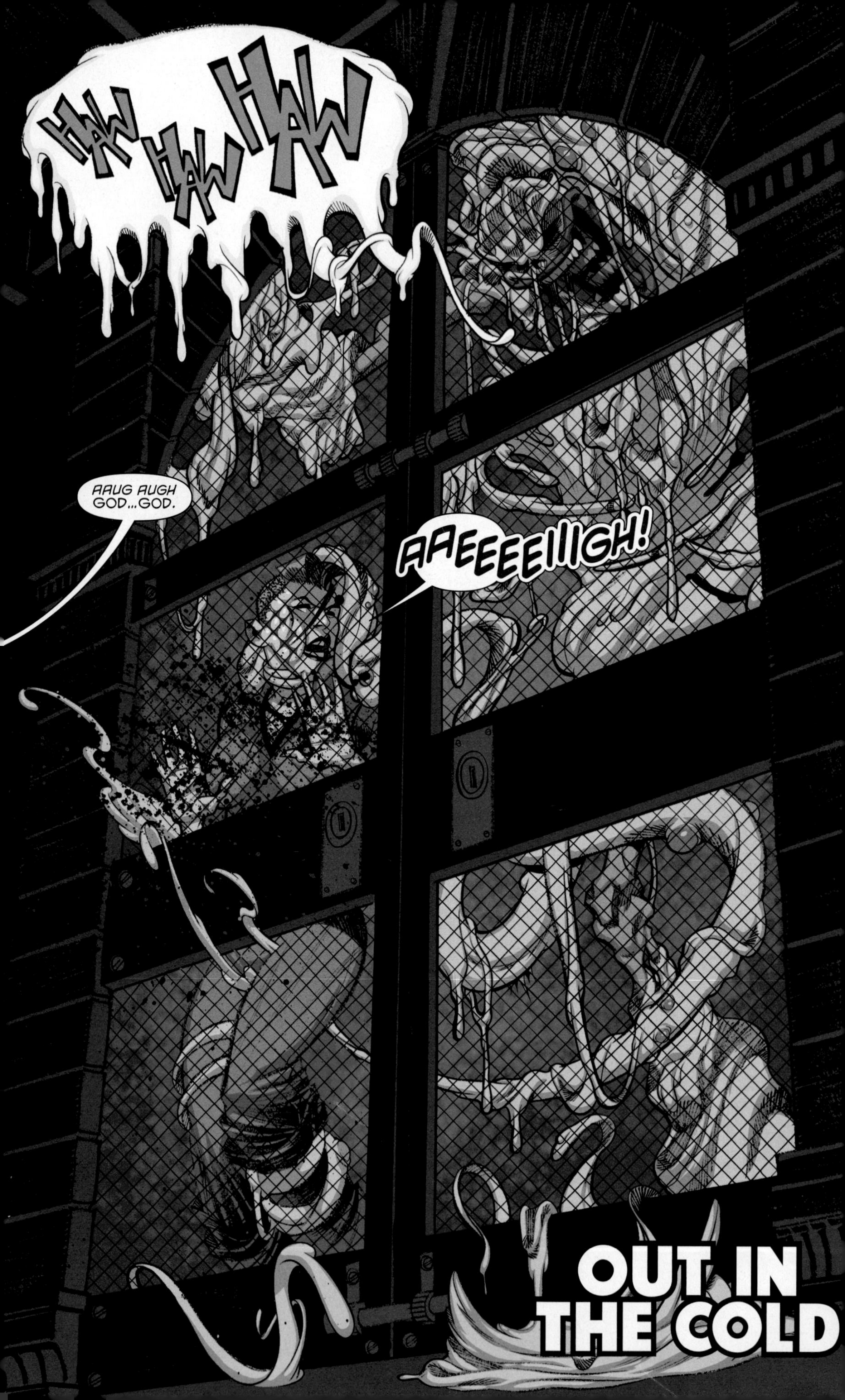
HAW HAW HAW
AAUG AUGH GOD...GOD.
AAEEEEEIIIIGH!
OUT IN THE COLD

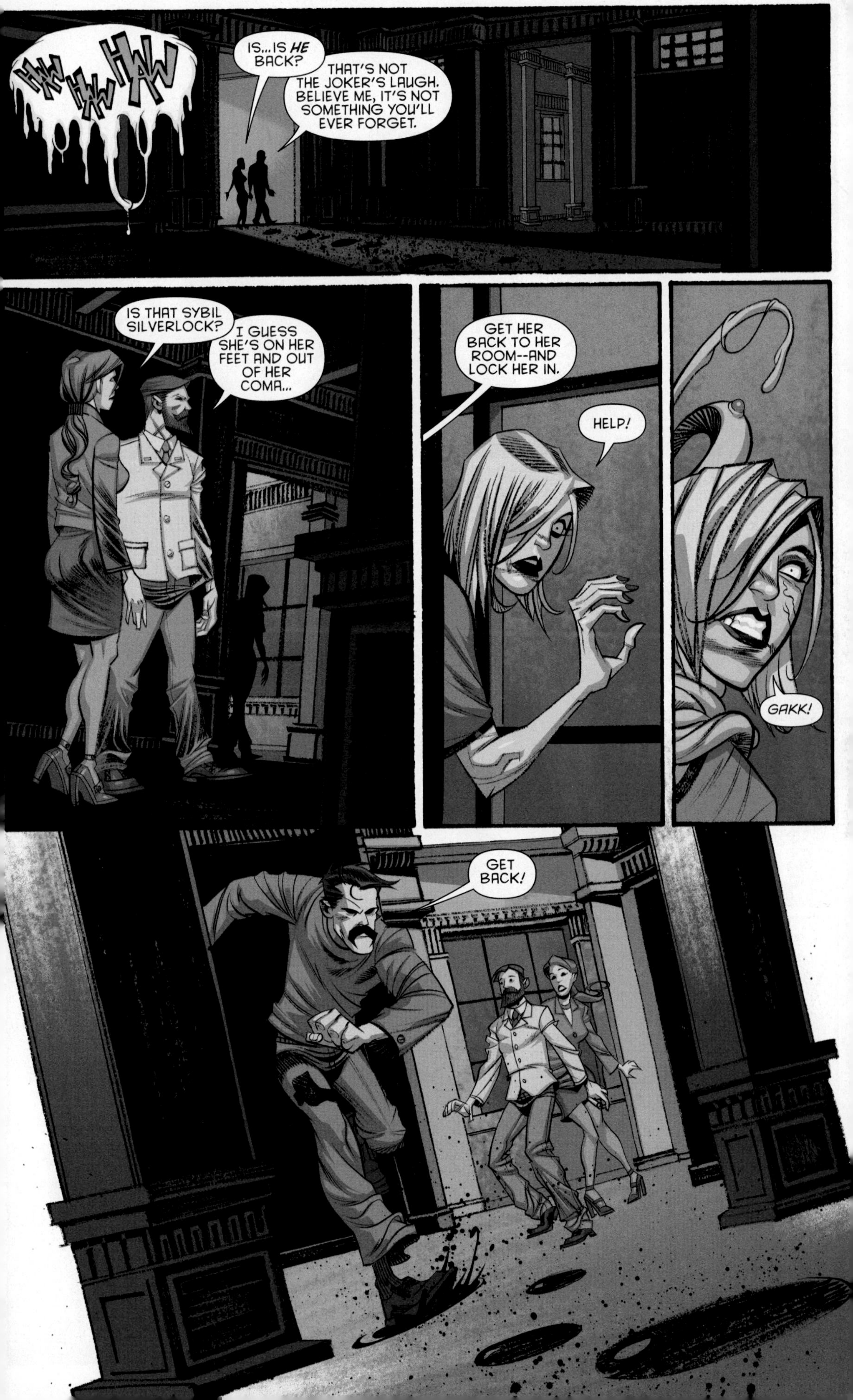
HAW HAW HAW
IS...IS HE BACK?
THAT'S NOT THE JOKER'S LAUGH. BELIEVE ME, IT'S NOT SOMETHING YOU'LL EVER FORGET.
IS THAT SYBIL SILVERLOCK?
I GUESS SHE'S ON HER FEET AND OUT OF HER COMA...
GET HER BACK TO HER ROOM--AND LOCK HER IN.
HELP!
GAKK!
GET BACK!

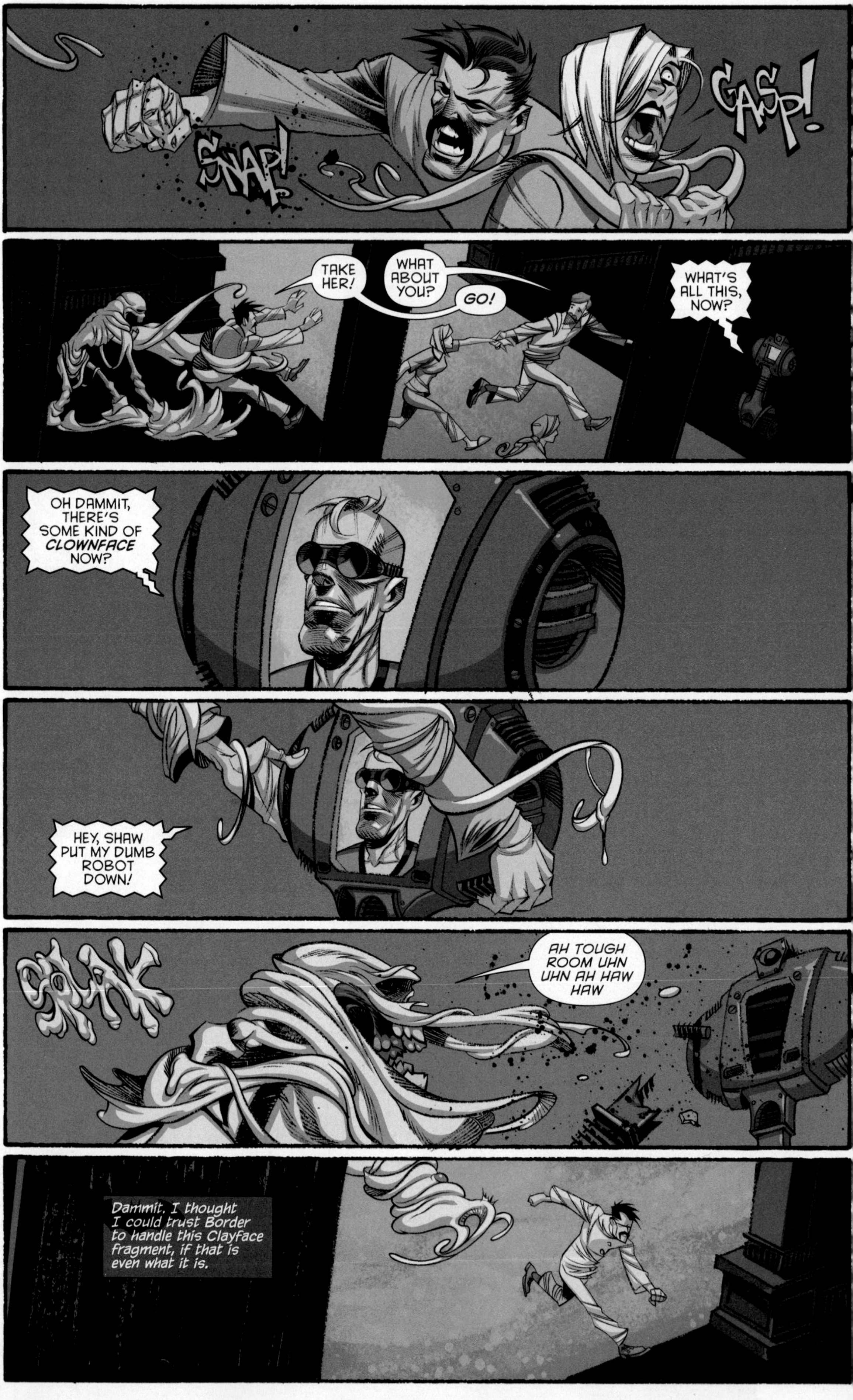
SNAP!
GASP!
TAKE HER!
WHAT ABOUT YOU?
GO!
WHAT'S ALL THIS, NOW?
OH DAMMIT, THERE'S SOME KIND OF CLOWNFACE NOW?
HEY, SHAW PUT MY DUMB ROBOT DOWN!
SPLAK
AH TOUGH ROOM UHN UHN AH HAW HAW
Dammit. I thought I could trust Border to handle this Clayface fragment, if that is even what it is.

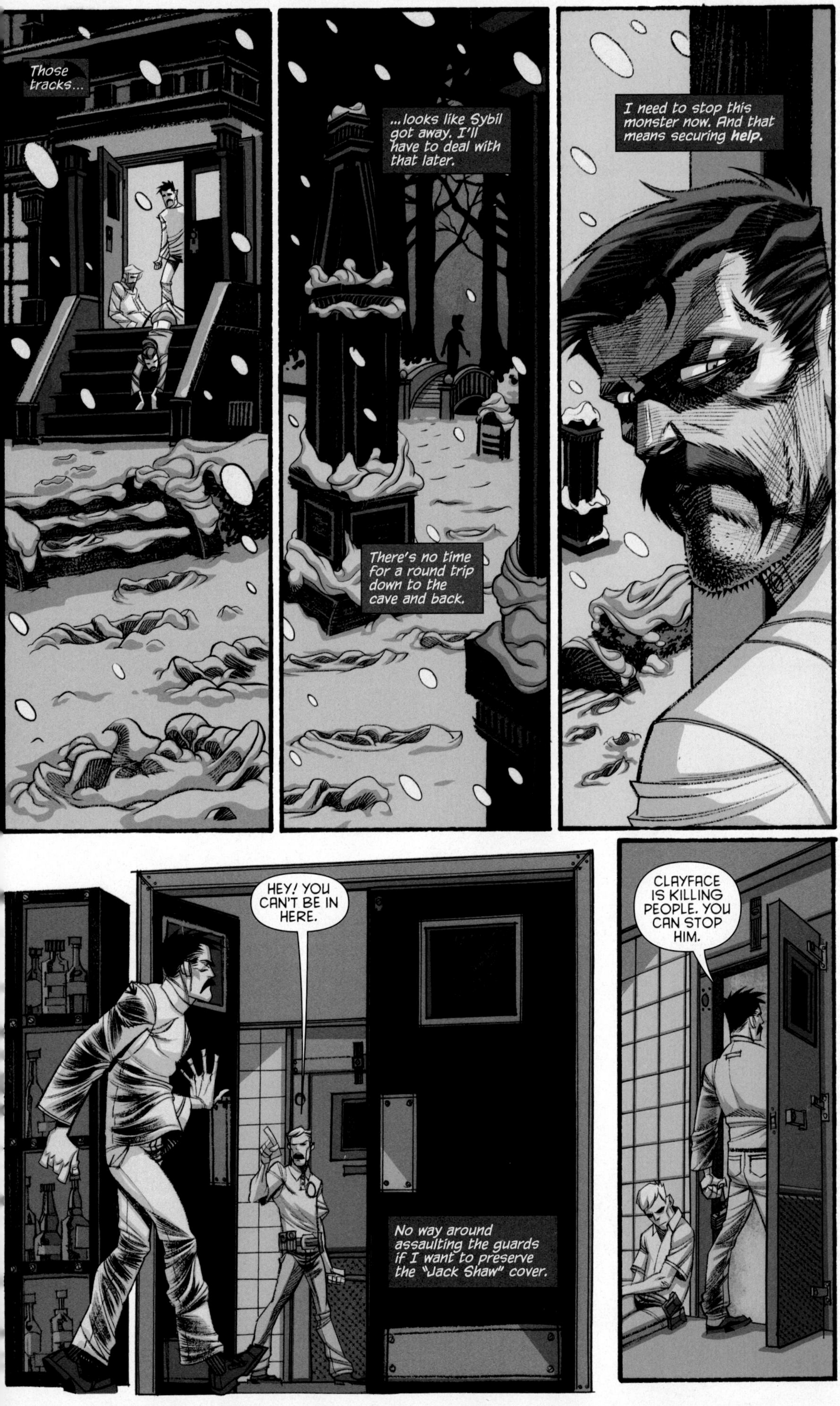
Those tracks...
...looks like Sybil got away. I'll have to deal with that later.
There's no time for a round trip down to the cave and back.
I need to stop this monster now. And that means securing **help.**
HEY! YOU CAN'T BE IN HERE.
No way around assaulting the guards if I want to preserve the "Jack Shaw" cover.
CLAYFACE IS KILLING PEOPLE. YOU CAN STOP HIM.

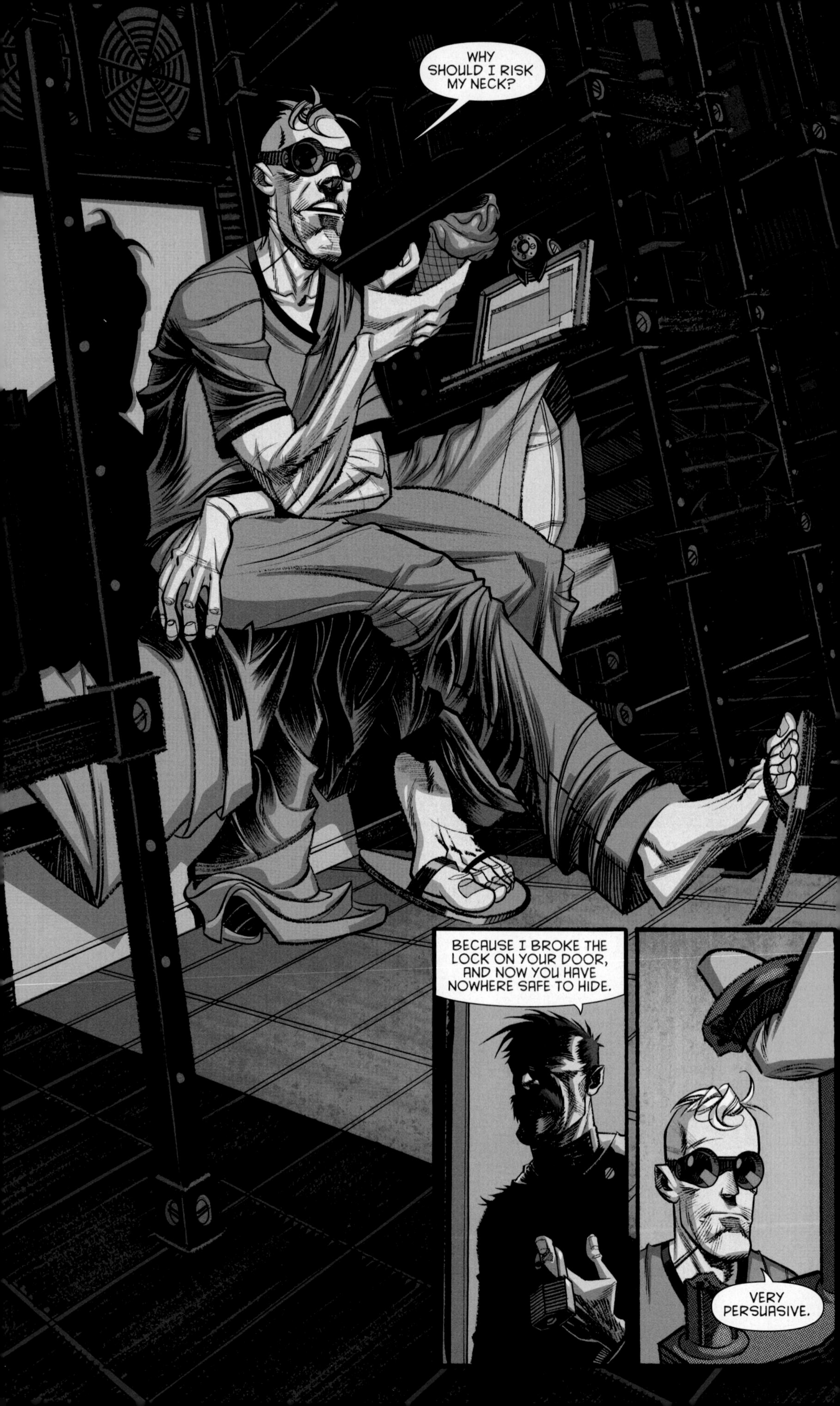
WHY SHOULD I RISK MY NECK?
BECAUSE I BROKE THE LOCK ON YOUR DOOR, AND NOW YOU HAVE NOWHERE SAFE TO HIDE.
VERY PERSUASIVE.

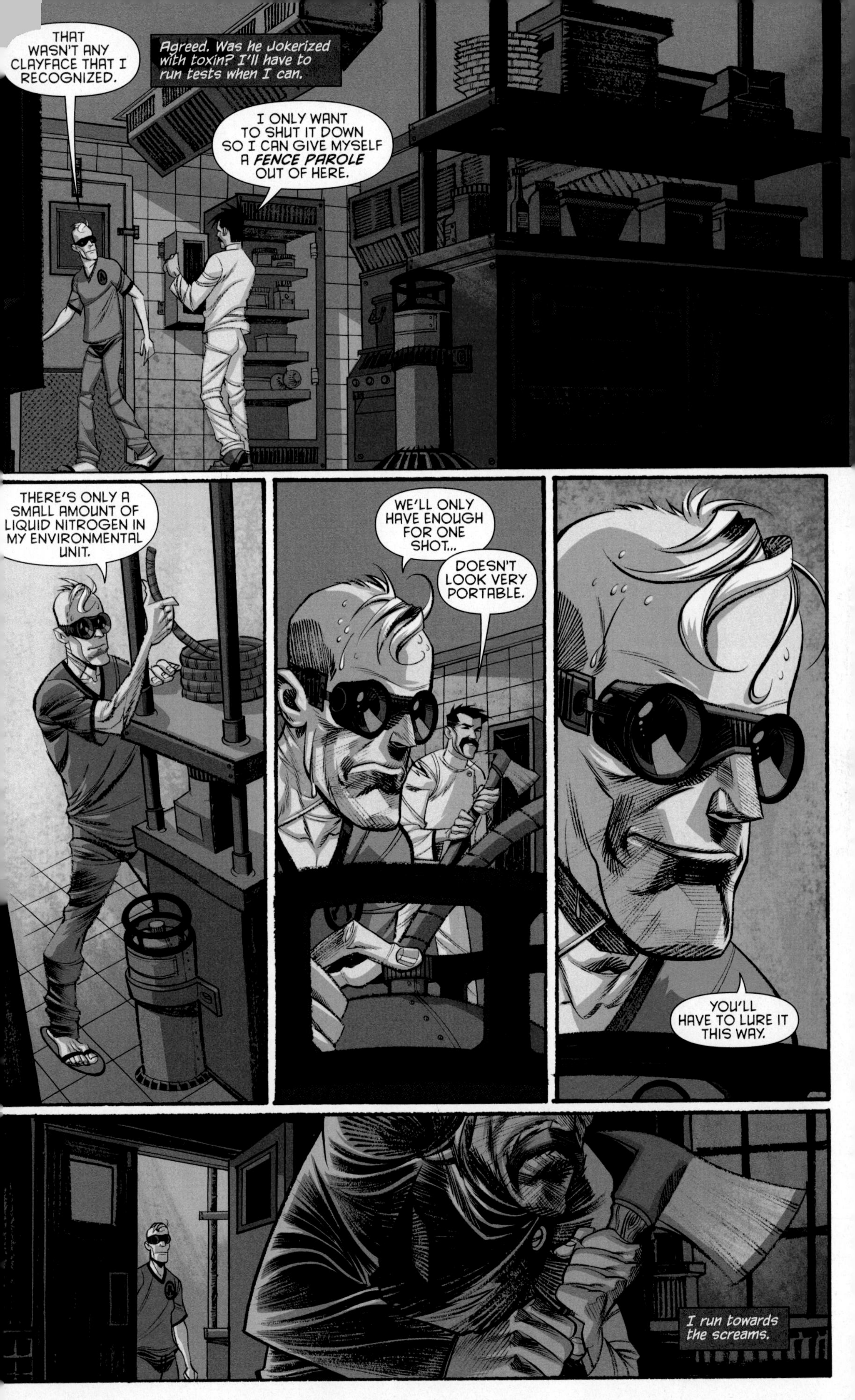
THAT WASN'T ANY CLAYFACE THAT I RECOGNIZED.
Agreed. Was he Jokerized with toxin? I'll have to run tests when I can.
I ONLY WANT TO SHUT IT DOWN SO I CAN GIVE MYSELF A FENCE PAROLE OUT OF HERE.
THERE'S ONLY A SMALL AMOUNT OF LIQUID NITROGEN IN MY ENVIRONMENTAL UNIT.
WE'LL ONLY HAVE ENOUGH FOR ONE SHOT...
DOESN'T LOOK VERY PORTABLE.
YOU'LL HAVE TO LURE IT THIS WAY.
I run towards the screams.

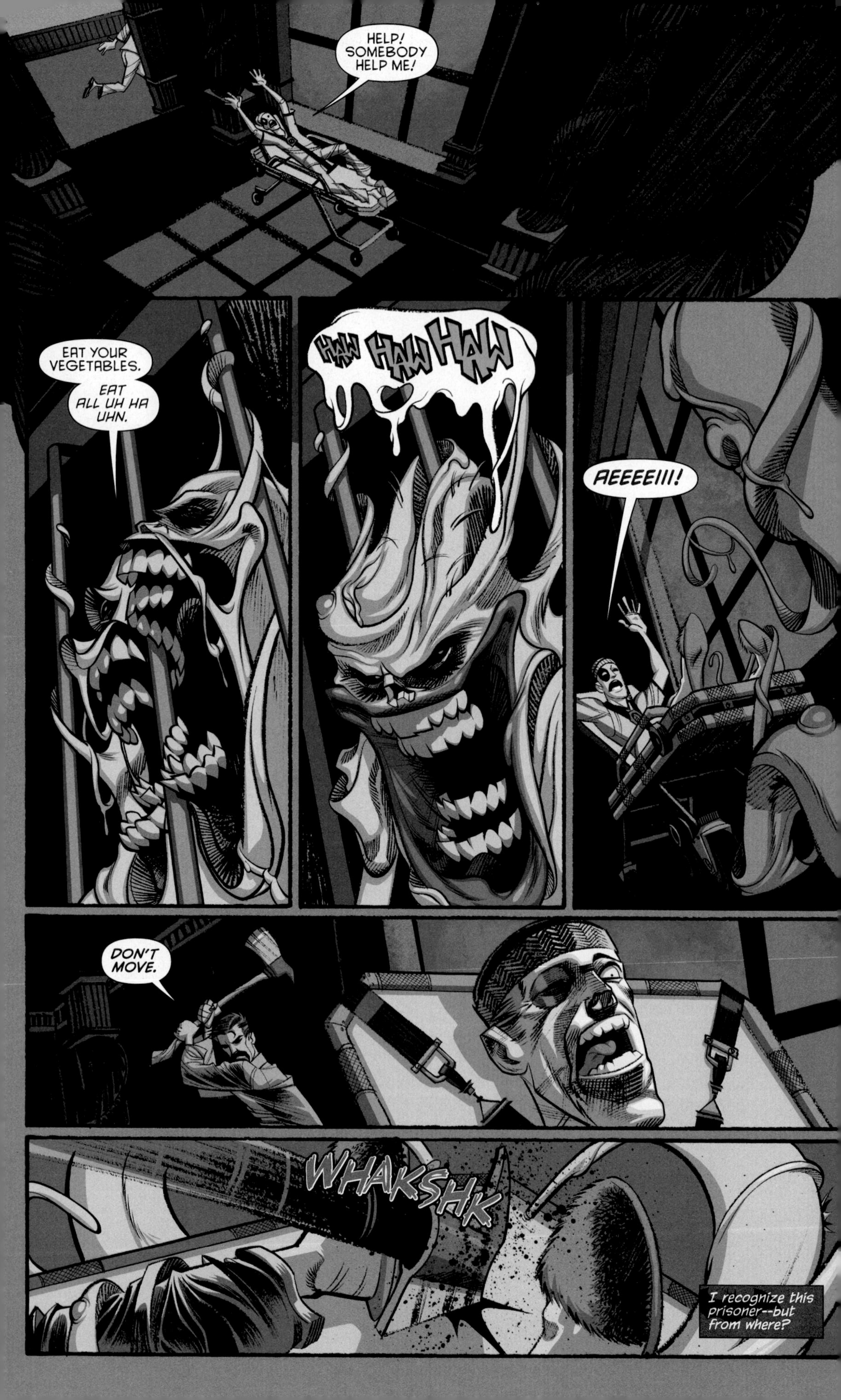

HELP! SOMEBODY HELP ME!
EAT YOUR VEGETABLES.
EAT ALL UH HA UHN.
HAW HAW HAW
AEEEEIII!
DON'T MOVE.
WHAKSHK
I recognize this prisoner--but from where?

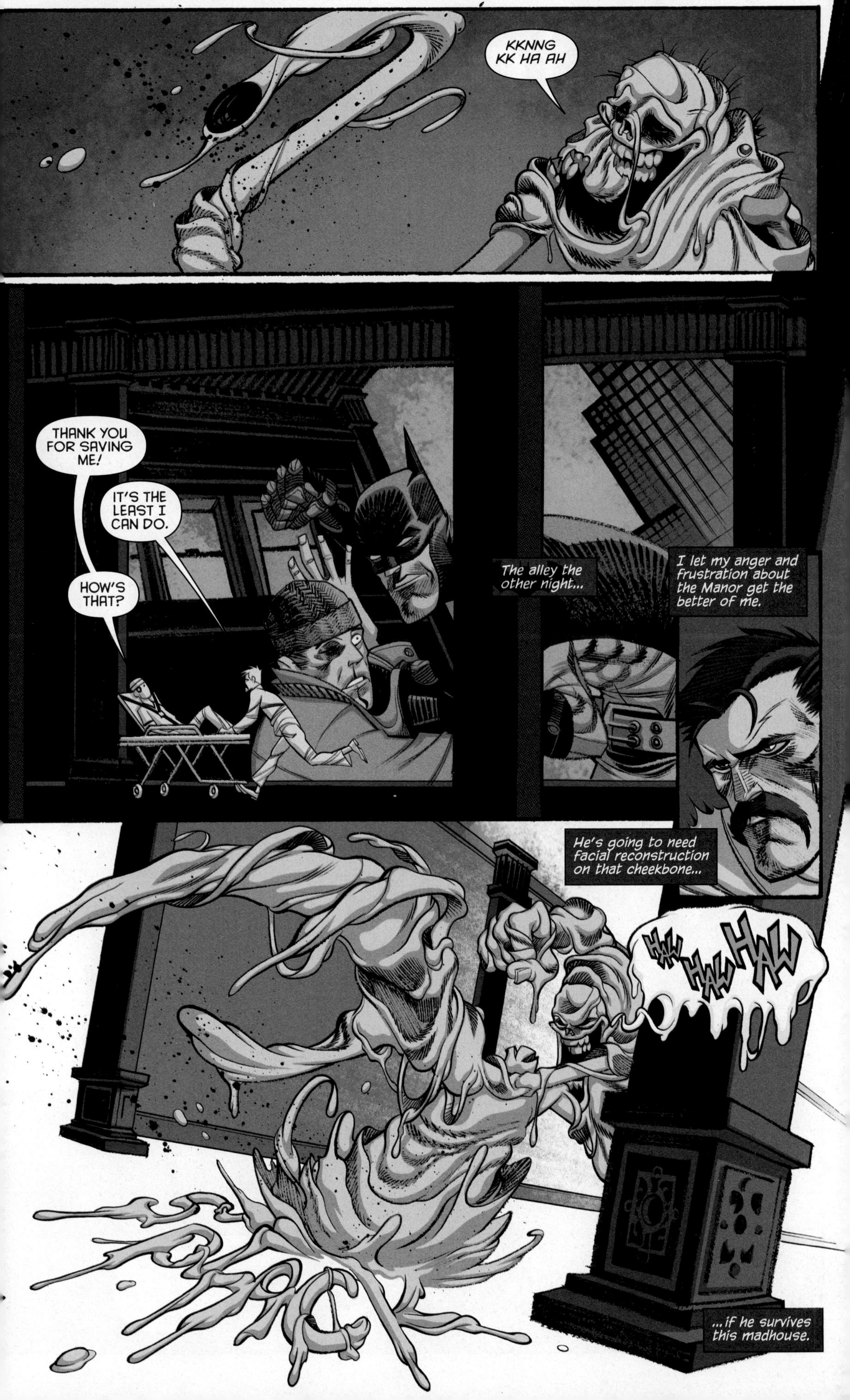
KKNNG KK HA AH
THANK YOU FOR SAVING ME!
IT'S THE LEAST I CAN DO.
HOW'S THAT?
The alley the other night...
I let my anger and frustration about the Manor get the better of me.
He's going to need facial reconstruction on that cheekbone...
HAW HAW HAW
...if he survives this madhouse.

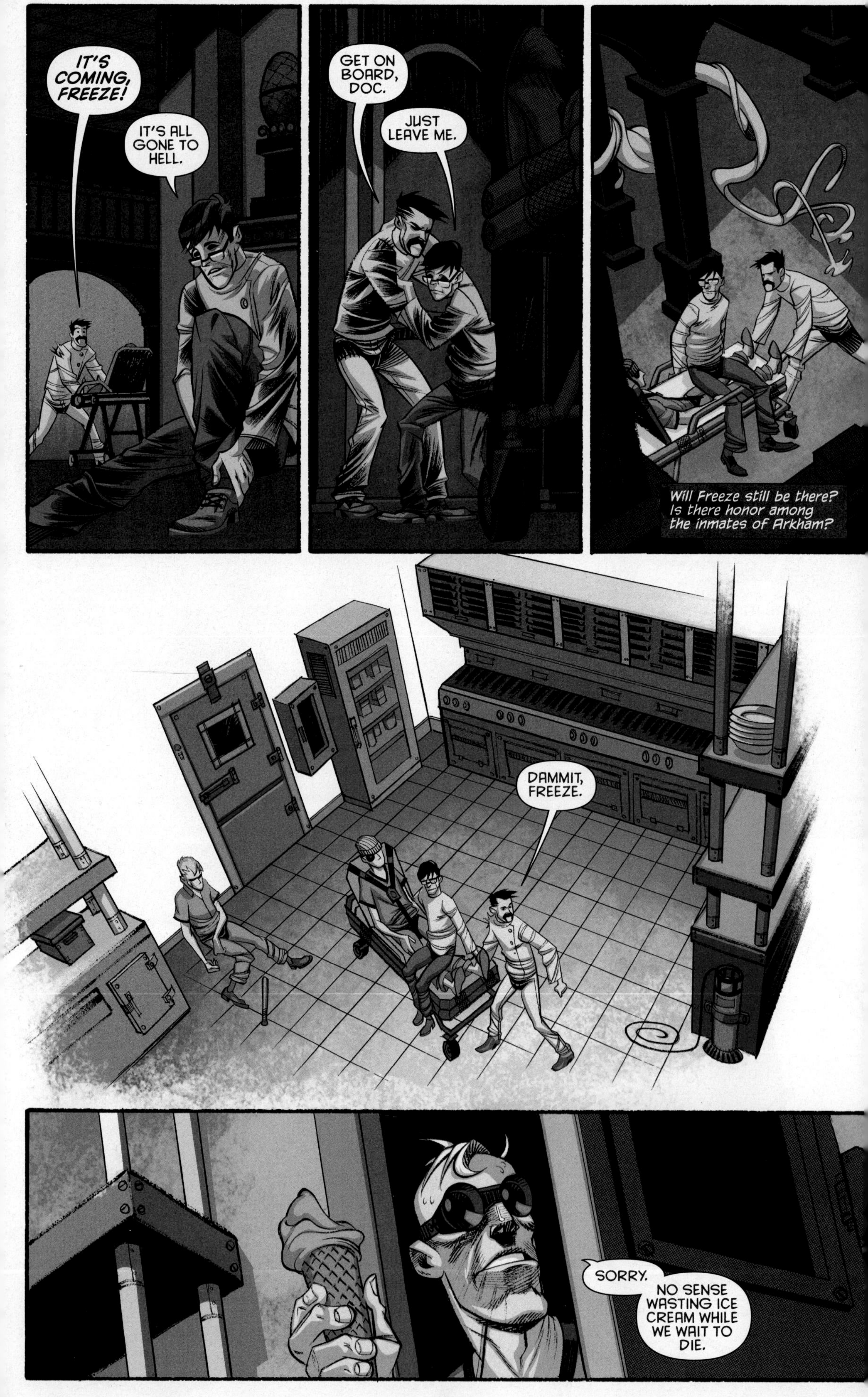
IT'S COMING, FREEZE!
IT'S ALL GONE TO HELL.
GET ON BOARD, DOC.
JUST LEAVE ME.
Will Freeze still be there? Is there honor among the inmates of Arkham?
DAMMIT, FREEZE.
SORRY.
NO SENSE WASTING ICE CREAM WHILE WE WAIT TO DIE.

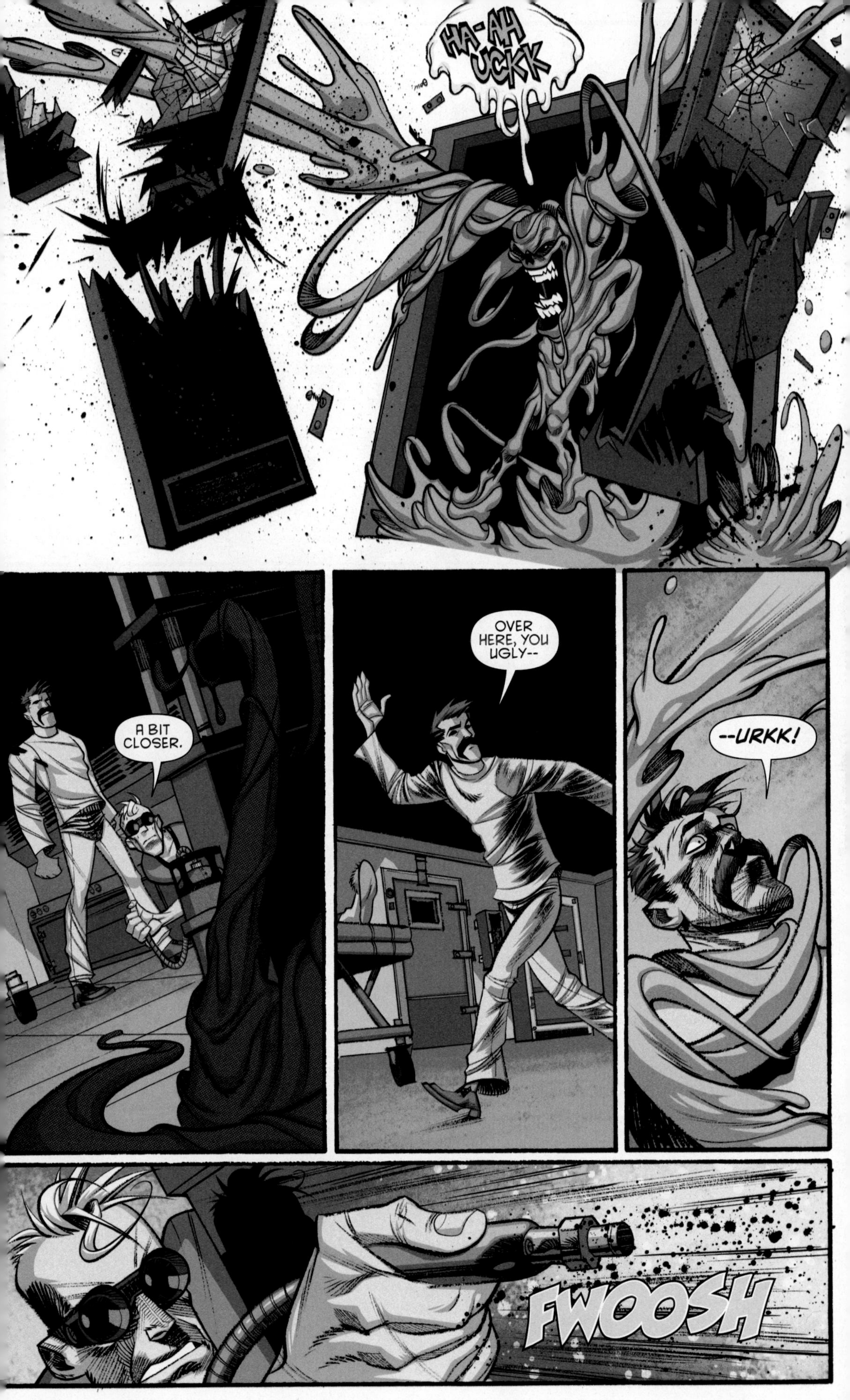
HA-AH UCKK
A BIT CLOSER.
OVER HERE, YOU UGLY--
--URKK!
FWOOSH

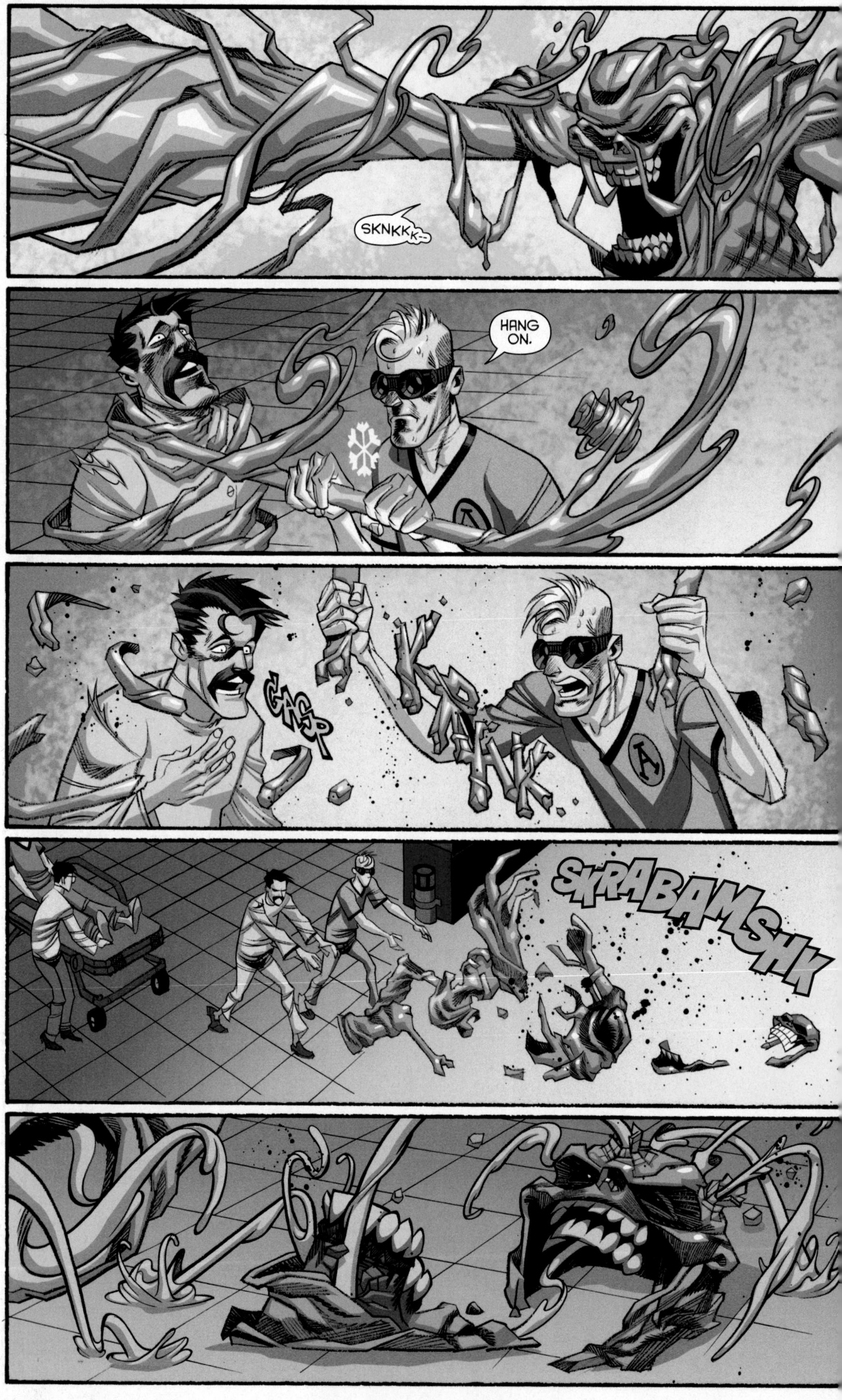

SKNKKK--
HANG ON.
GASP
KRAKK
SKRABAMSHK

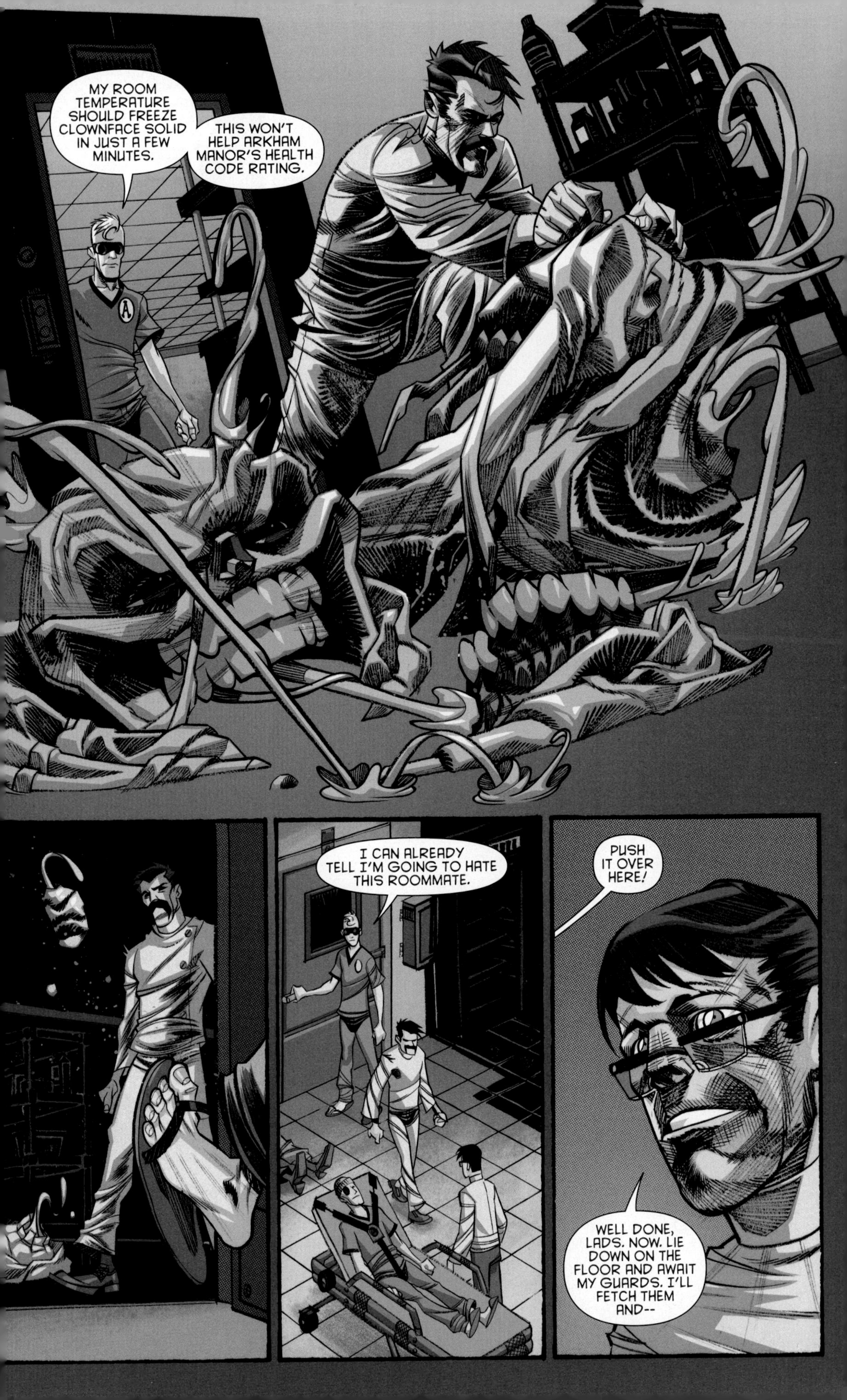
MY ROOM TEMPERATURE SHOULD FREEZE CLOWNFACE SOLID IN JUST A FEW MINUTES.
THIS WON'T HELP ARKHAM MANOR'S HEALTH CODE RATING.
I CAN ALREADY TELL I'M GOING TO HATE THIS ROOMMATE.
PUSH IT OVER HERE!
WELL DONE, LADS. NOW. LIE DOWN ON THE FLOOR AND AWAIT MY GUARDS. I'LL FETCH THEM AND--

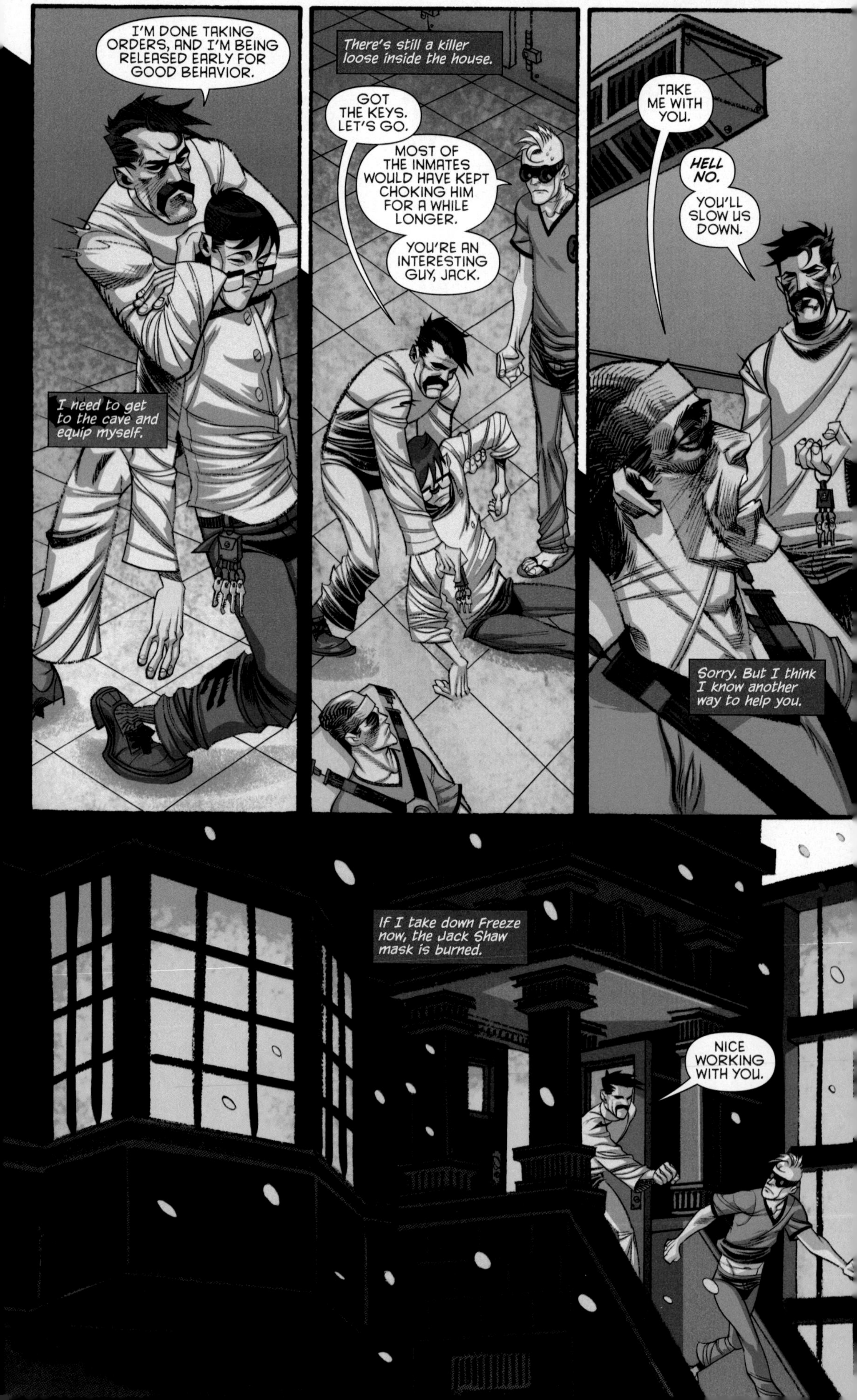
I'M DONE TAKING ORDERS, AND I'M BEING RELEASED EARLY FOR GOOD BEHAVIOR.
I need to get to the cave and equip myself.
There's still a killer loose inside the house.
GOT THE KEYS. LET'S GO.
MOST OF THE INMATES WOULD HAVE KEPT CHOKING HIM FOR A WHILE LONGER.
YOU'RE AN INTERESTING GUY, JACK.
TAKE ME WITH YOU.
HELL NO.
YOU'LL SLOW US DOWN.
Sorry. But I think I know another way to help you.
If I take down Freeze now, the Jack Shaw mask is burned.
NICE WORKING WITH YOU.

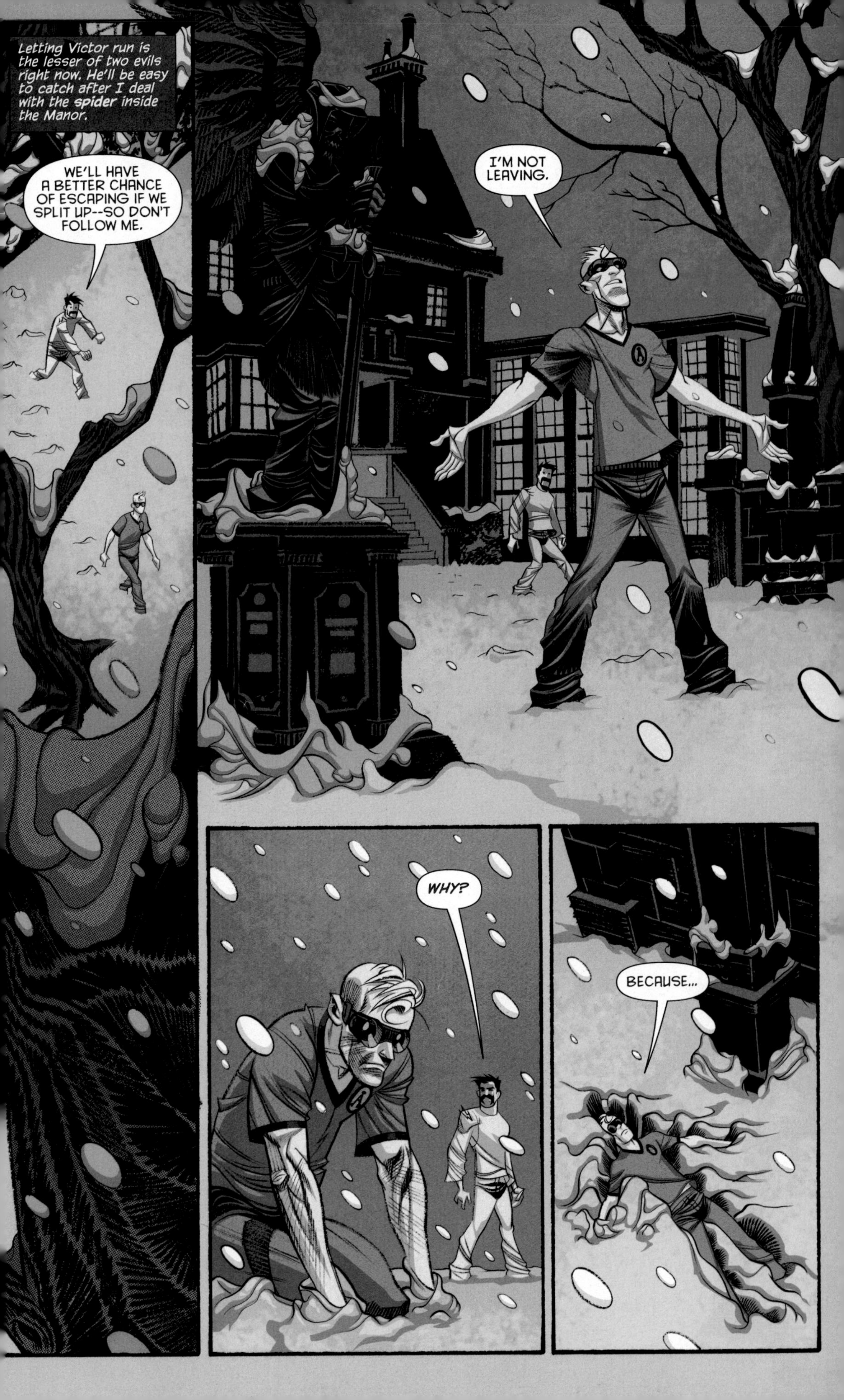
Letting Victor run is the lesser of two evils right now. He'll be easy to catch after I deal with the spider inside the Manor.
WE'LL HAVE A BETTER CHANCE OF ESCAPING IF WE SPLIT UP--SO DON'T FOLLOW ME.
I'M NOT LEAVING.
WHY?
BECAUSE...

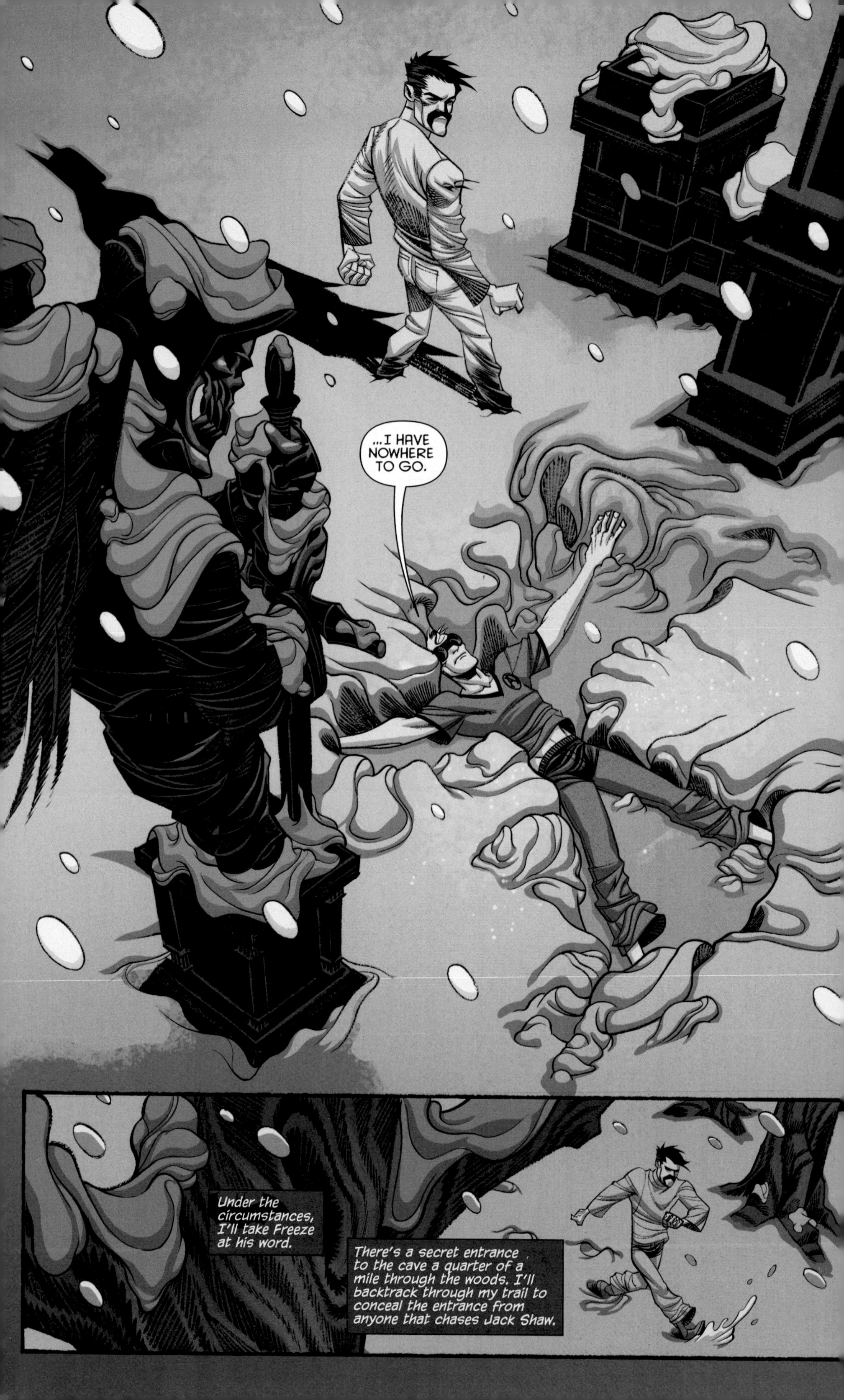
...I HAVE NOWHERE TO GO.
Under the circumstances, I'll take Freeze at his word.
There's a secret entrance to the cave a quarter of a mile through the woods. I'll backtrack through my trail to conceal the entrance from anyone that chases Jack Shaw.

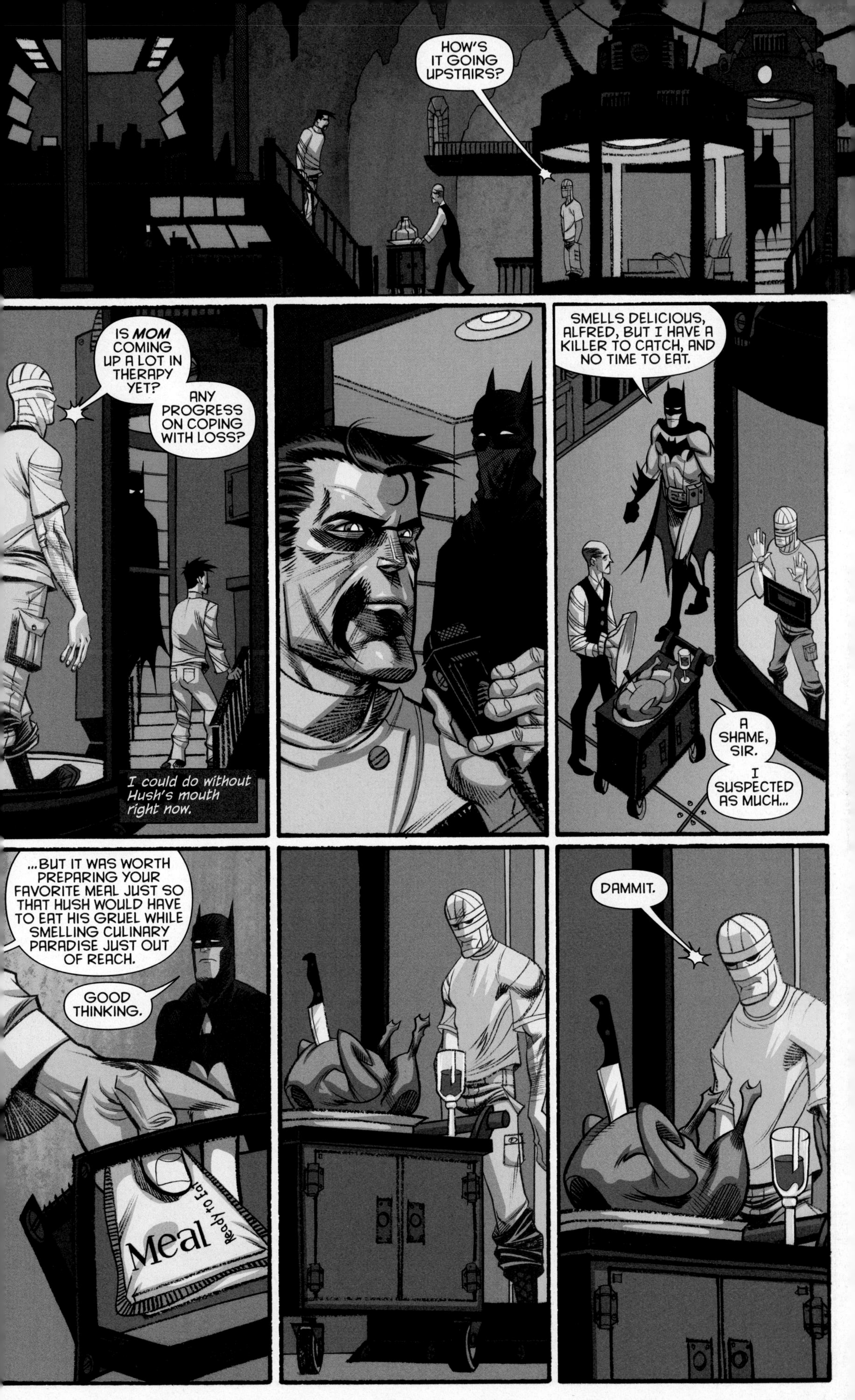
HOW'S IT GOING UPSTAIRS?
IS MOM COMING UP A LOT IN THERAPY YET?
ANY PROGRESS ON COPING WITH LOSS?
I could do without Hush's mouth right now.
SMELLS DELICIOUS, ALFRED, BUT I HAVE A KILLER TO CATCH, AND NO TIME TO EAT.
A SHAME, SIR.
I SUSPECTED AS MUCH...
...BUT IT WAS WORTH PREPARING YOUR FAVORITE MEAL JUST SO THAT HUSH WOULD HAVE TO EAT HIS GRUEL WHILE SMELLING CULINARY PARADISE JUST OUT OF REACH.
GOOD THINKING.
Meal
Ready to Eat
DAMMIT.

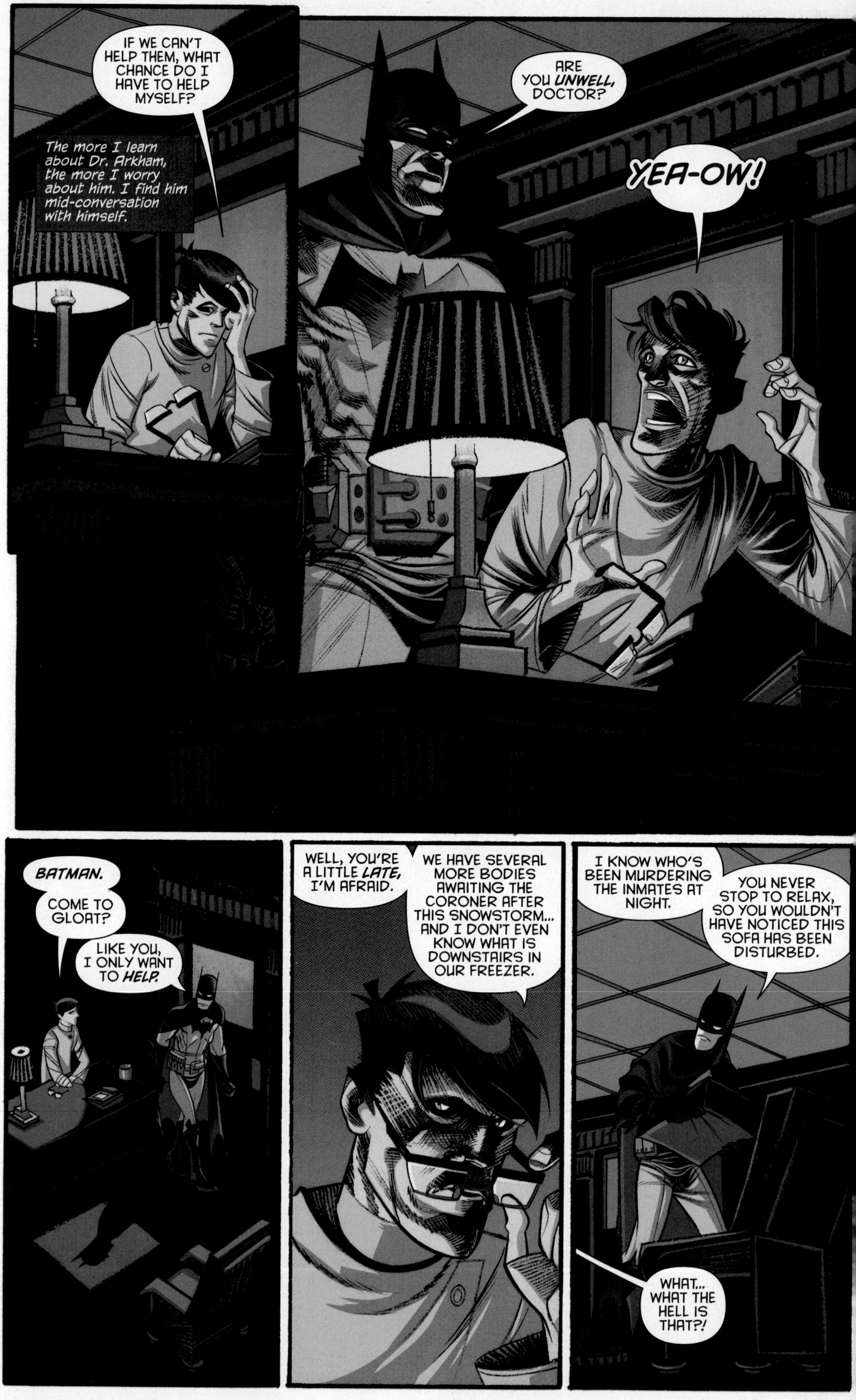
IF WE CAN'T HELP THEM, WHAT CHANCE DO I HAVE TO HELP MYSELF?
The more I learn about Dr. Arkham, the more I worry about him. I find him mid-conversation with himself.
ARE YOU UNWELL, DOCTOR?
YEA-OW!
BATMAN.
COME TO GLOAT?
LIKE YOU, I ONLY WANT TO HELP.
WELL, YOU'RE A LITTLE LATE, I'M AFRAID.
WE HAVE SEVERAL MORE BODIES AWAITING THE CORONER AFTER THIS SNOWSTORM... AND I DON'T EVEN KNOW WHAT IS DOWNSTAIRS IN OUR FREEZER.
I KNOW WHO'S BEEN MURDERING THE INMATES AT NIGHT.
YOU NEVER STOP TO RELAX, SO YOU WOULDN'T HAVE NOTICED THIS SOFA HAS BEEN DISTURBED.
WHAT... WHAT THE HELL IS THAT?!

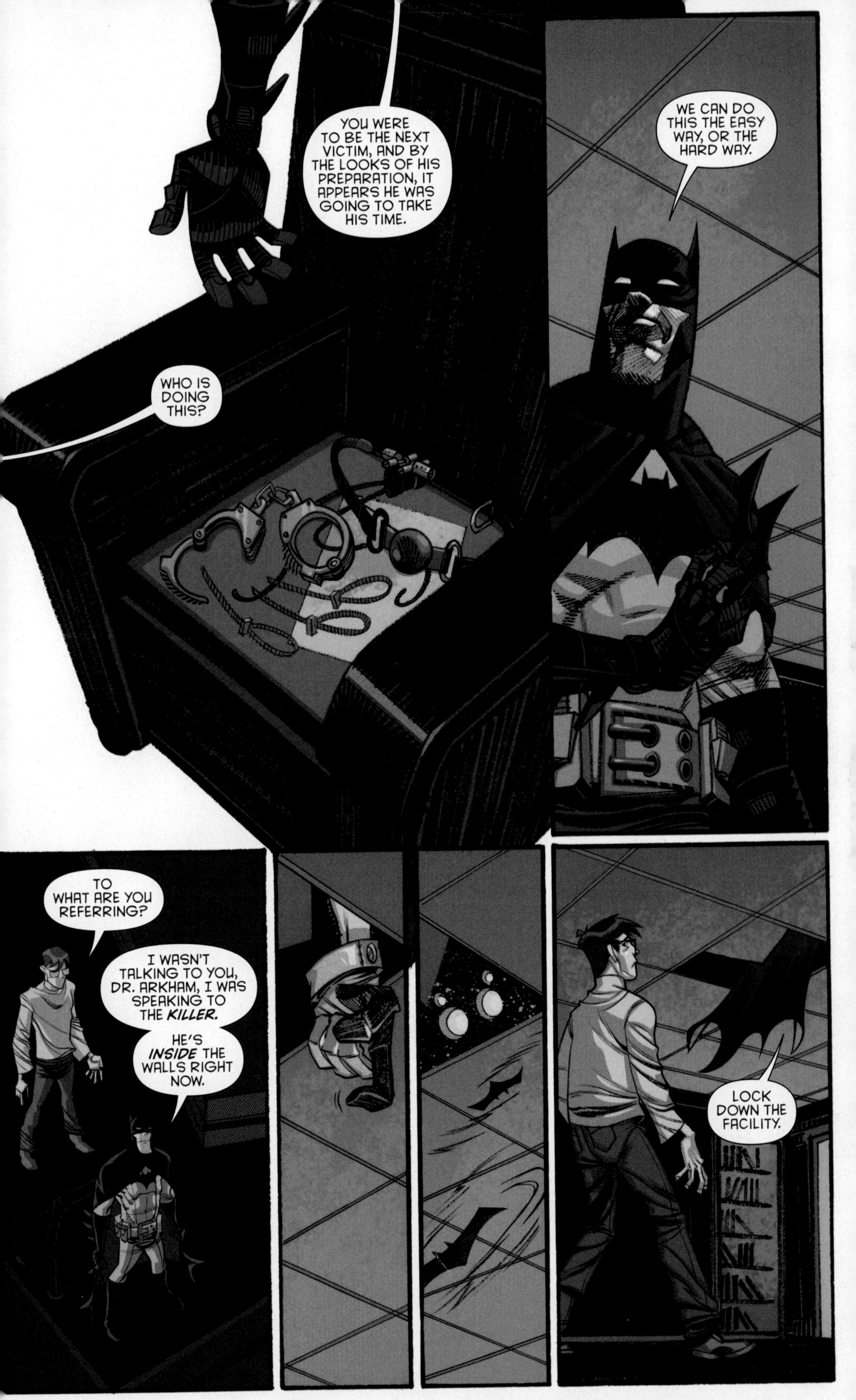

YOU WERE TO BE THE NEXT VICTIM, AND BY THE LOOKS OF HIS PREPARATION, IT APPEARS HE WAS GOING TO TAKE HIS TIME.
WHO IS DOING THIS?
WE CAN DO THIS THE EASY WAY, OR THE HARD WAY.
TO WHAT ARE YOU REFERRING?
I WASN'T TALKING TO YOU, DR. ARKHAM, I WAS SPEAKING TO THE *KILLER.*
HE'S *INSIDE* THE WALLS RIGHT NOW.
LOCK DOWN THE FACILITY.

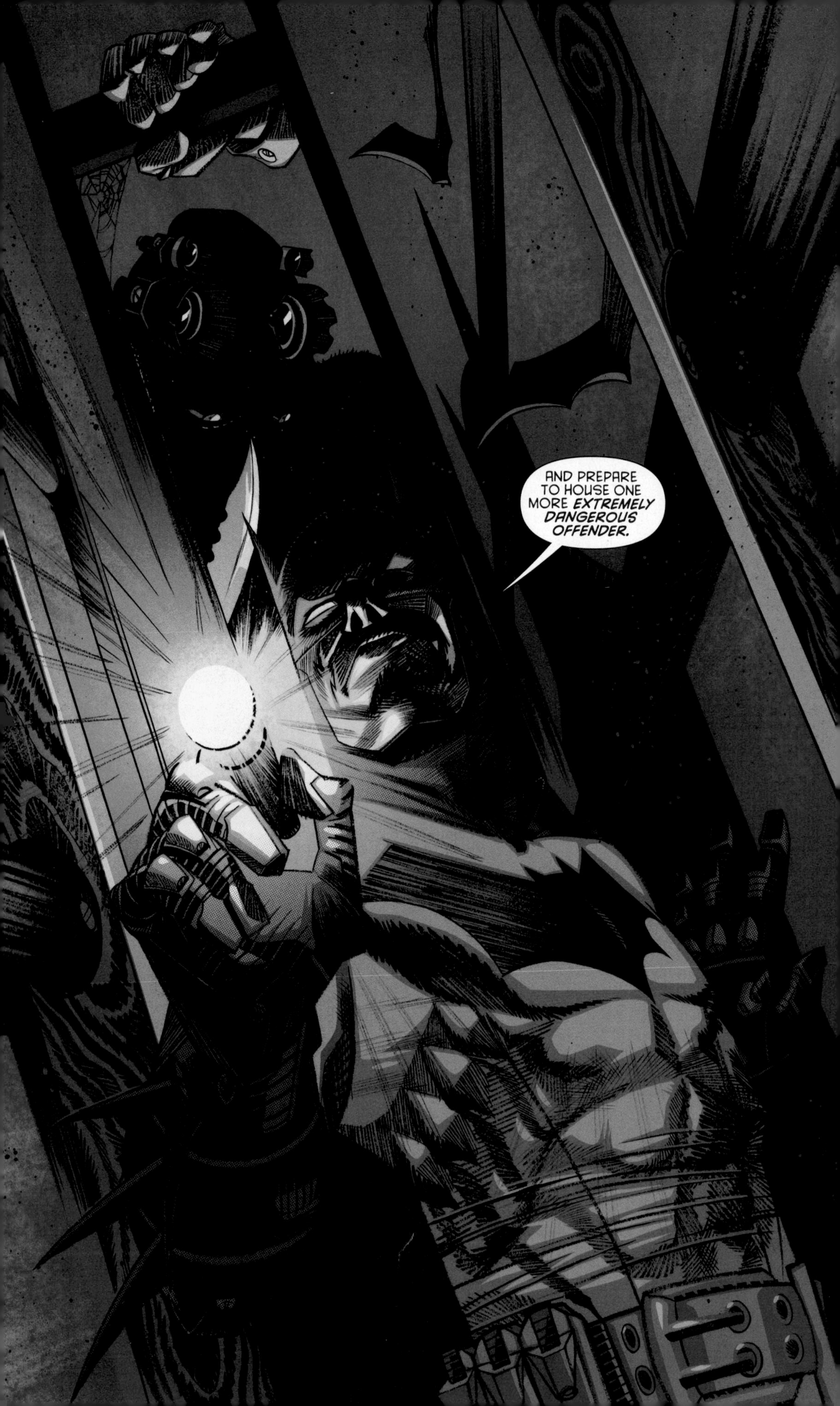
AND PREPARE TO HOUSE ONE MORE *EXTREMELY DANGEROUS* OFFENDER.

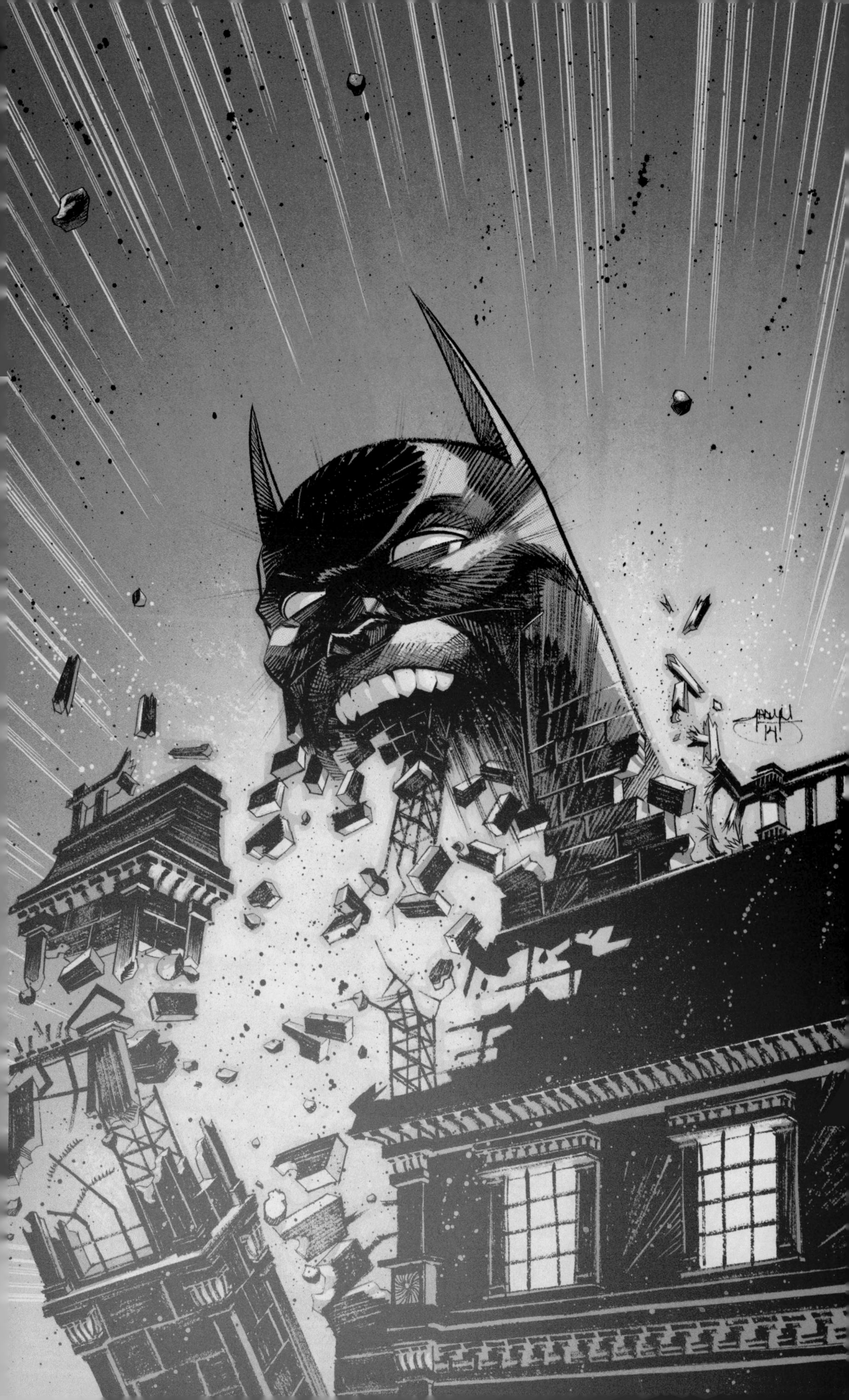

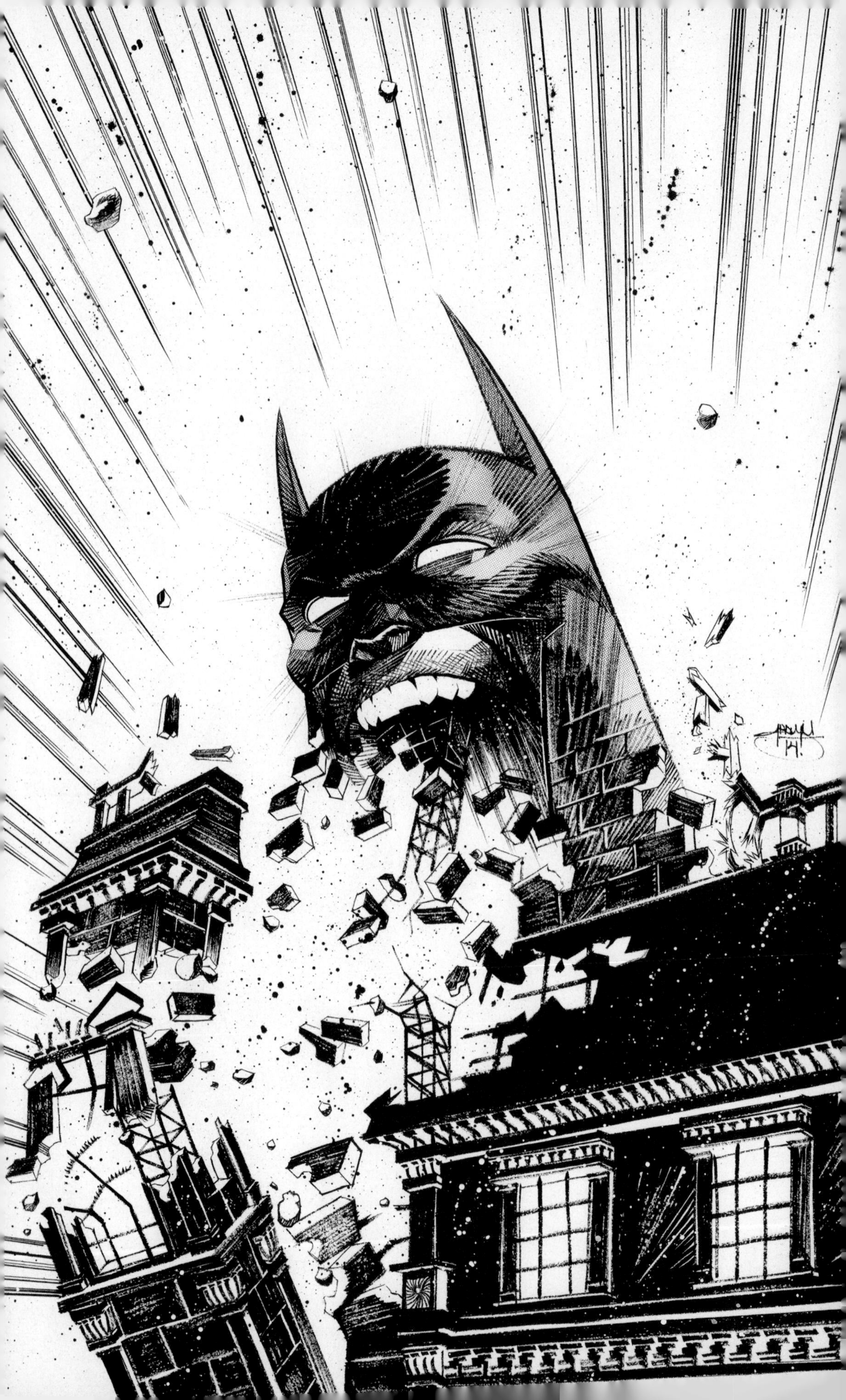

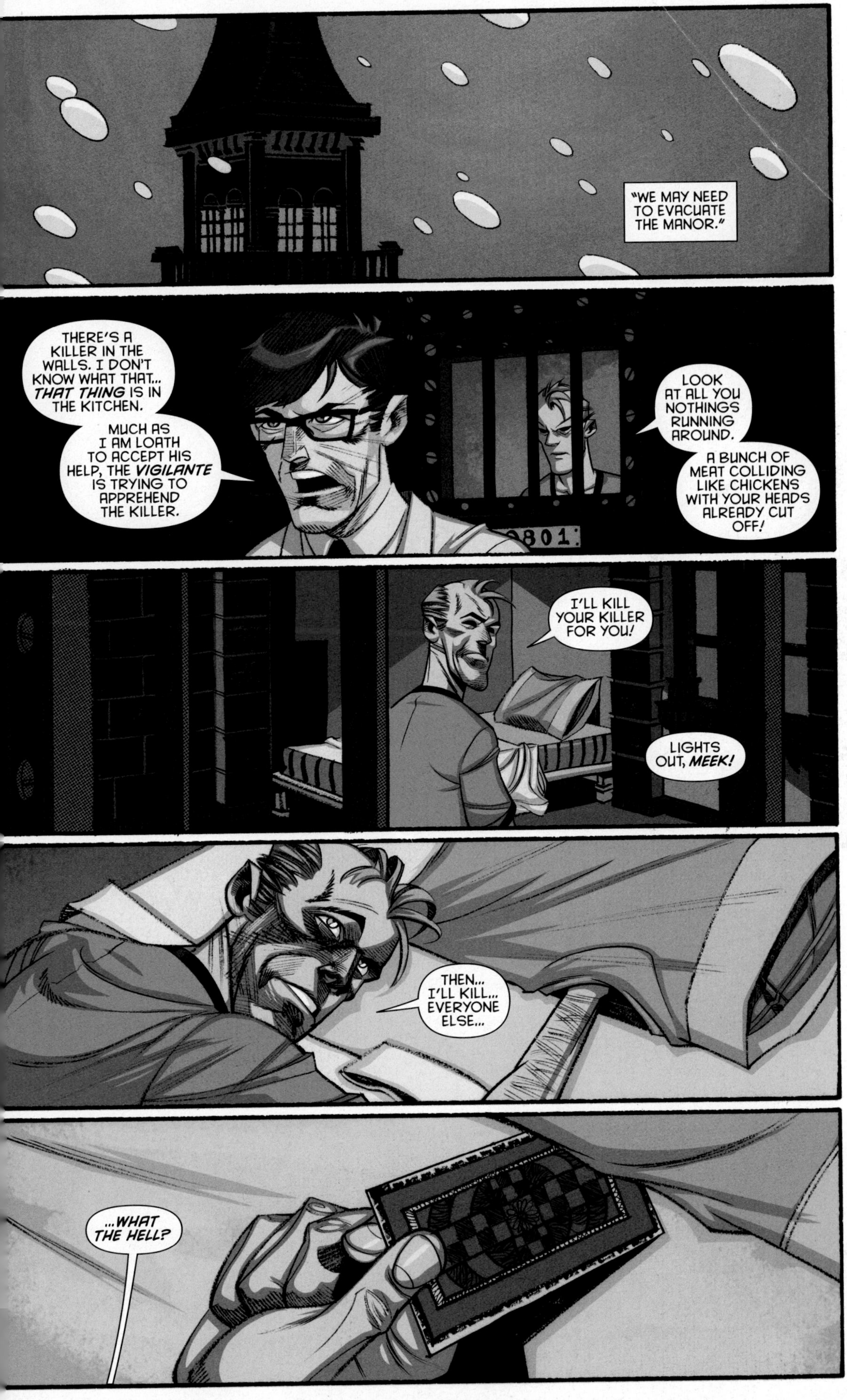
"WE MAY NEED TO EVACUATE THE MANOR."
THERE'S A KILLER IN THE WALLS. I DON'T KNOW WHAT THAT... THAT THING IS IN THE KITCHEN.
MUCH AS I AM LOATH TO ACCEPT HIS HELP, THE VIGILANTE IS TRYING TO APPREHEND THE KILLER.
LOOK AT ALL YOU NOTHINGS RUNNING AROUND.
A BUNCH OF MEAT COLLIDING LIKE CHICKENS WITH YOUR HEADS ALREADY CUT OFF!
0801
I'LL KILL YOUR KILLER FOR YOU!
LIGHTS OUT, MEEK!
THEN... I'LL KILL... EVERYONE ELSE...
...WHAT THE HELL?

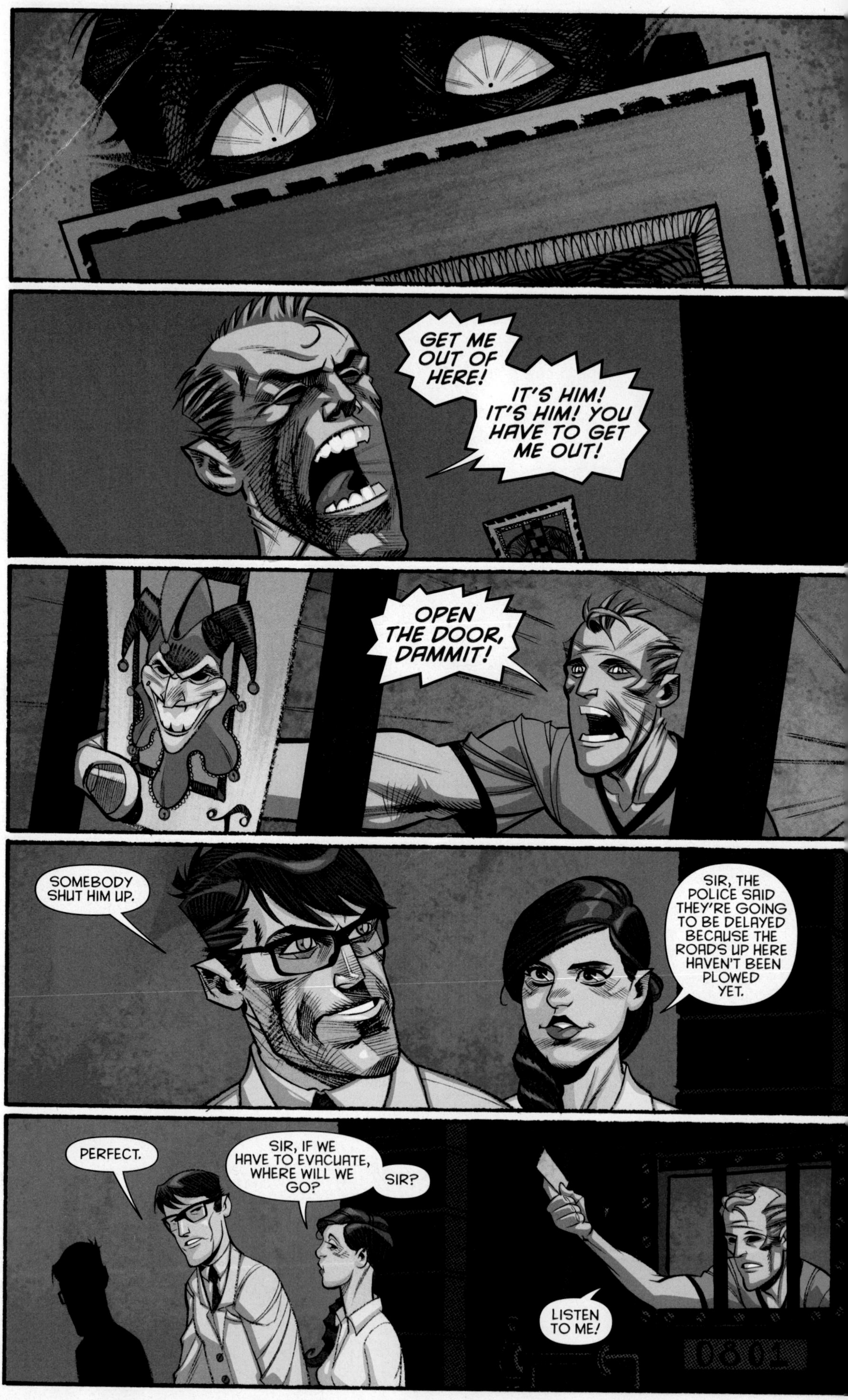
GET ME OUT OF HERE!
IT'S HIM! IT'S HIM! YOU HAVE TO GET ME OUT!
OPEN THE DOOR, DAMMIT!
SOMEBODY SHUT HIM UP.
SIR, THE POLICE SAID THEY'RE GOING TO BE DELAYED BECAUSE THE ROADS UP HERE HAVEN'T BEEN PLOWED YET.
PERFECT.
SIR, IF WE HAVE TO EVACUATE, WHERE WILL WE GO?
SIR?
LISTEN TO ME!

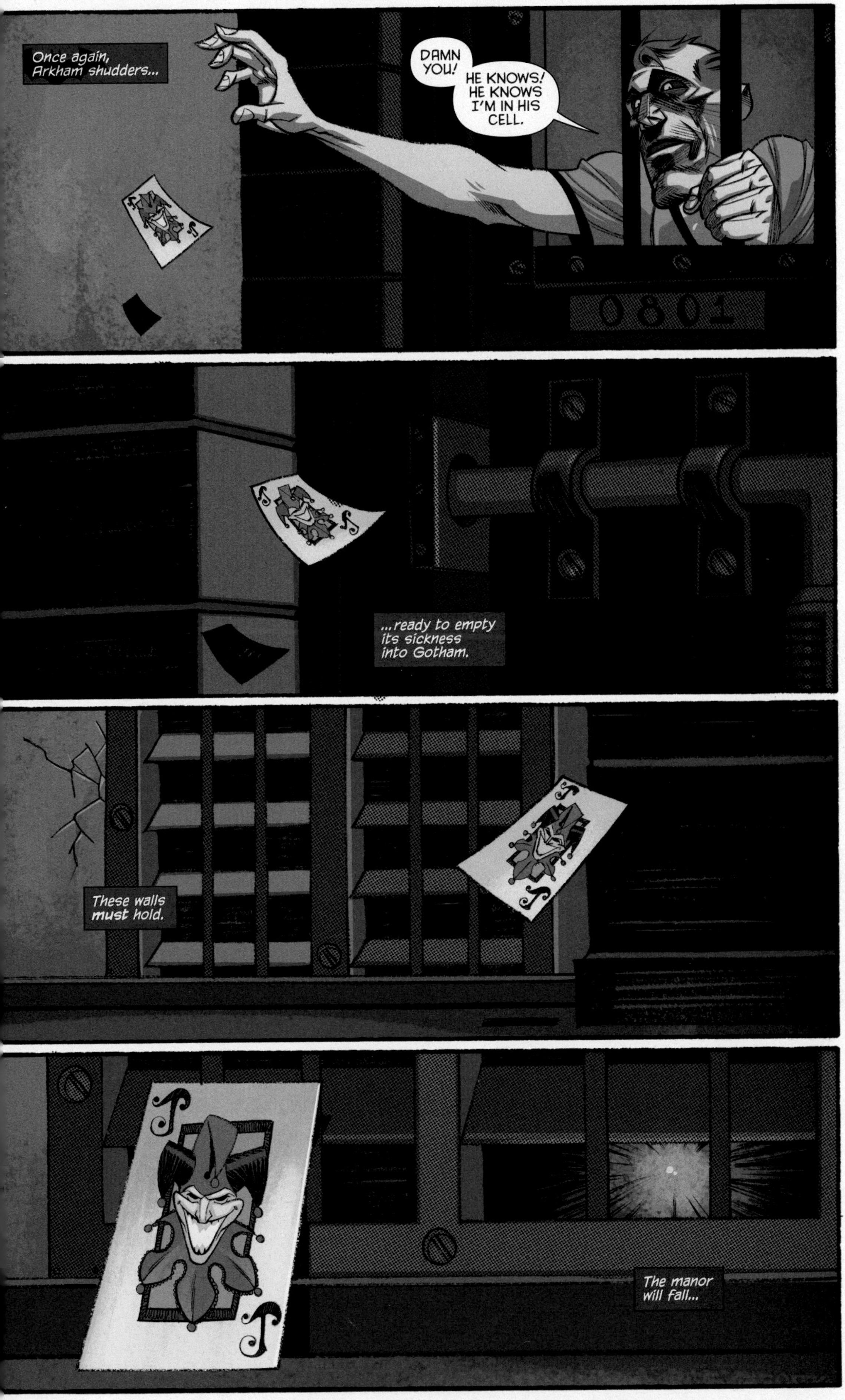
Once again, Arkham shudders...
DAMN YOU!
HE KNOWS! HE KNOWS I'M IN HIS CELL.
0801
...ready to empty its sickness into Gotham.
These walls **must** hold.
The manor will fall...

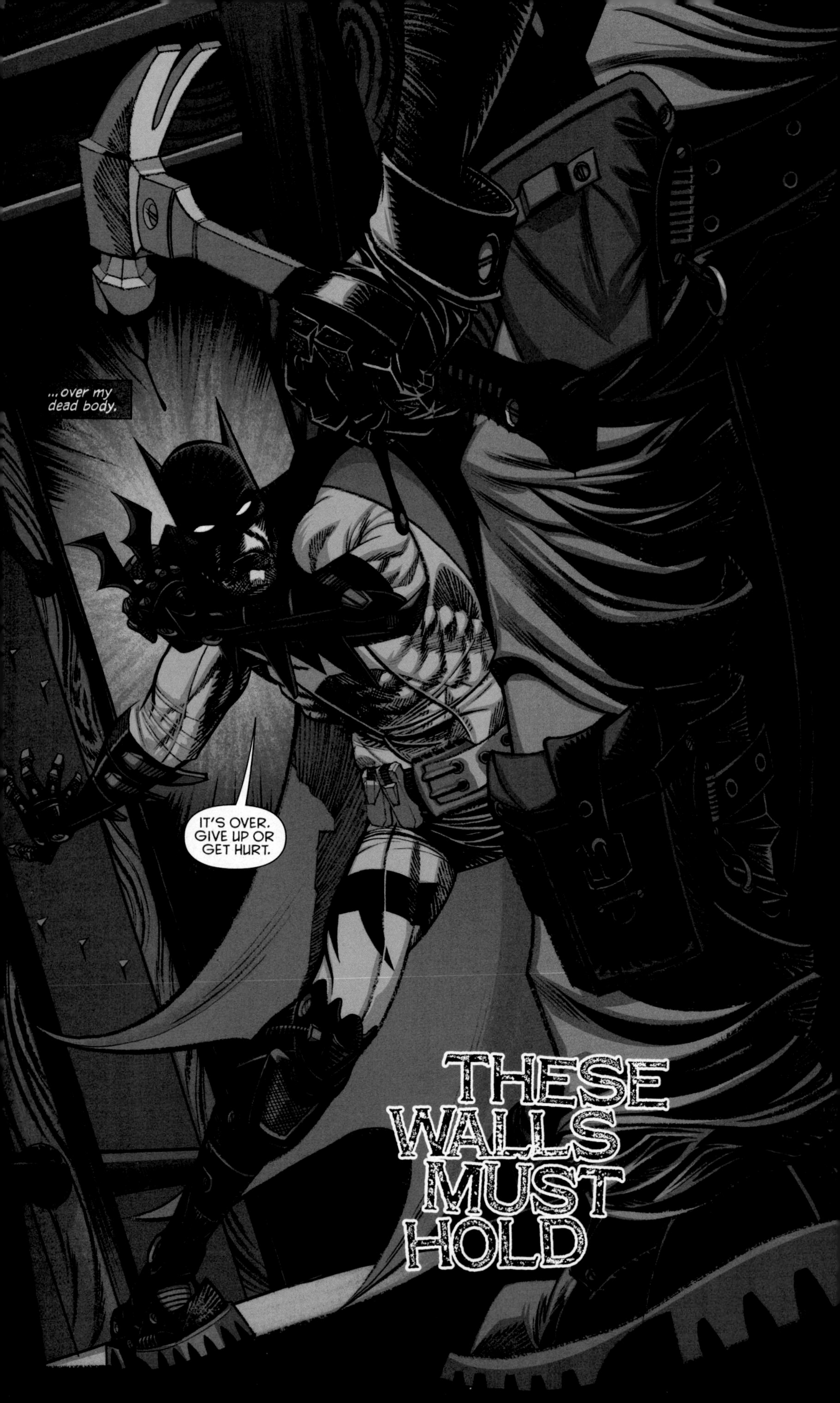

...over my dead body.
IT'S OVER. GIVE UP OR GET HURT.
THESE WALLS MUST HOLD

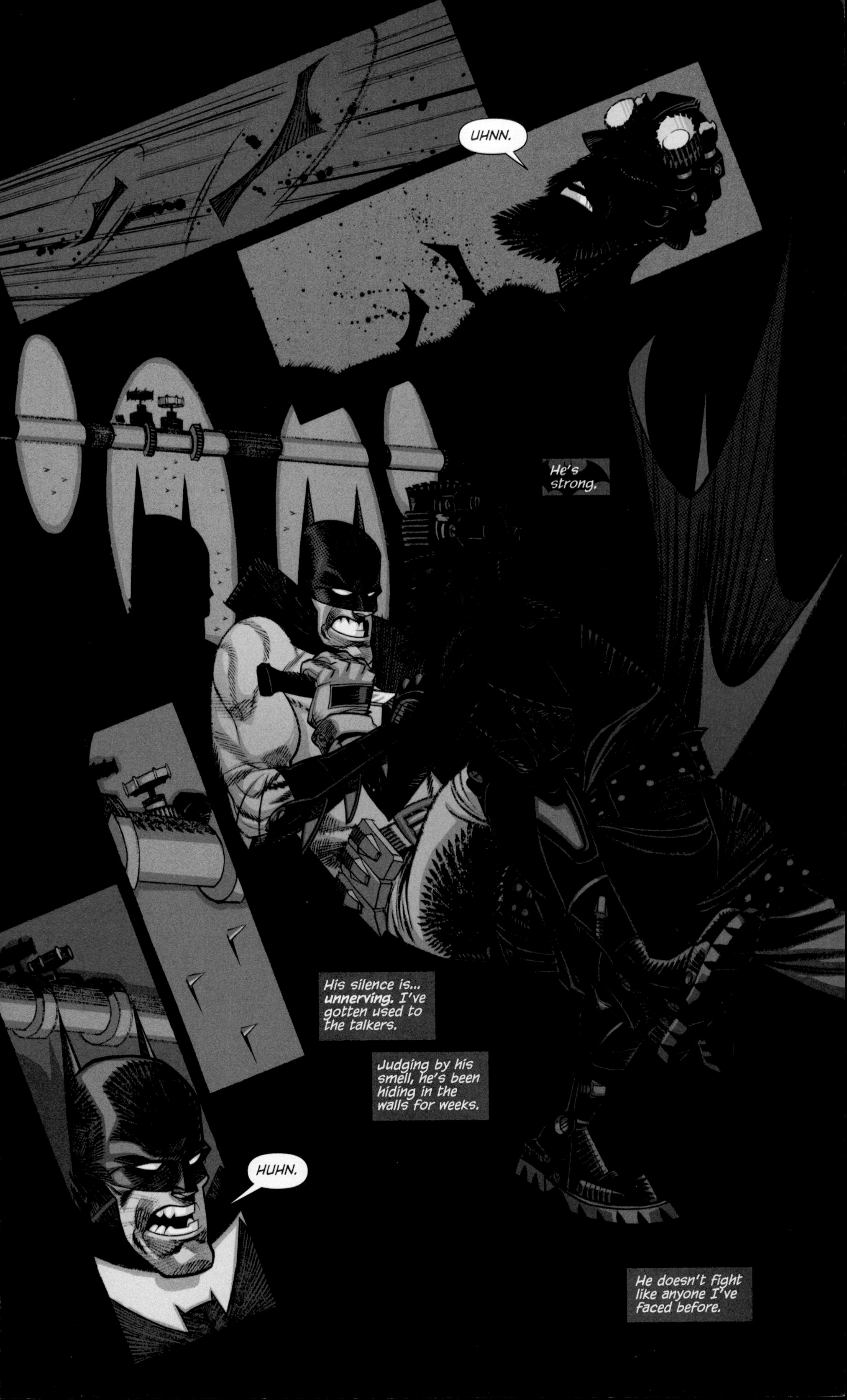
UHNN.
He's strong.
His silence is... unnerving. I've gotten used to the talkers.
Judging by his smell, he's been hiding in the walls for weeks.
HUHN.
He doesn't fight like anyone I've faced before.

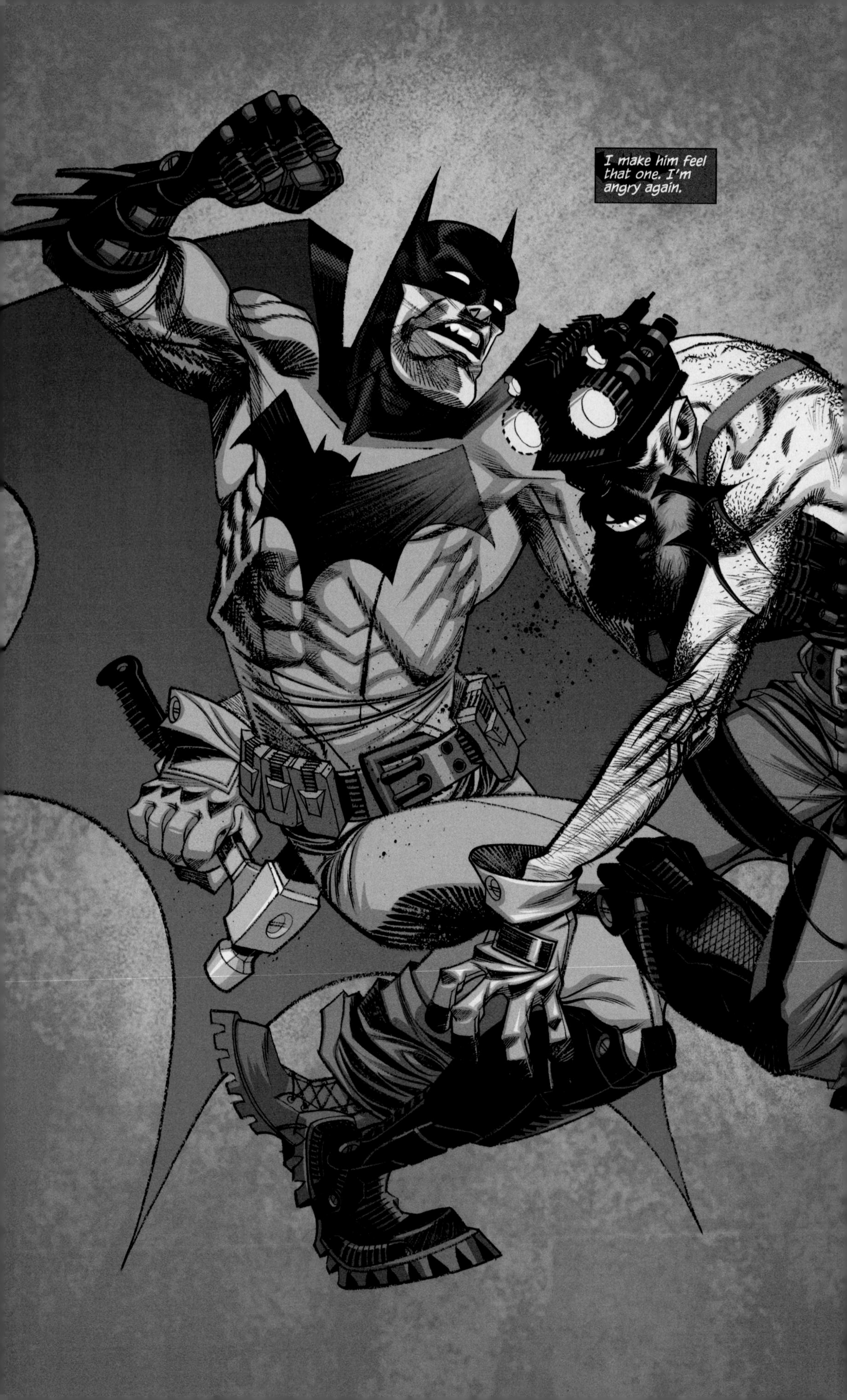
I make him feel that one. I'm angry again.

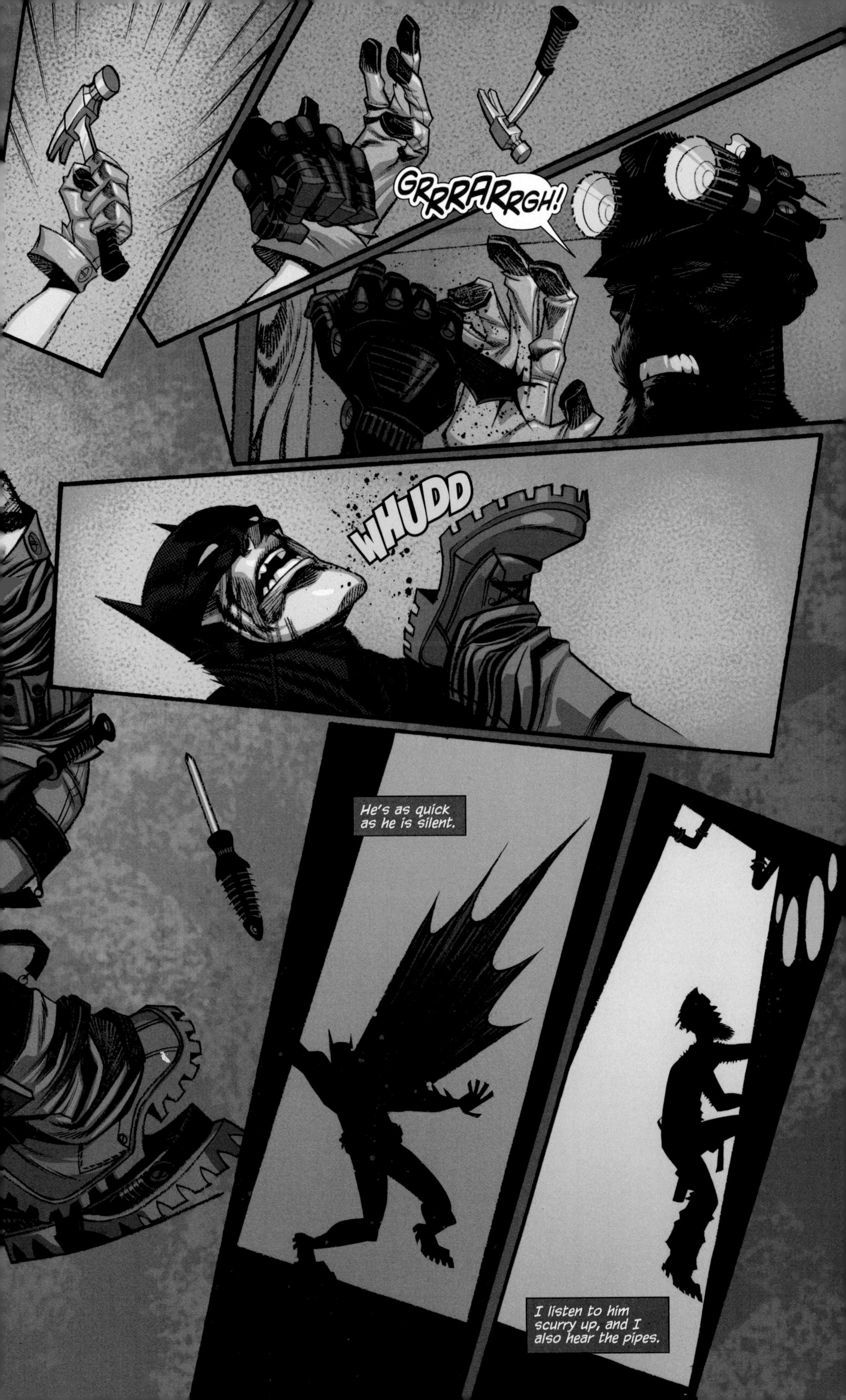
GRRRARRRGH!
WHUDD
He's as quick as he is silent.
I listen to him scurry up, and I also hear the pipes.

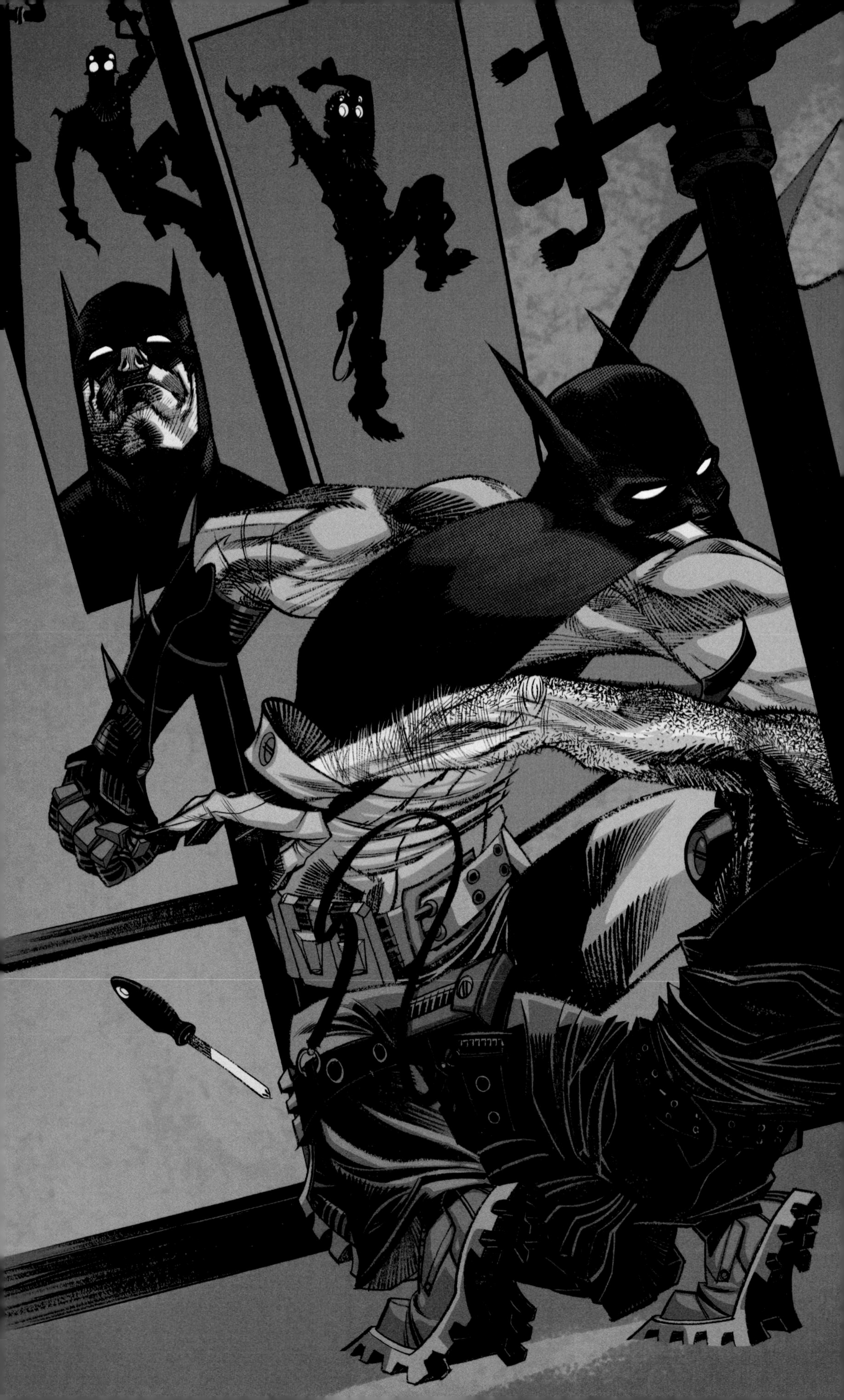

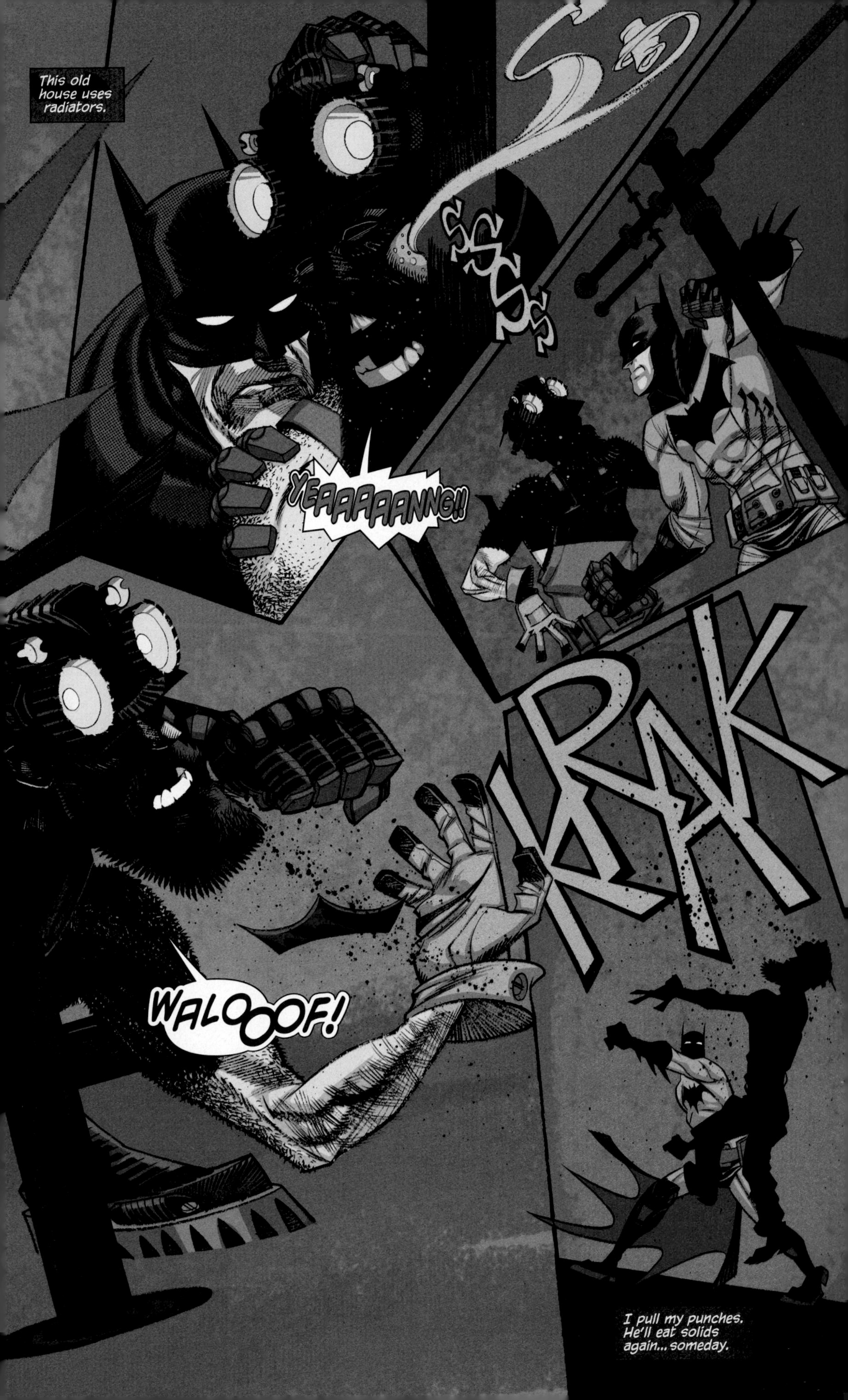
This old house uses radiators.
SSSSSS
YEAAAAAANNG!!
KRAK
WALOOOOF!
I pull my punches. He'll eat solids again... someday.

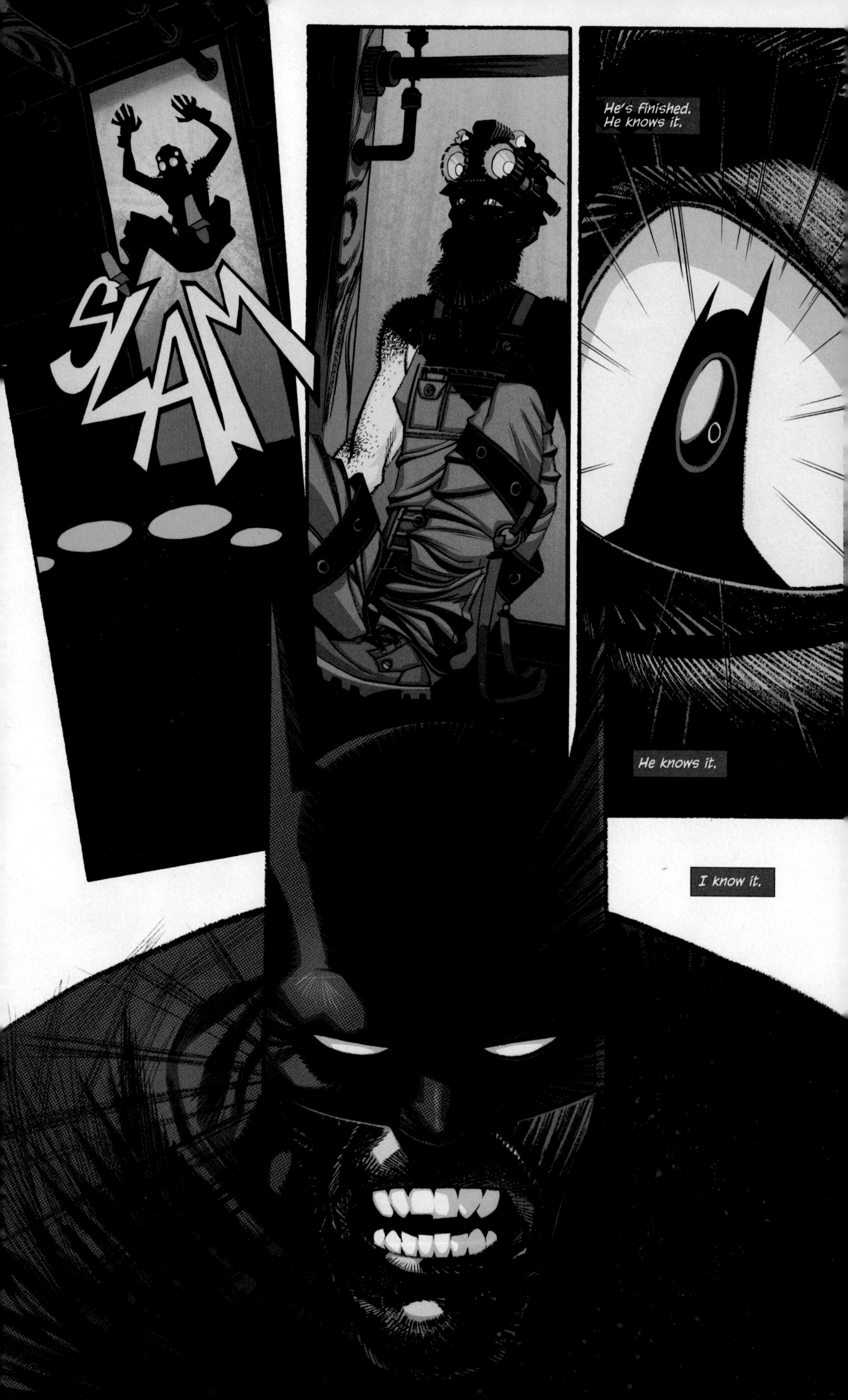
SLAM
He's finished.
He knows it.
He knows it.
I know it.

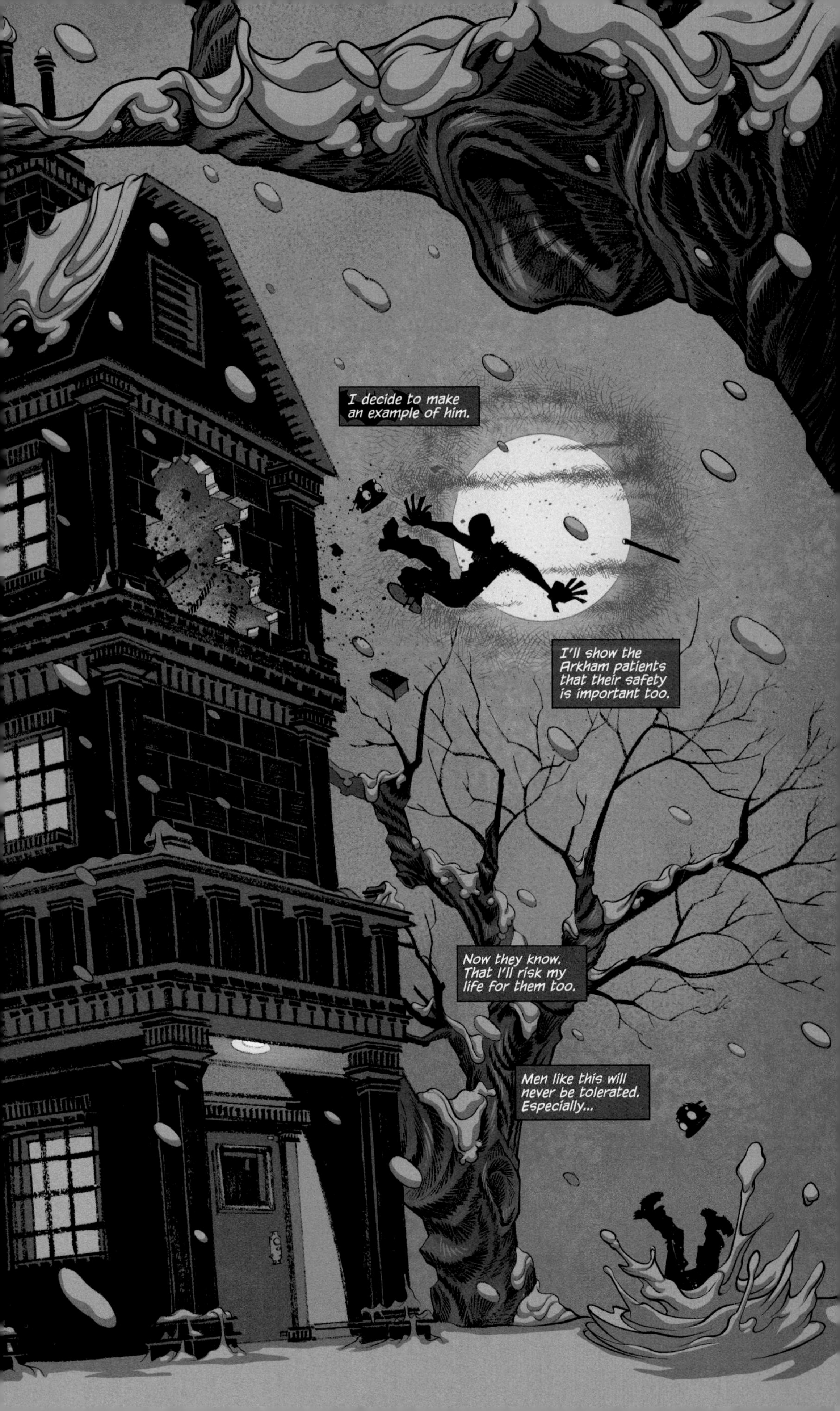
I decide to make an example of him.
I'll show the Arkham patients that their safety is important too.
Now they know. That I'll risk my life for them too.
Men like this will never be tolerated. Especially...

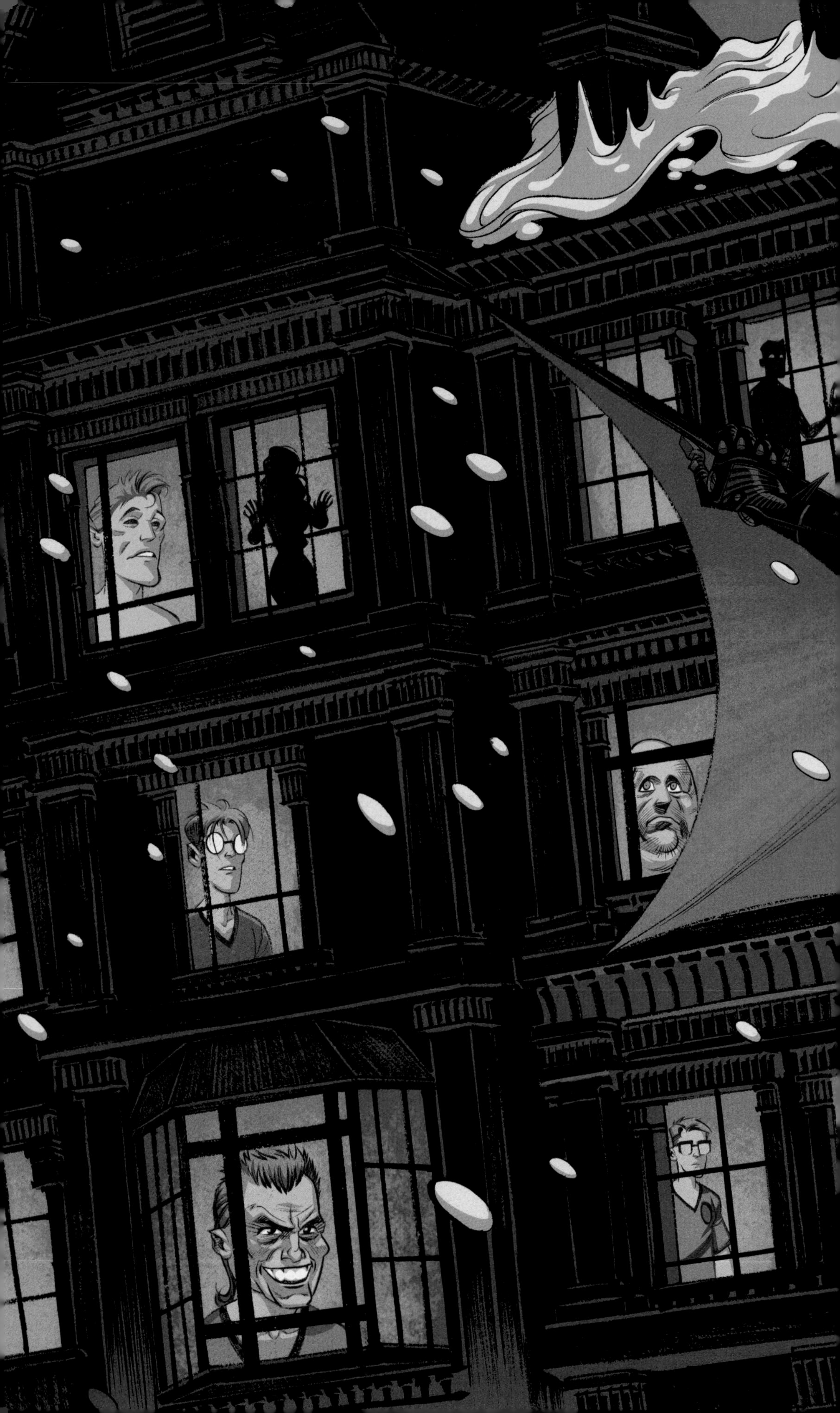

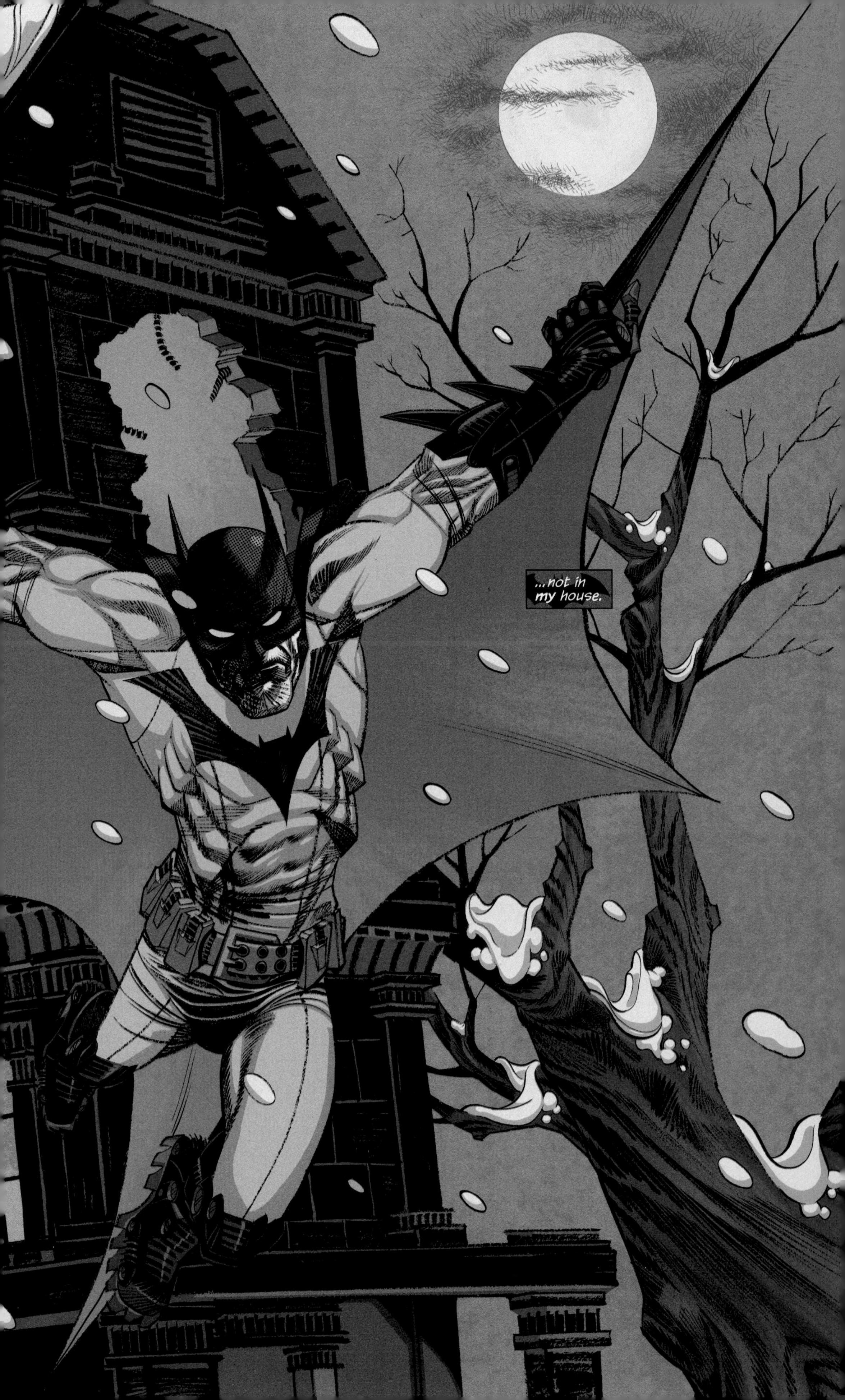
...not in my house.

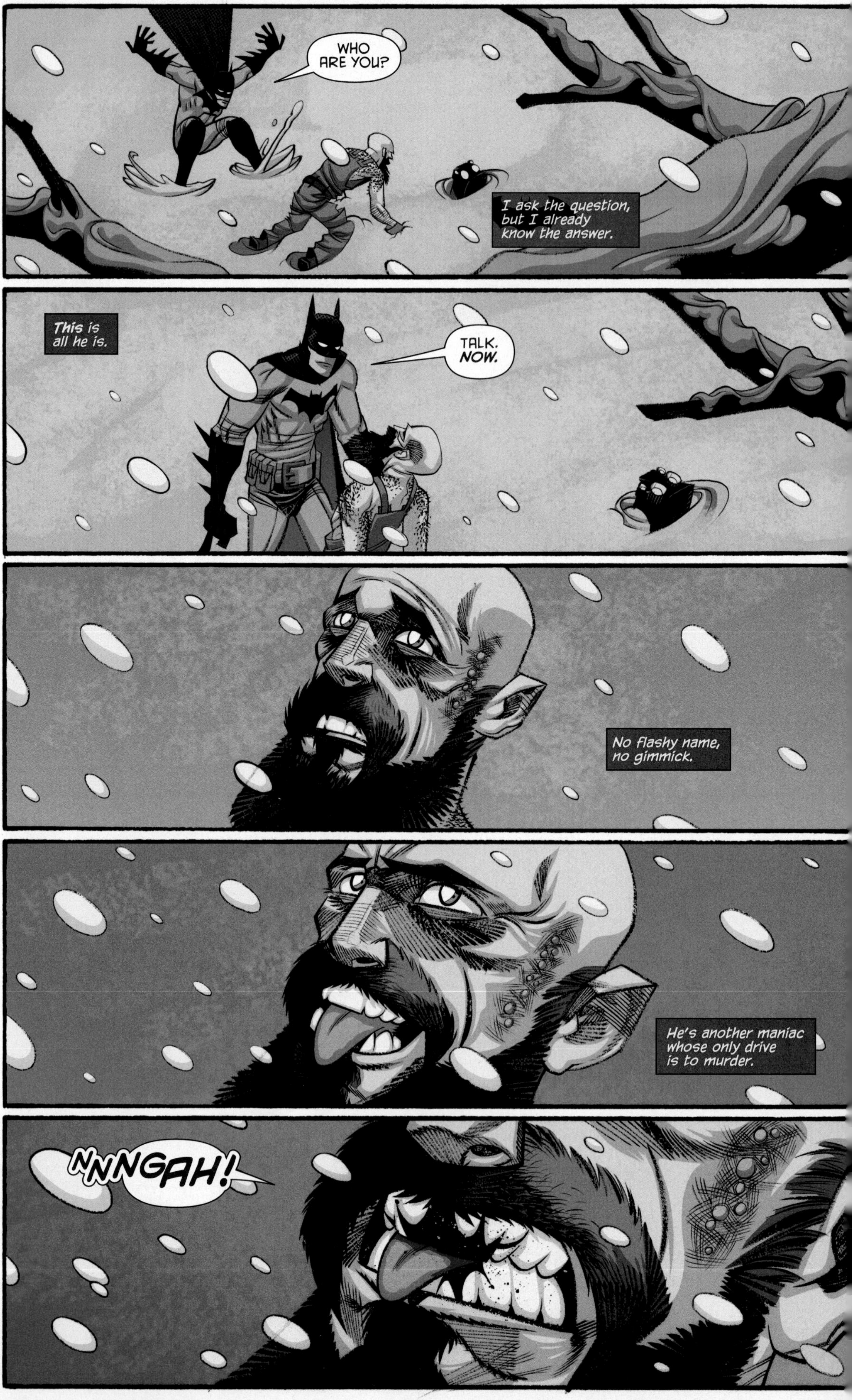
WHO ARE YOU?
I ask the question, but I already know the answer.
This is all he is.
TALK. NOW.
No flashy name, no gimmick.
He's another maniac whose only drive is to murder.
NNNGAH!

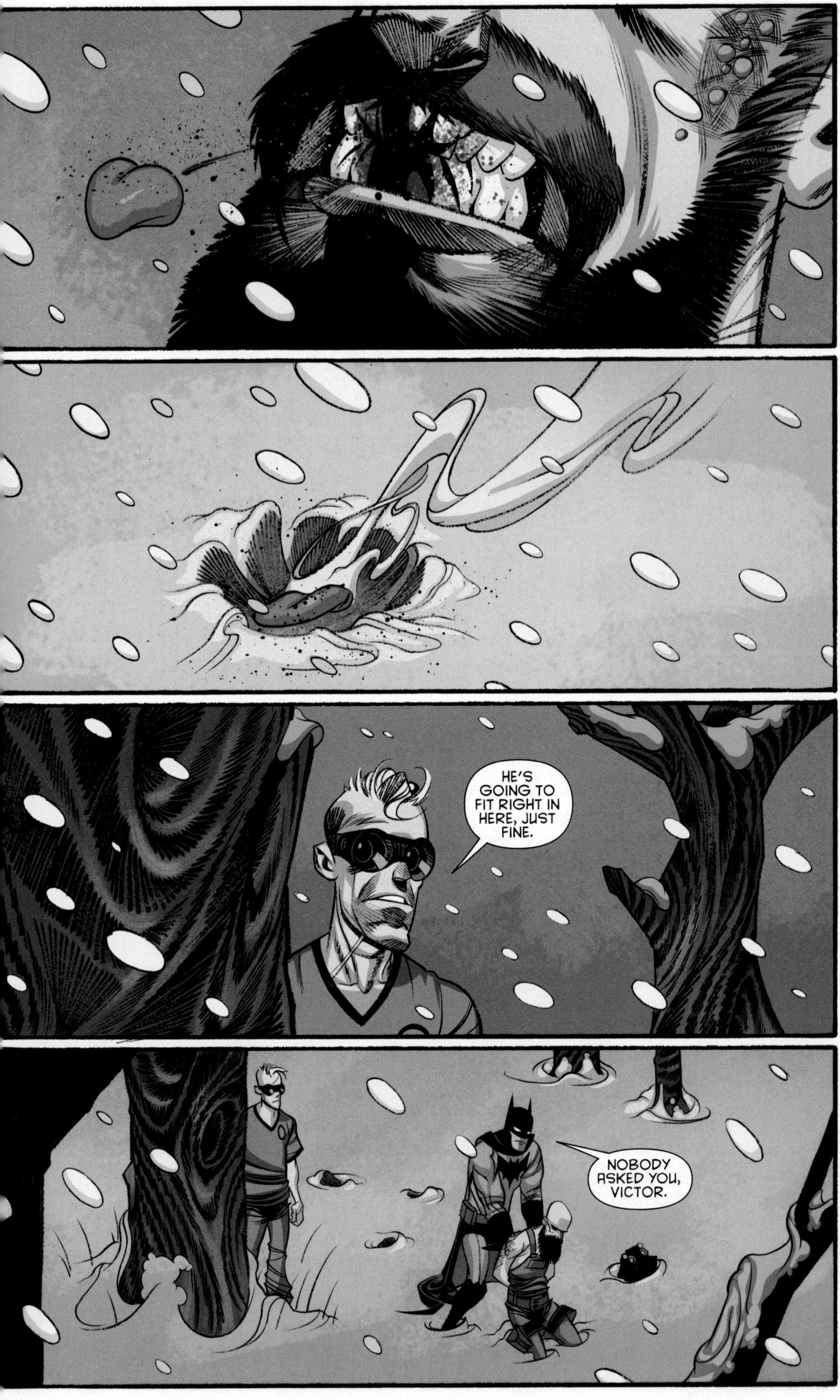

HE'S GOING TO FIT RIGHT IN HERE, JUST FINE.
NOBODY ASKED YOU, VICTOR.

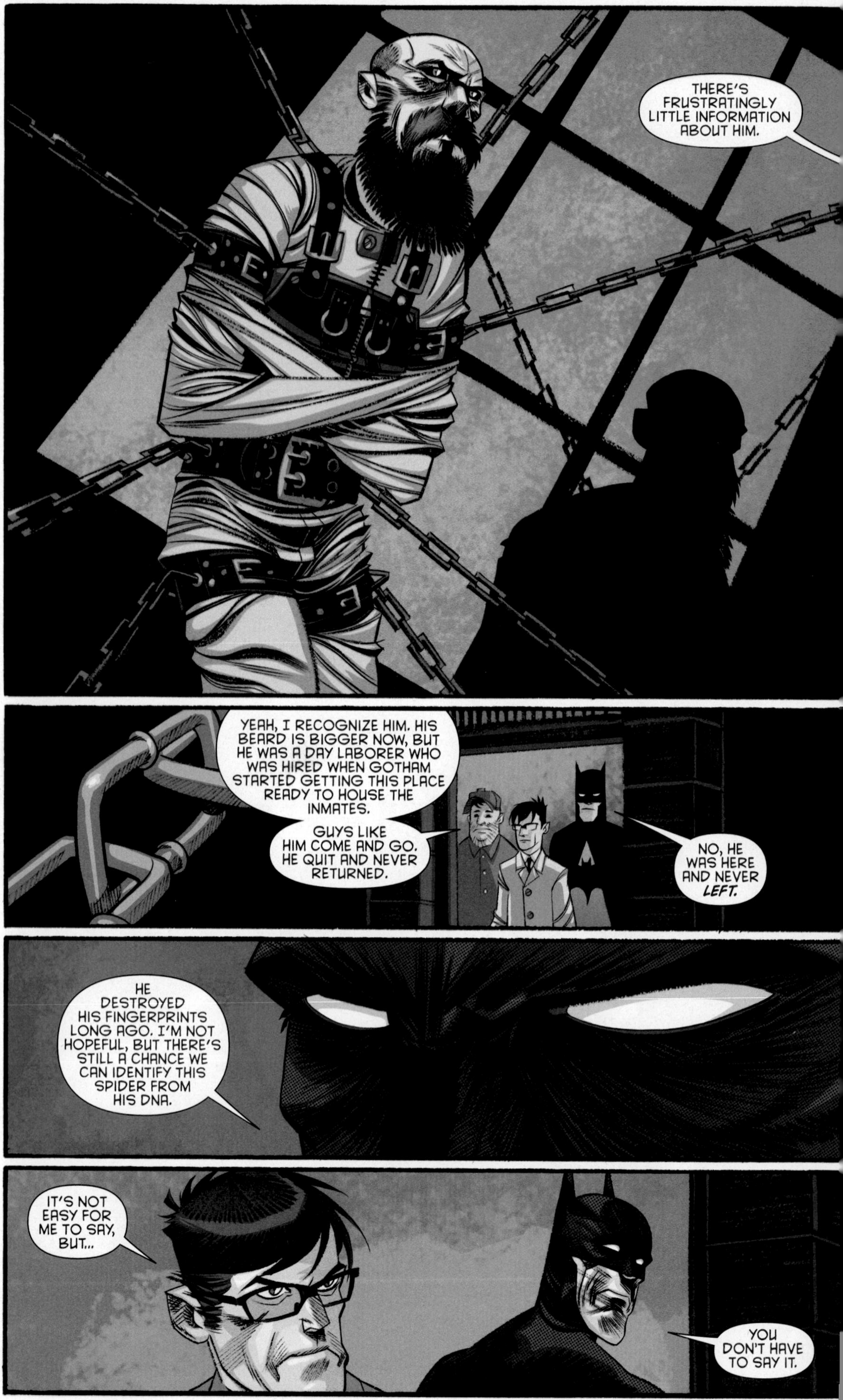
THERE'S FRUSTRATINGLY LITTLE INFORMATION ABOUT HIM.
YEAH, I RECOGNIZE HIM. HIS BEARD IS BIGGER NOW, BUT HE WAS A DAY LABORER WHO WAS HIRED WHEN GOTHAM STARTED GETTING THIS PLACE READY TO HOUSE THE INMATES.
GUYS LIKE HIM COME AND GO. HE QUIT AND NEVER RETURNED.
NO, HE WAS HERE AND NEVER *LEFT.*
HE DESTROYED HIS FINGERPRINTS LONG AGO. I'M NOT HOPEFUL, BUT THERE'S STILL A CHANCE WE CAN IDENTIFY THIS SPIDER FROM HIS DNA.
IT'S NOT EASY FOR ME TO SAY, BUT...
YOU DON'T HAVE TO SAY IT.

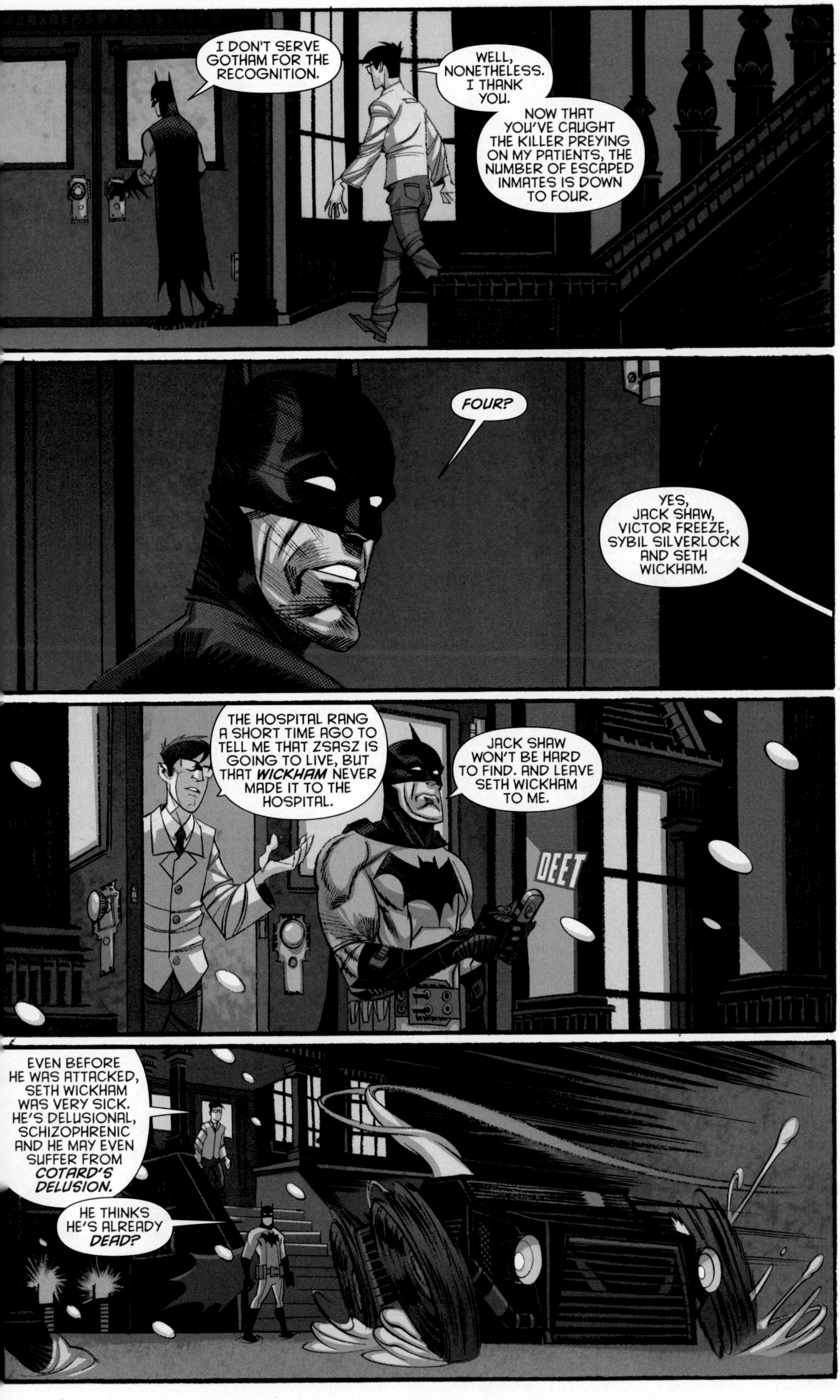
I DON'T SERVE GOTHAM FOR THE RECOGNITION.
WELL, NONETHELESS. I THANK YOU.
NOW THAT YOU'VE CAUGHT THE KILLER PREYING ON MY PATIENTS, THE NUMBER OF ESCAPED INMATES IS DOWN TO FOUR.
FOUR?
YES, JACK SHAW, VICTOR FREEZE, SYBIL SILVERLOCK AND SETH WICKHAM.
THE HOSPITAL RANG A SHORT TIME AGO TO TELL ME THAT ZSASZ IS GOING TO LIVE, BUT THAT ***WICKHAM*** NEVER MADE IT TO THE HOSPITAL.
JACK SHAW WON'T BE HARD TO FIND. AND LEAVE SETH WICKHAM TO ME.
DEET
EVEN BEFORE HE WAS ATTACKED, SETH WICKHAM WAS VERY SICK. HE'S DELUSIONAL, SCHIZOPHRENIC AND HE MAY EVEN SUFFER FROM ***COTARD'S DELUSION.***
HE THINKS HE'S ALREADY ***DEAD?***

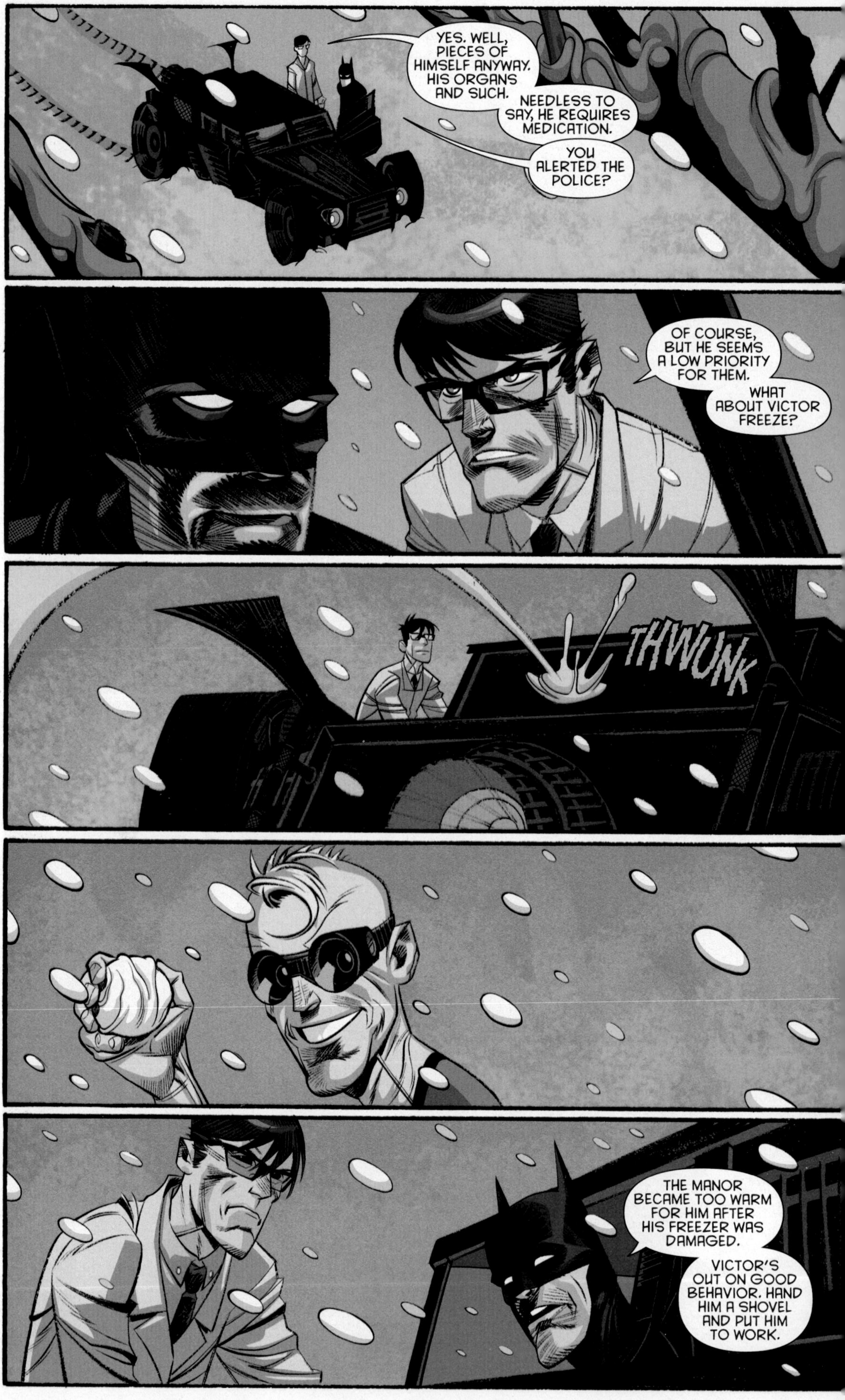

YES. WELL, PIECES OF HIMSELF ANYWAY. HIS ORGANS AND SUCH.
NEEDLESS TO SAY, HE REQUIRES MEDICATION.
YOU ALERTED THE POLICE?
OF COURSE, BUT HE SEEMS A LOW PRIORITY FOR THEM.
WHAT ABOUT VICTOR FREEZE?
THWUNK
THE MANOR BECAME TOO WARM FOR HIM AFTER HIS FREEZER WAS DAMAGED.
VICTOR'S OUT ON GOOD BEHAVIOR. HAND HIM A SHOVEL AND PUT HIM TO WORK.

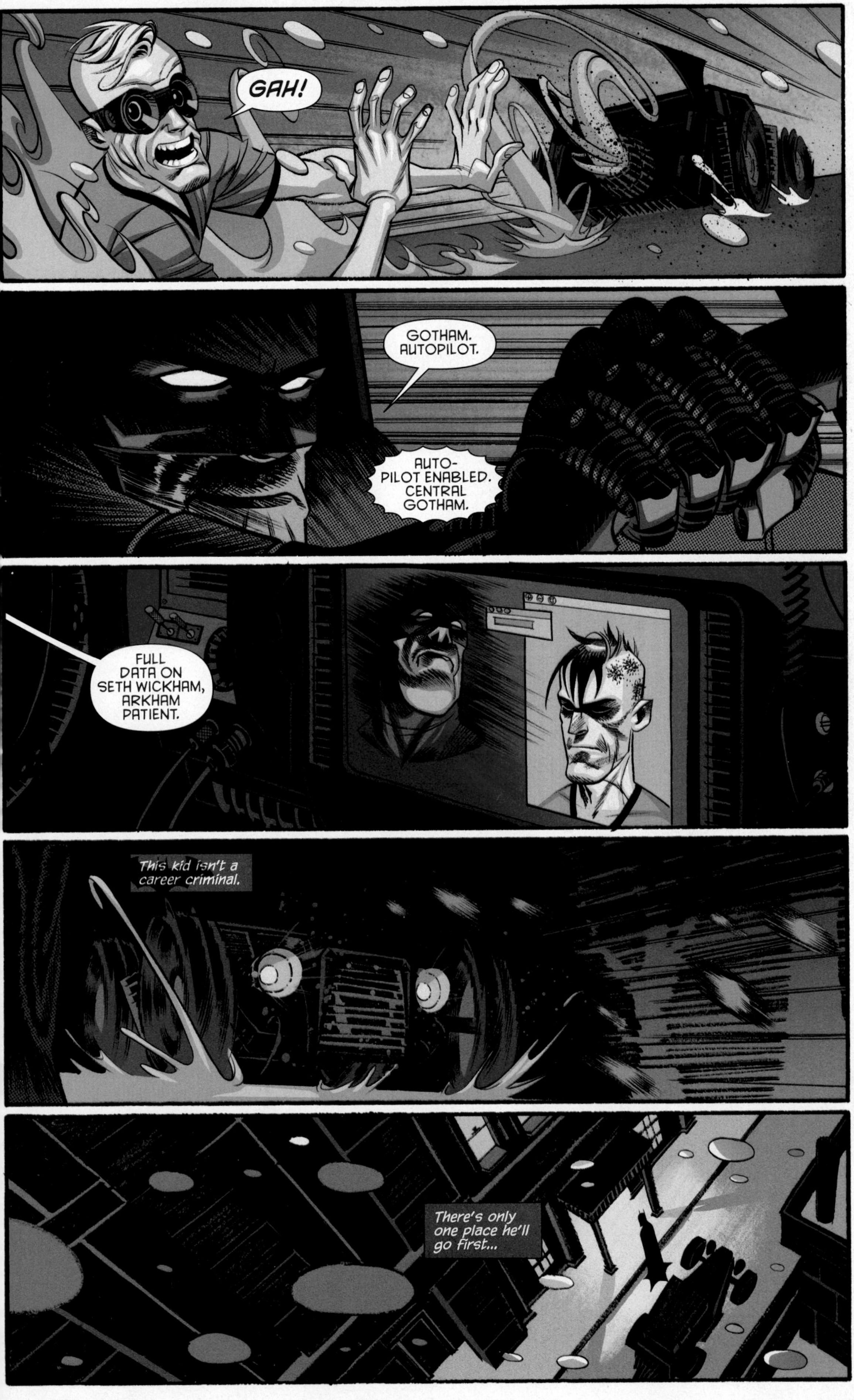
GAH!
GOTHAM. AUTOPILOT.
AUTO-PILOT ENABLED. CENTRAL GOTHAM.
FULL DATA ON SETH WICKHAM, ARKHAM PATIENT.
This kid isn't a career criminal.
There's only one place he'll go first...

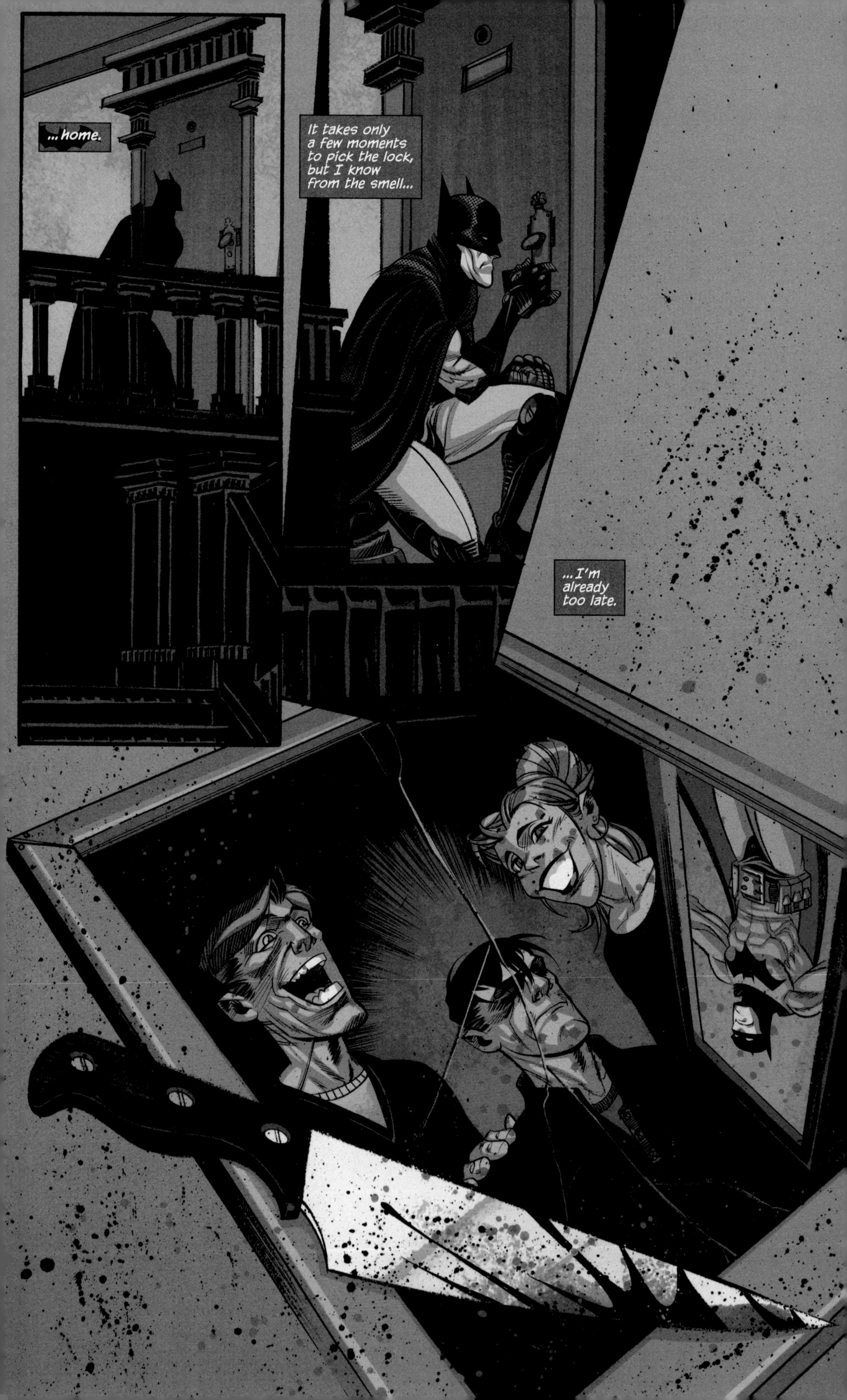
...home.
It takes only a few moments to pick the lock, but I know from the smell...
...I'm already too late.

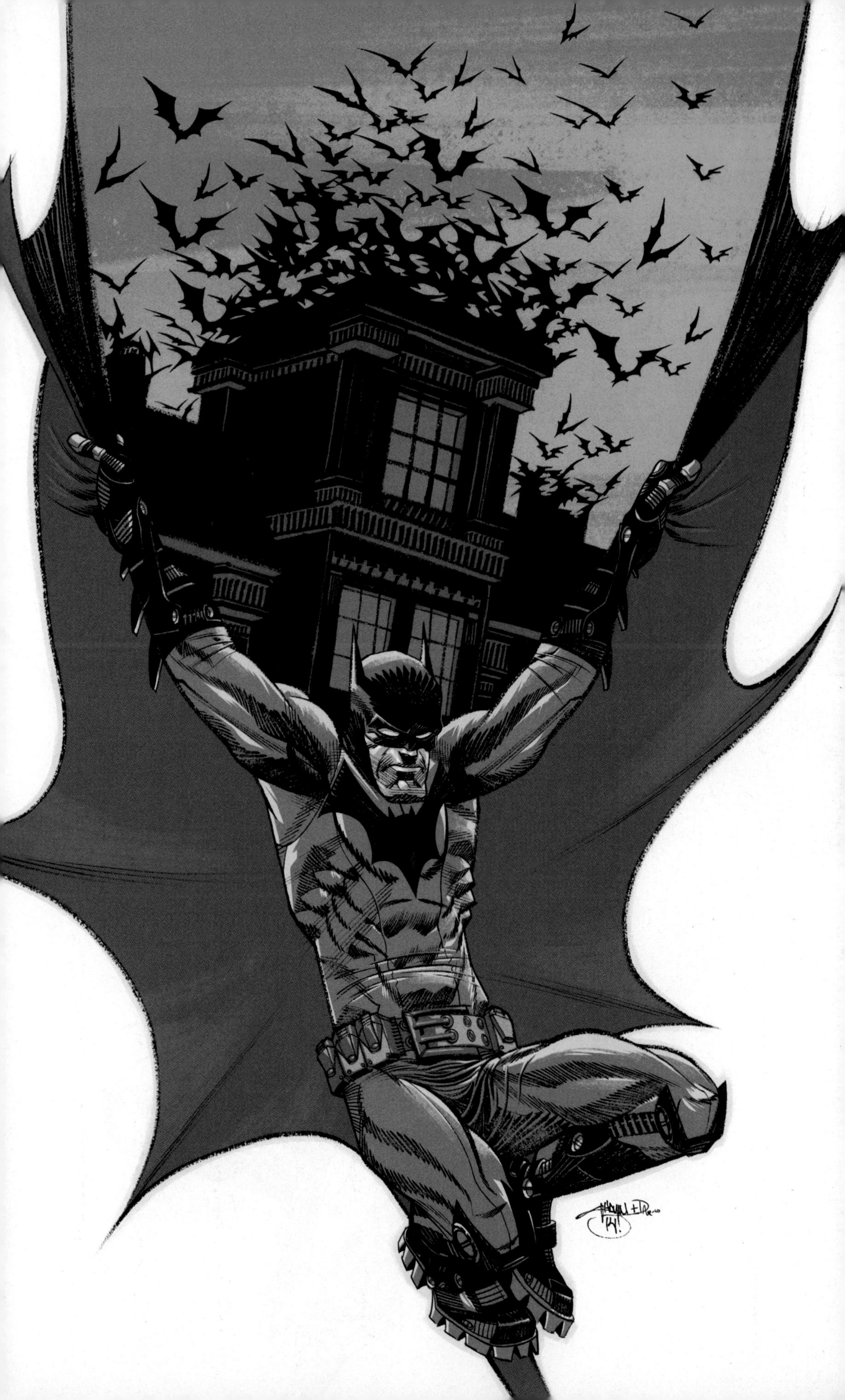

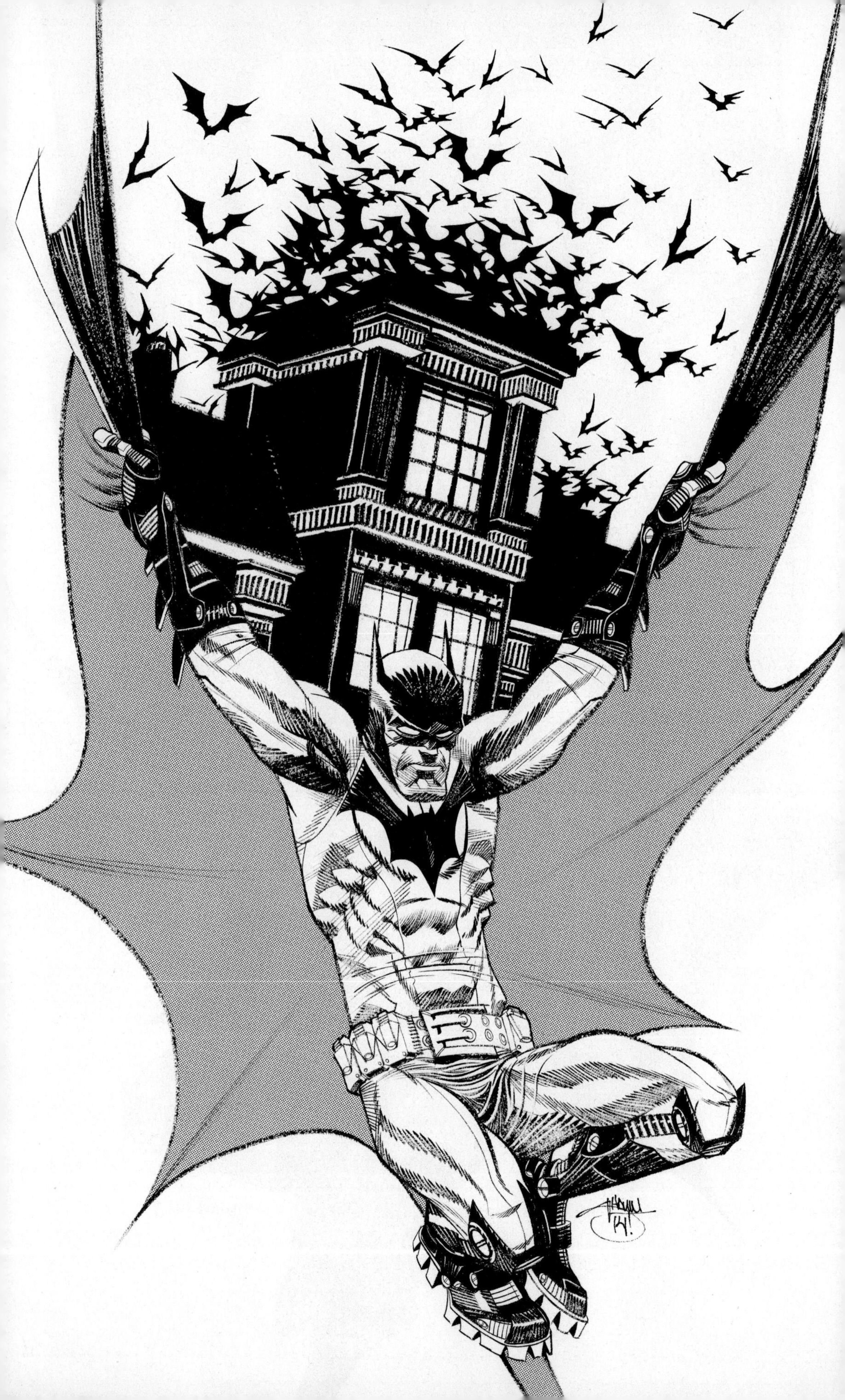

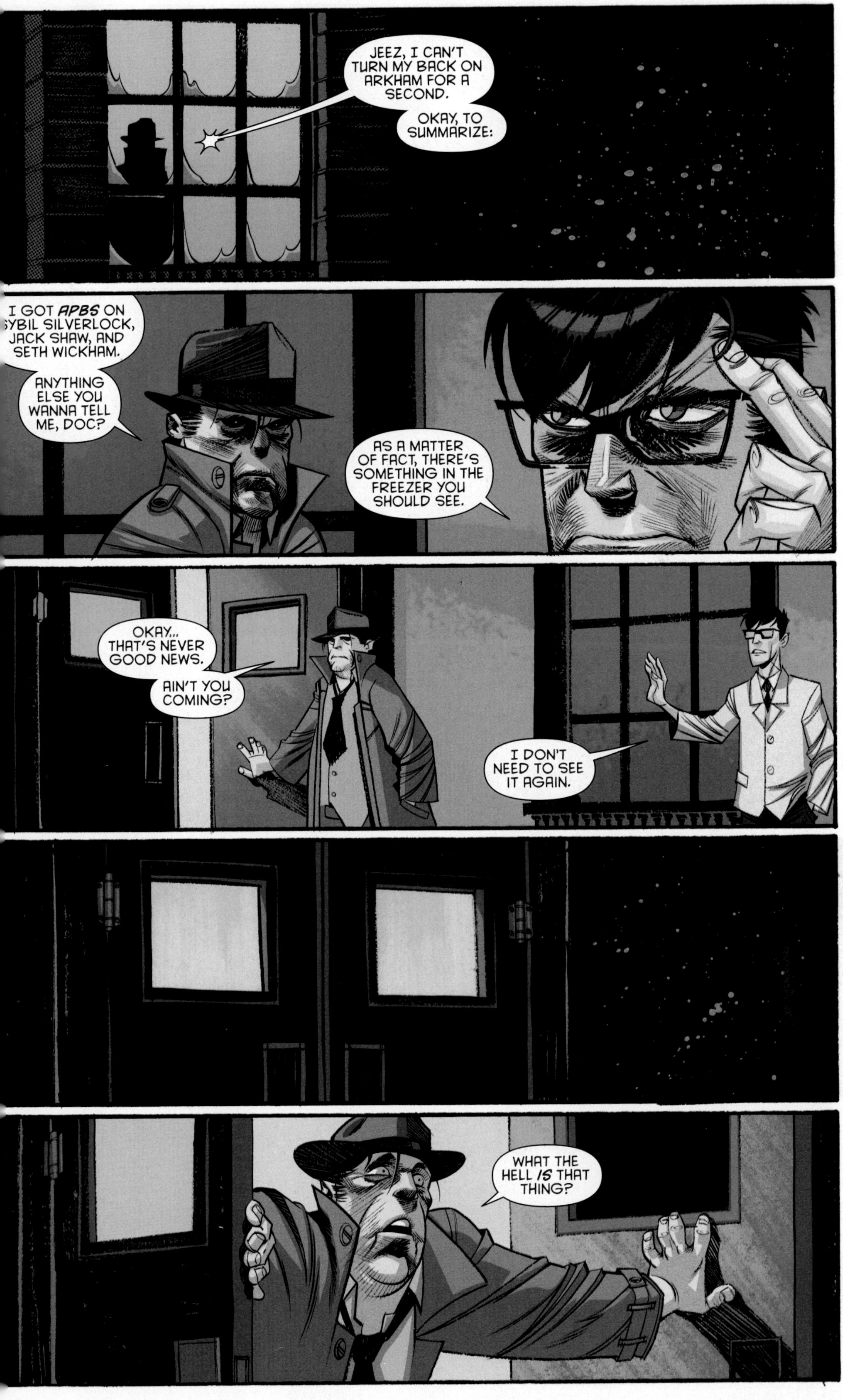
JEEZ, I CAN'T TURN MY BACK ON ARKHAM FOR A SECOND.
OKAY, TO SUMMARIZE:
I GOT APBS ON SYBIL SILVERLOCK, JACK SHAW, AND SETH WICKHAM.
ANYTHING ELSE YOU WANNA TELL ME, DOC?
AS A MATTER OF FACT, THERE'S SOMETHING IN THE FREEZER YOU SHOULD SEE.
OKAY... THAT'S NEVER GOOD NEWS.
AIN'T YOU COMING?
I DON'T NEED TO SEE IT AGAIN.
WHAT THE HELL IS THAT THING?

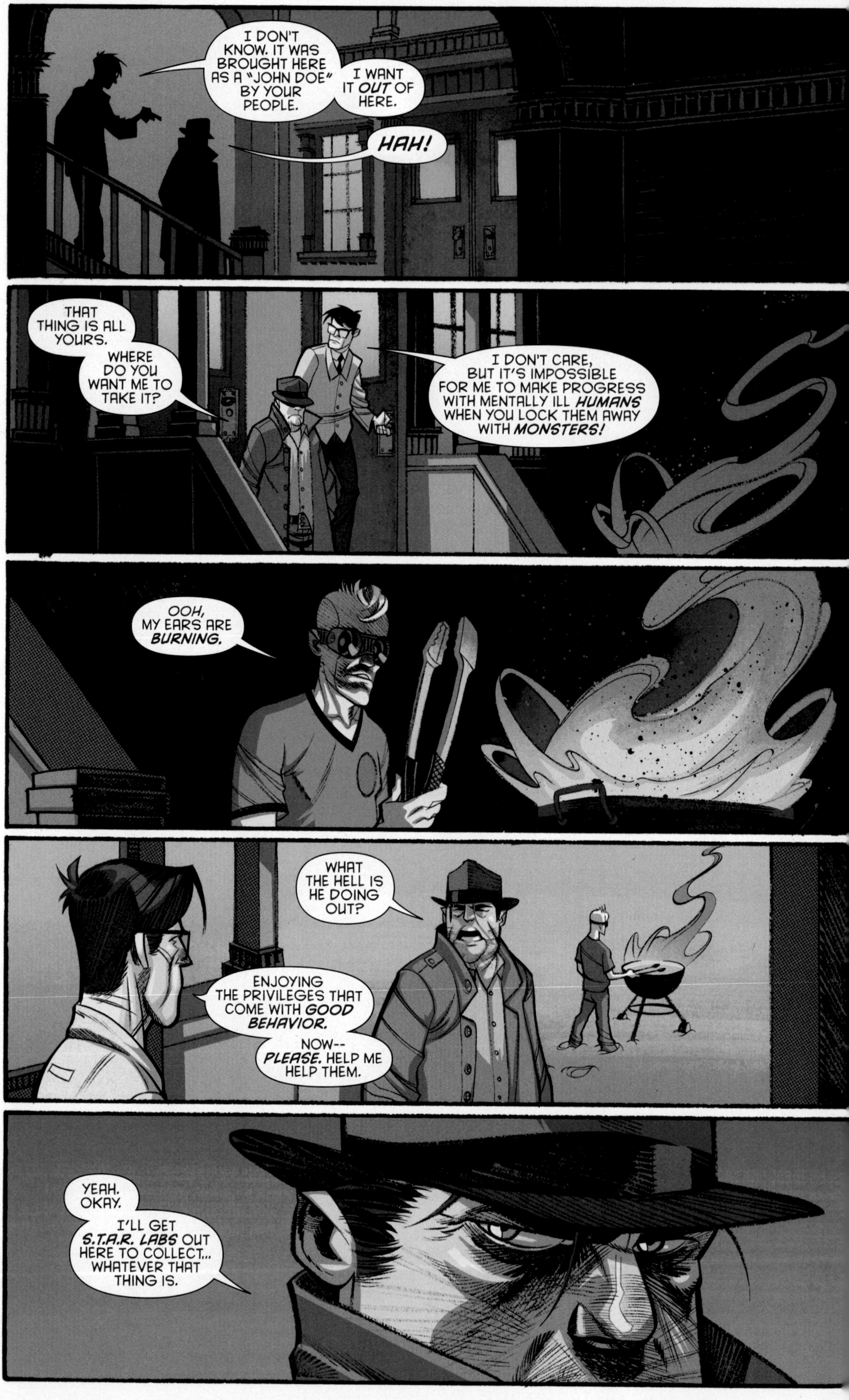
I DON'T KNOW. IT WAS BROUGHT HERE AS A "JOHN DOE" BY YOUR PEOPLE.
I WANT IT OUT OF HERE.
HAH!
THAT THING IS ALL YOURS.
WHERE DO YOU WANT ME TO TAKE IT?
I DON'T CARE, BUT IT'S IMPOSSIBLE FOR ME TO MAKE PROGRESS WITH MENTALLY ILL HUMANS WHEN YOU LOCK THEM AWAY WITH MONSTERS!
OOH, MY EARS ARE BURNING.
WHAT THE HELL IS HE DOING OUT?
ENJOYING THE PRIVILEGES THAT COME WITH GOOD BEHAVIOR.
NOW-- PLEASE. HELP ME HELP THEM.
YEAH. OKAY.
I'LL GET S.T.A.R. LABS OUT HERE TO COLLECT... WHATEVER THAT THING IS.

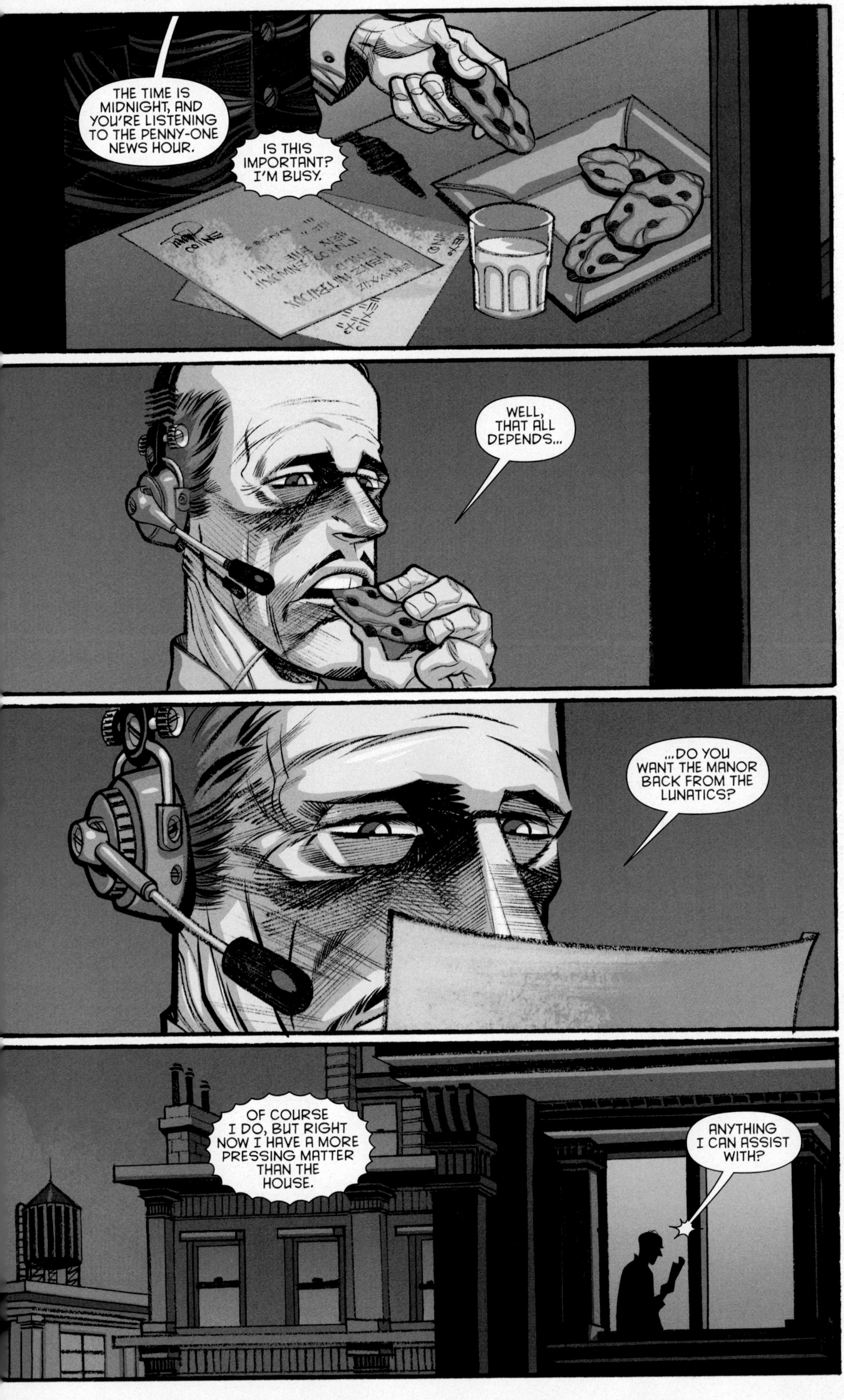
THE TIME IS MIDNIGHT, AND YOU'RE LISTENING TO THE PENNY-ONE NEWS HOUR.
IS THIS IMPORTANT? I'M BUSY.
WELL, THAT ALL DEPENDS...
...DO YOU WANT THE MANOR BACK FROM THE LUNATICS?
OF COURSE I DO, BUT RIGHT NOW I HAVE A MORE PRESSING MATTER THAN THE HOUSE.
ANYTHING I CAN ASSIST WITH?

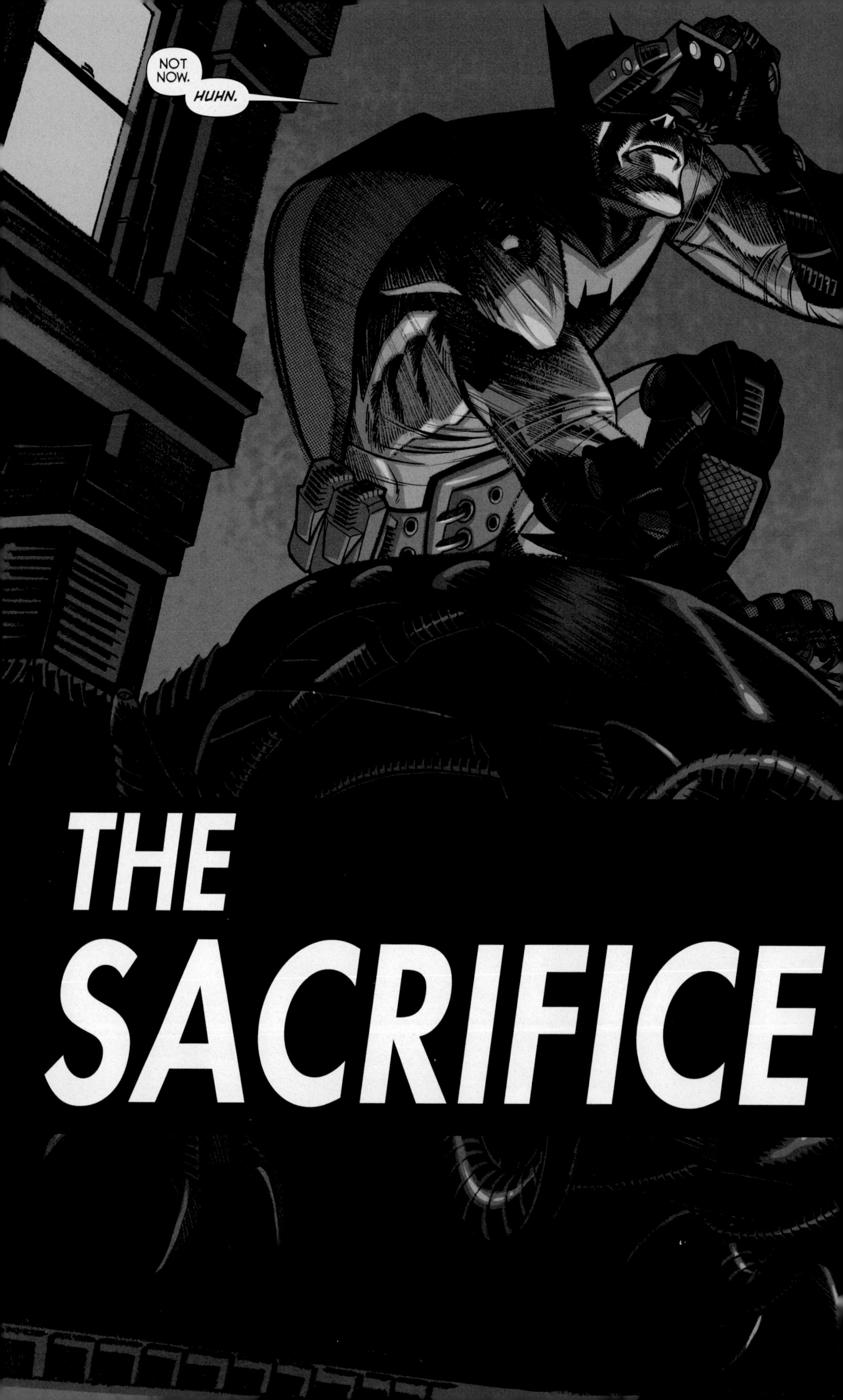
NOT NOW.
HUHN.
THE SACRIFICE

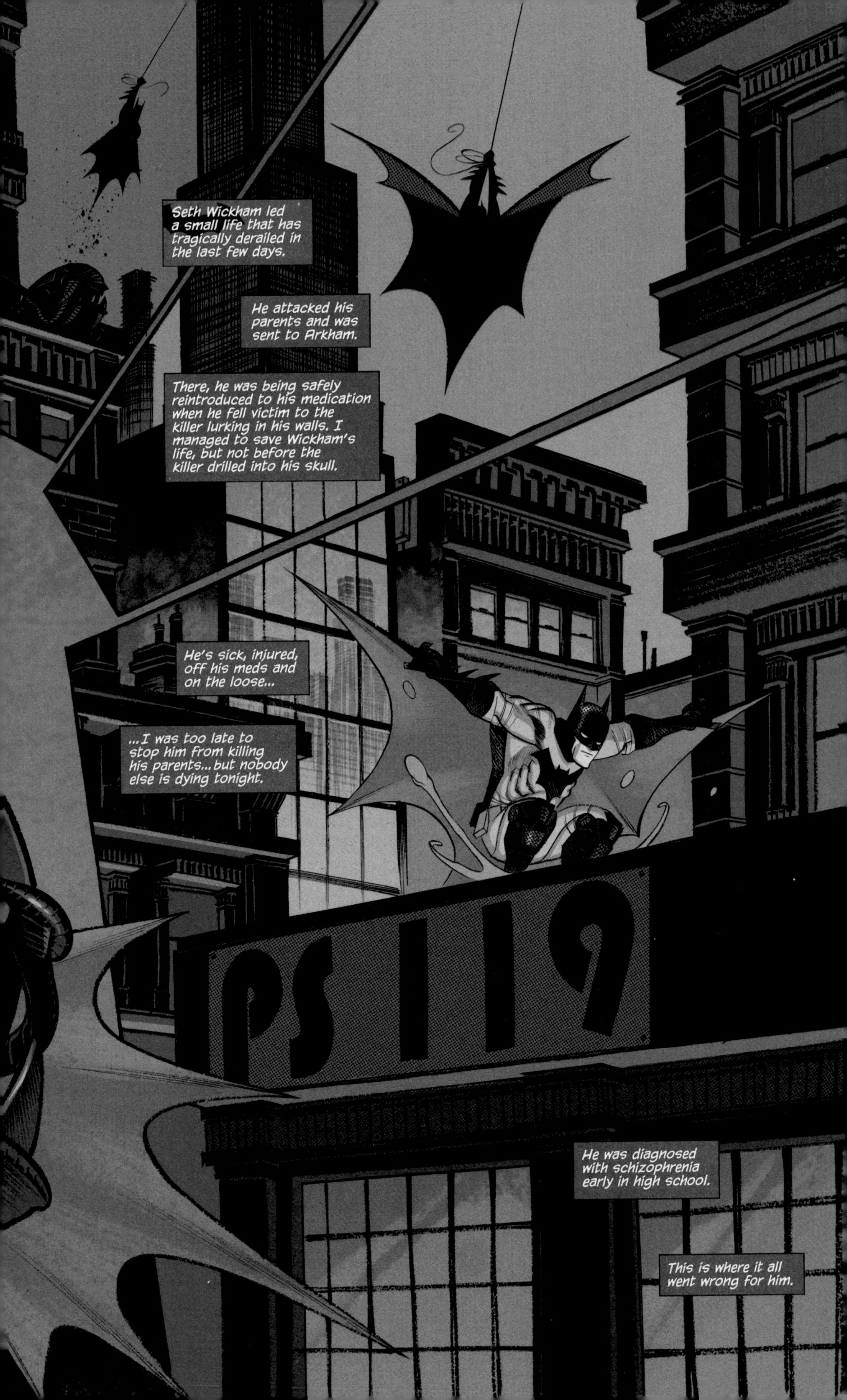
Seth Wickham led a small life that has tragically derailed in the last few days.
He attacked his parents and was sent to Arkham.
There, he was being safely reintroduced to his medication when he fell victim to the killer lurking in his walls. I managed to save Wickham's life, but not before the killer drilled into his skull.
He's sick, injured, off his meds and on the loose...
...I was too late to stop him from killing his parents...but nobody else is dying tonight.
PS 119
He was diagnosed with schizophrenia early in high school.
This is where it all went wrong for him.

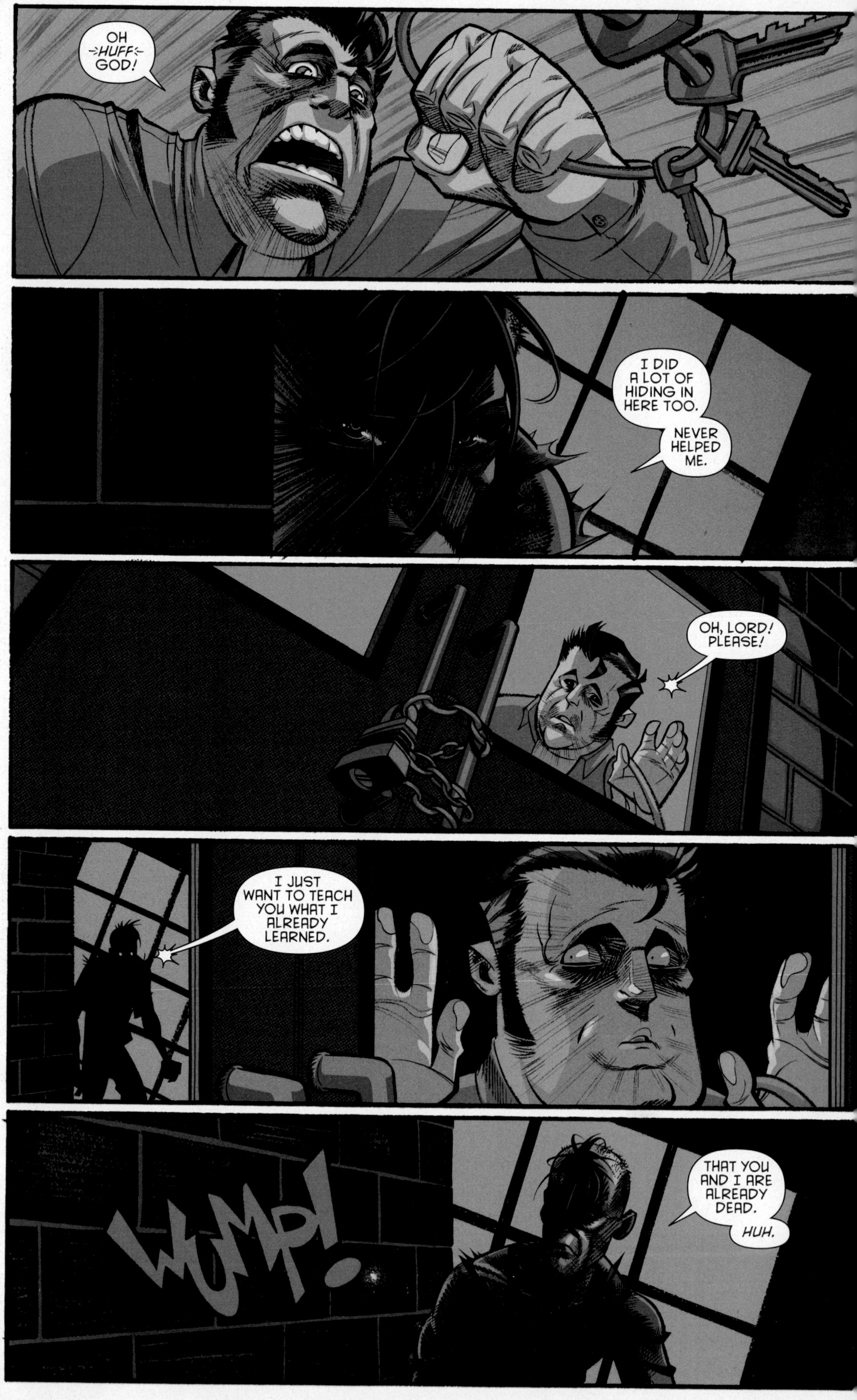
OH -HUFF- GOD!
I DID A LOT OF HIDING IN HERE TOO.
NEVER HELPED ME.
OH, LORD! PLEASE!
I JUST WANT TO TEACH YOU WHAT I ALREADY LEARNED.
WUMP!
THAT YOU AND I ARE ALREADY DEAD.
HUH.

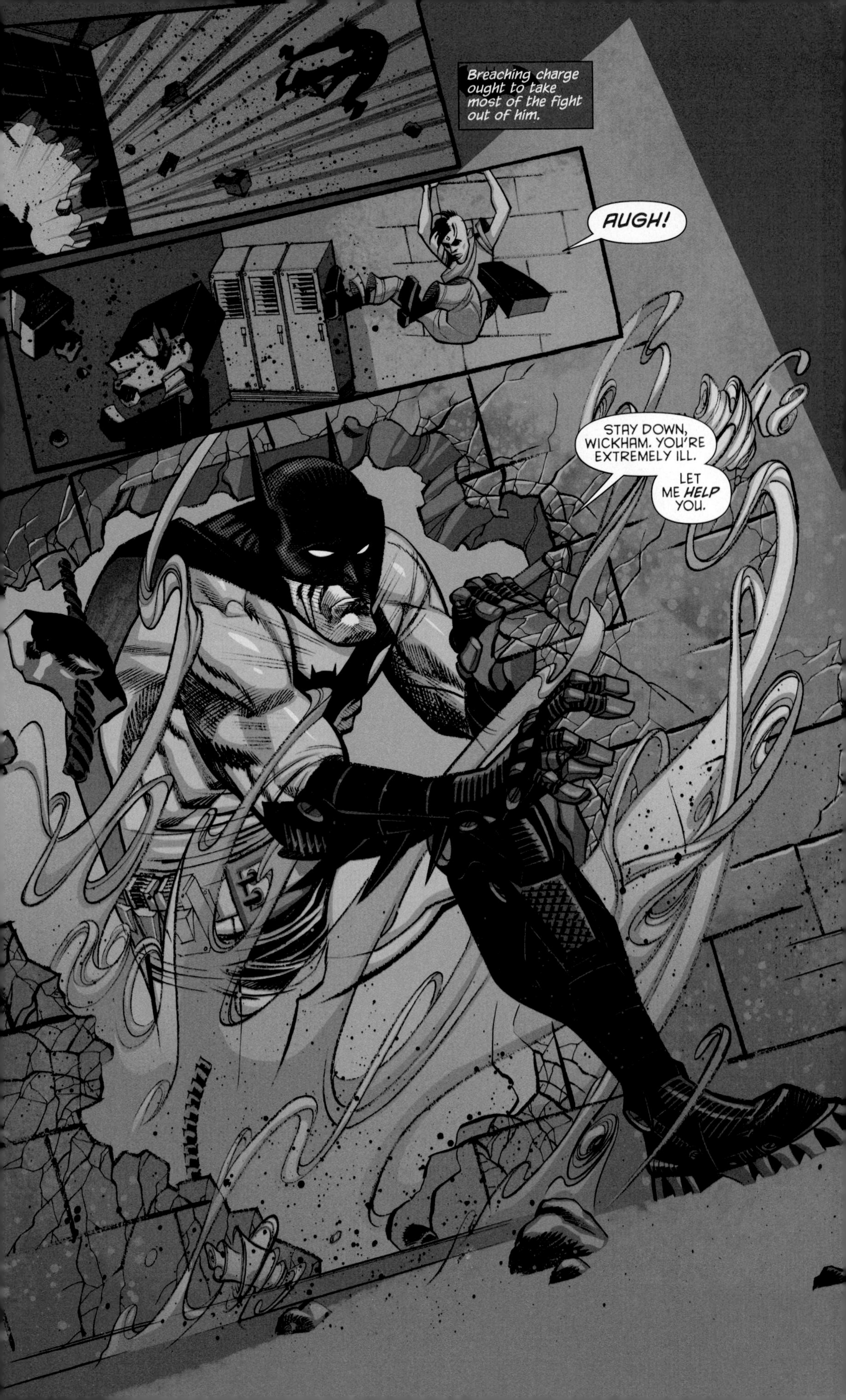
Breaching charge ought to take most of the fight out of him.
AUGH!
STAY DOWN, WICKHAM. YOU'RE EXTREMELY ILL.
LET ME HELP YOU.

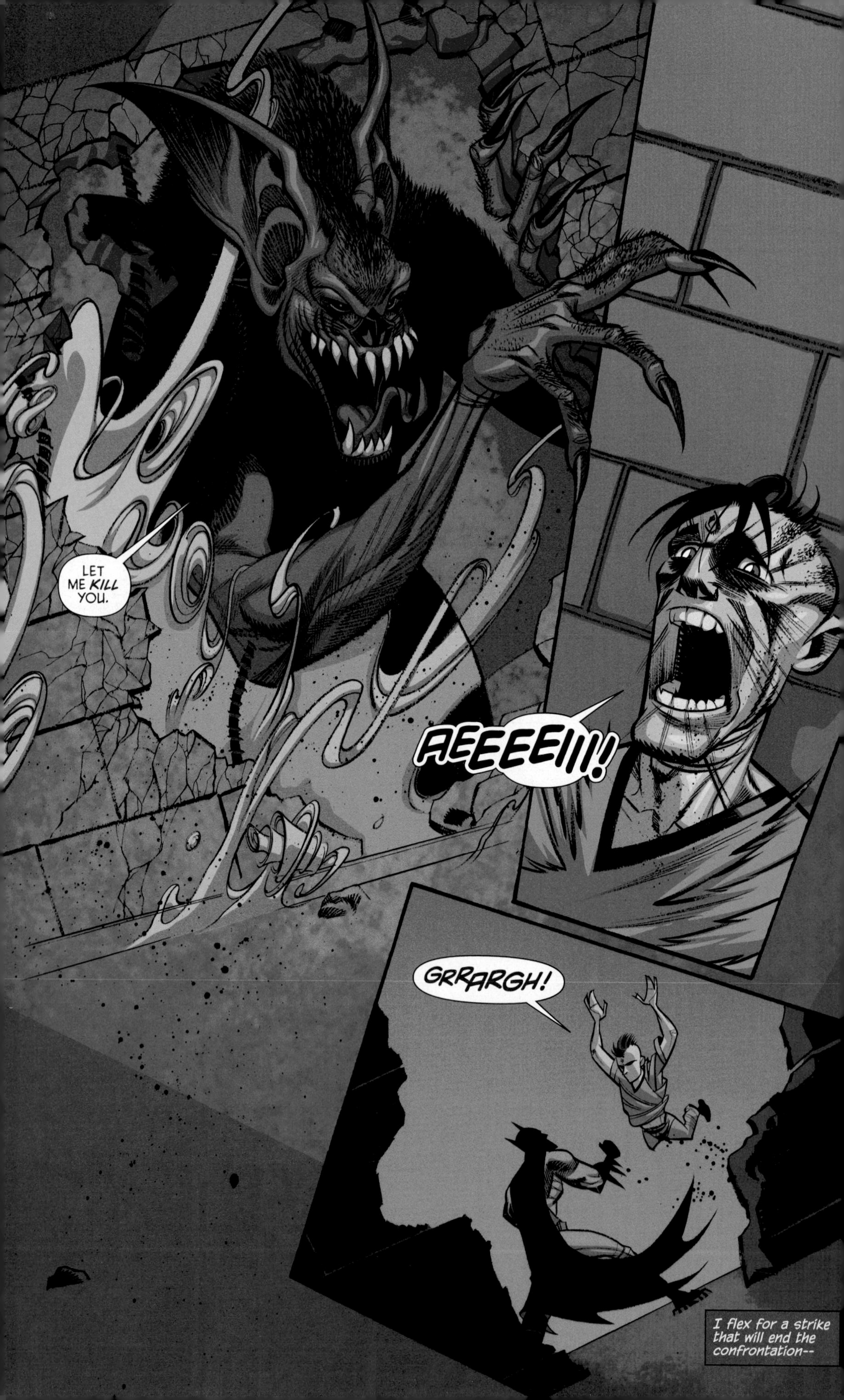
LET ME KILL YOU.
AEEEEIII!
GRRARGH!
I flex for a strike that will end the confrontation--

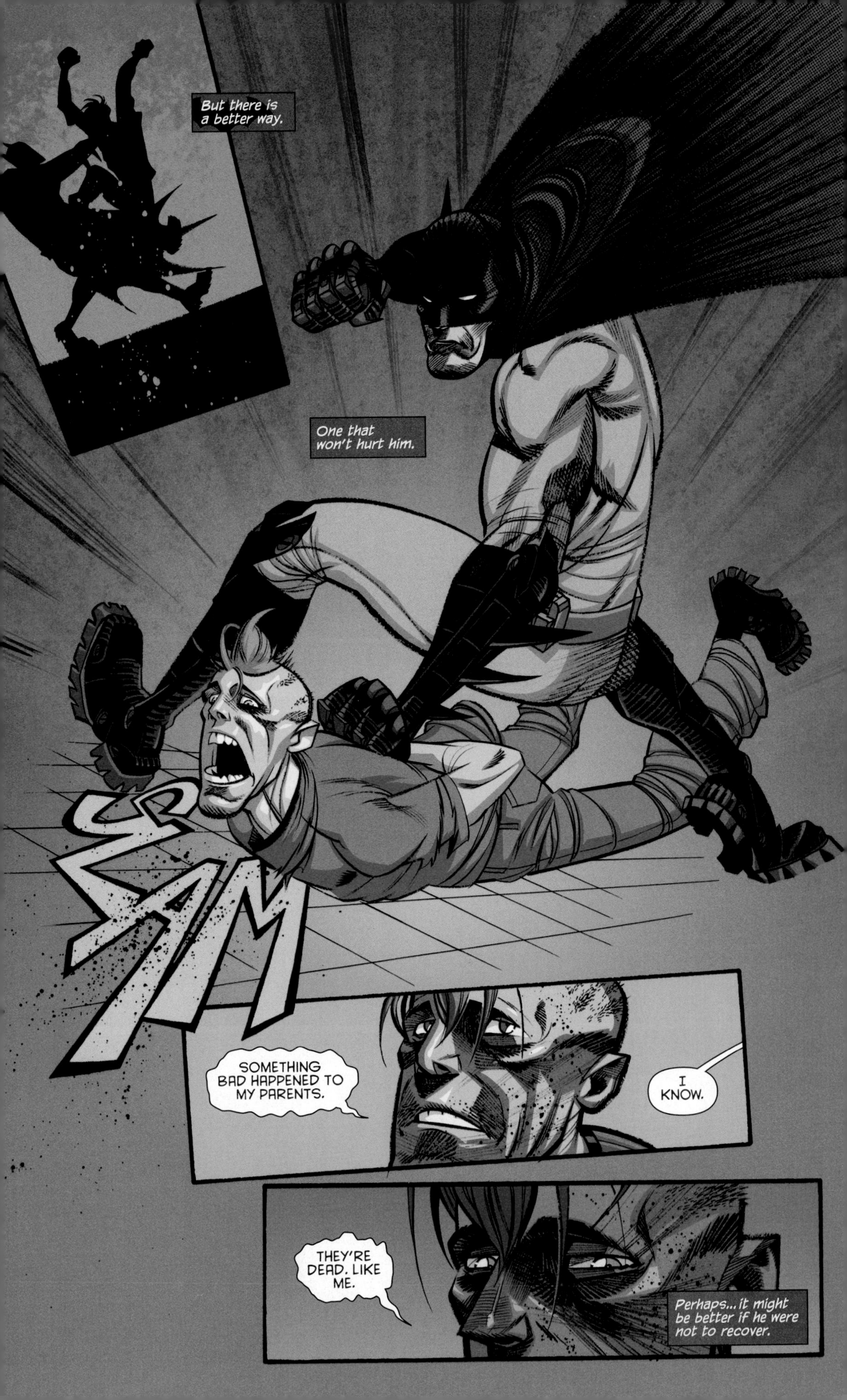
But there is a better way.
One that won't hurt him.
SLAM
SOMETHING BAD HAPPENED TO MY PARENTS.
I KNOW.
THEY'RE DEAD. LIKE ME.
Perhaps...it might be better if he were not to recover.

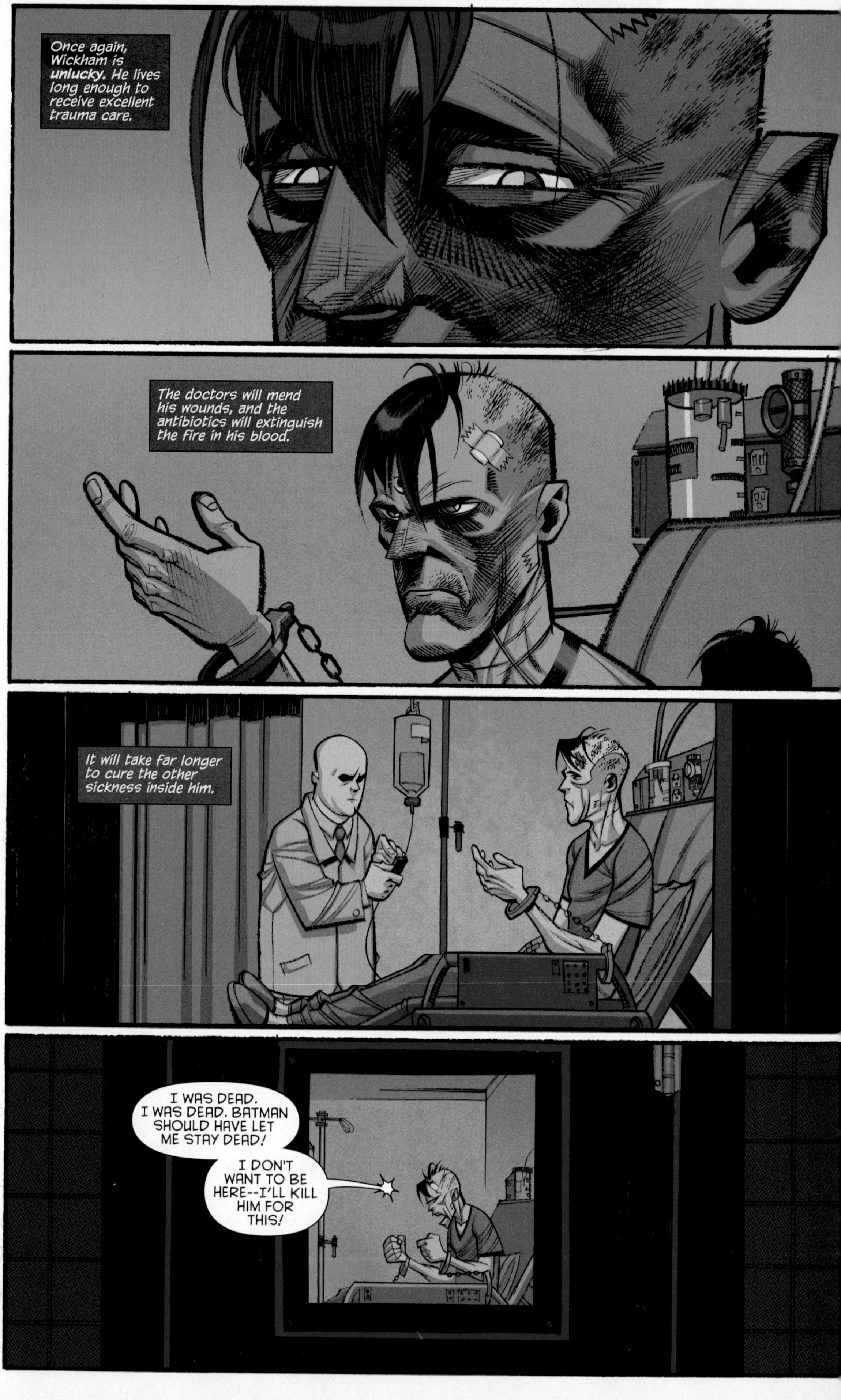
Once again, Wickham is **unlucky.** He lives long enough to receive excellent trauma care.
The doctors will mend his wounds, and the antibiotics will extinguish the fire in his blood.
It will take far longer to cure the other sickness inside him.
I WAS DEAD. I WAS DEAD. BATMAN SHOULD HAVE LET ME STAY DEAD!
I DON'T WANT TO BE HERE--I'LL KILL HIM FOR THIS!

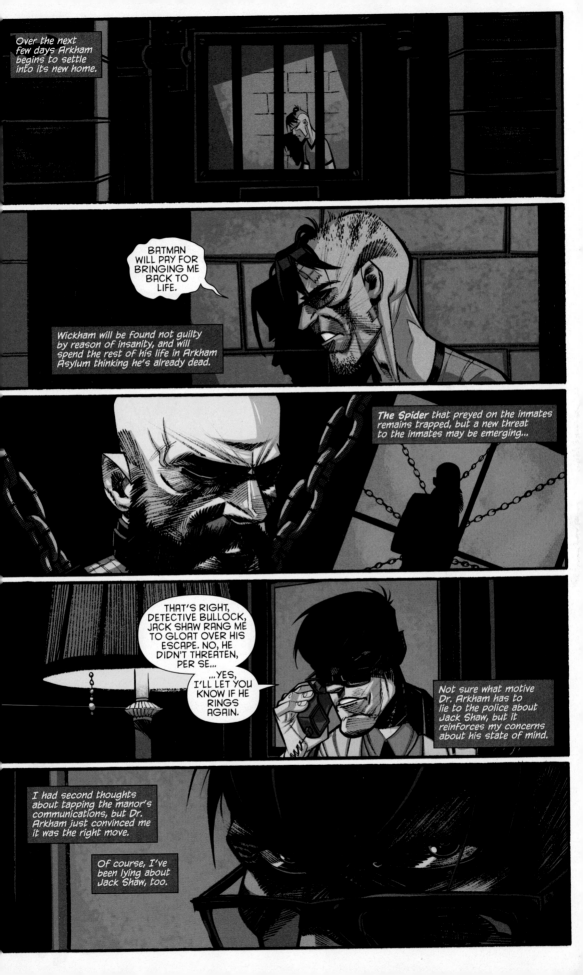

Over the next few days Arkham begins to settle into its new home.

BATMAN WILL PAY FOR BRINGING ME BACK TO LIFE.

Wickham will be found not guilty by reason of insanity, and will spend the rest of his life in Arkham Asylum thinking he's already dead.

The Spider that preyed on the inmates remains trapped, but a new threat to the inmates may be emerging...

THAT'S RIGHT, DETECTIVE BULLOCK, JACK SHAW RANG ME TO GLOAT OVER HIS ESCAPE. NO, HE DIDN'T THREATEN, PER SE...

...YES, I'LL LET YOU KNOW IF HE RINGS AGAIN.

Not sure what motive Dr. Arkham has to lie to the police about Jack Shaw, but it reinforces my concerns about his state of mind.

I had second thoughts about tapping the manor's communications, but Dr. Arkham just convinced me it was the right move.

Of course, I've been lying about Jack Shaw, too.

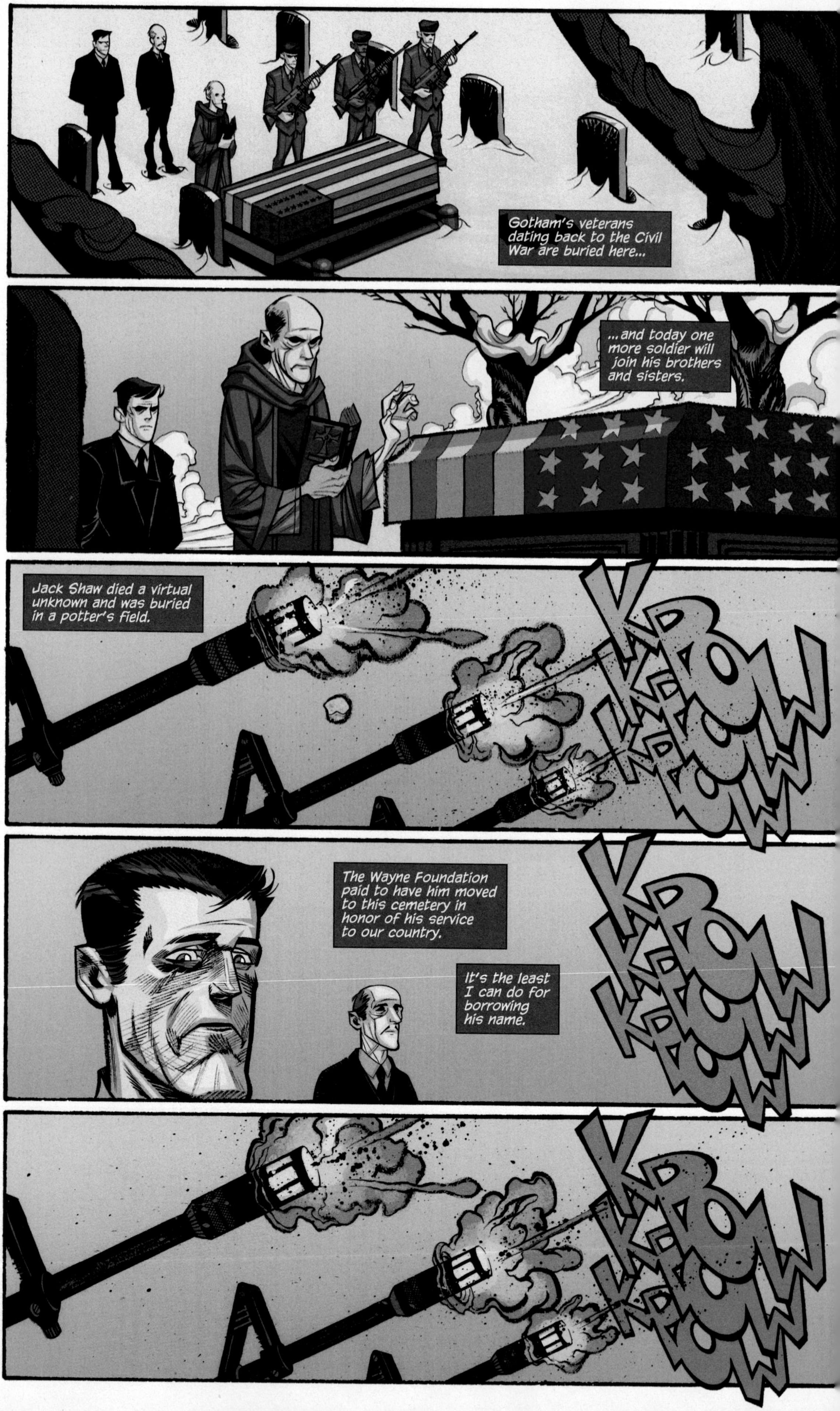

Gotham's veterans dating back to the Civil War are buried here...
...and today one more soldier will join his brothers and sisters.
Jack Shaw died a virtual unknown and was buried in a potter's field.
KBOW KBOW KBOW
The Wayne Foundation paid to have him moved to this cemetery in honor of his service to our country.
It's the least I can do for borrowing his name.
KBOW KBOW KBOW
KBOW KBOW KBOW

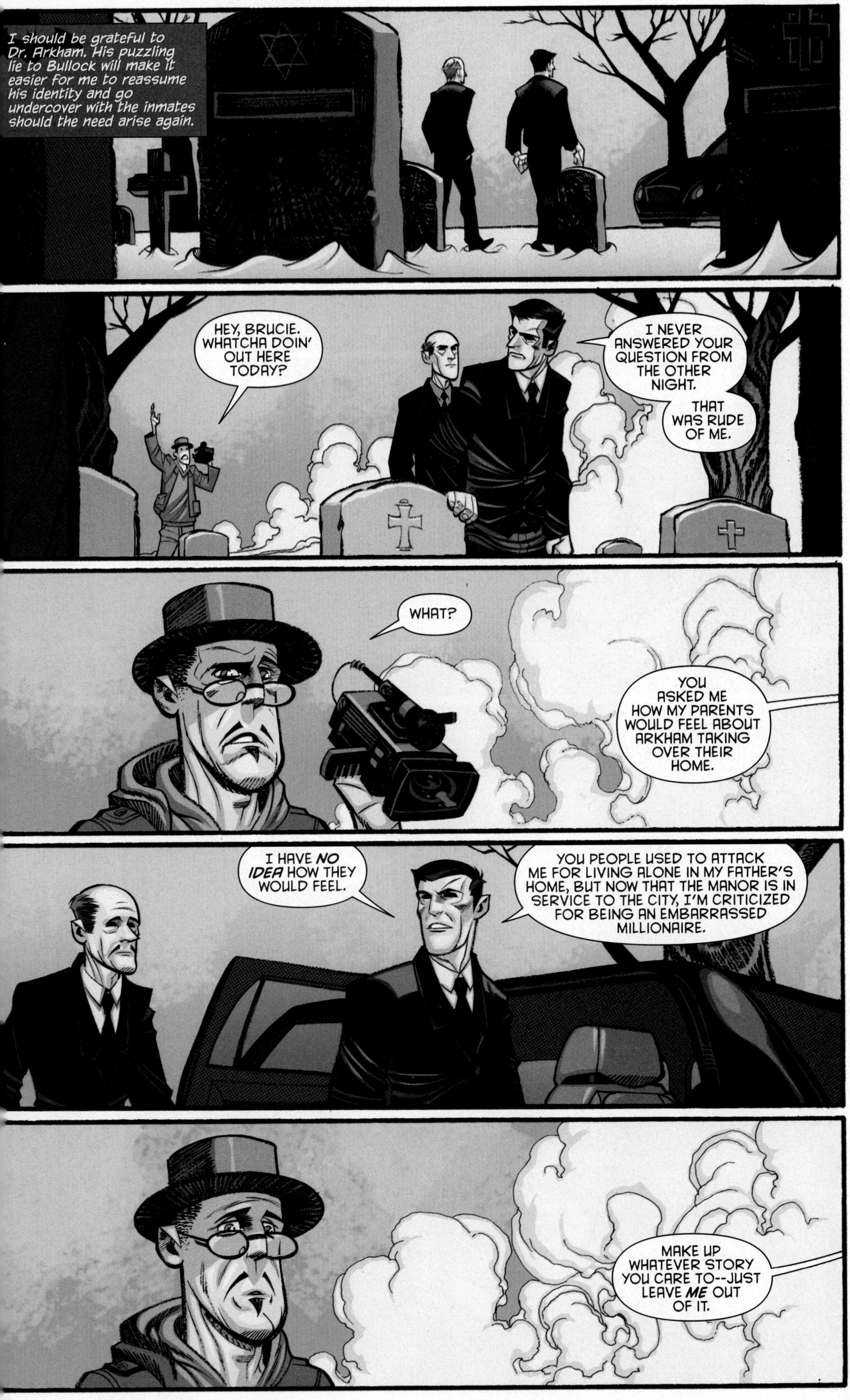
I should be grateful to Dr. Arkham. His puzzling lie to Bullock will make it easier for me to reassume his identity and go undercover with the inmates should the need arise again.
HEY, BRUCIE. WHATCHA DOIN' OUT HERE TODAY?
I NEVER ANSWERED YOUR QUESTION FROM THE OTHER NIGHT.
THAT WAS RUDE OF ME.
WHAT?
YOU ASKED ME HOW MY PARENTS WOULD FEEL ABOUT ARKHAM TAKING OVER THEIR HOME.
I HAVE NO IDEA HOW THEY WOULD FEEL.
YOU PEOPLE USED TO ATTACK ME FOR LIVING ALONE IN MY FATHER'S HOME, BUT NOW THAT THE MANOR IS IN SERVICE TO THE CITY, I'M CRITICIZED FOR BEING AN EMBARRASSED MILLIONAIRE.
MAKE UP WHATEVER STORY YOU CARE TO--JUST LEAVE ME OUT OF IT.

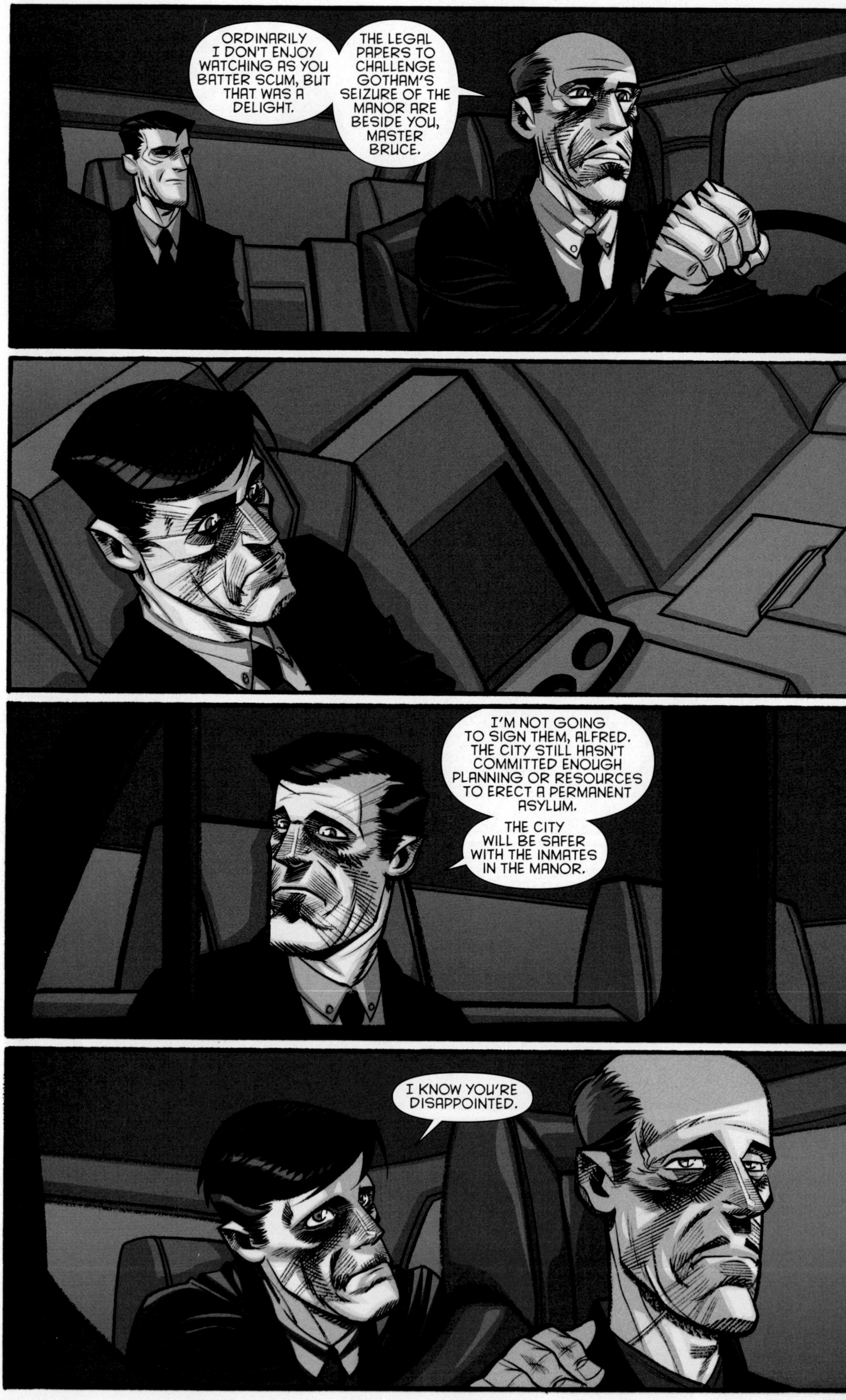
ORDINARILY I DON'T ENJOY WATCHING AS YOU BATTER SCUM, BUT THAT WAS A DELIGHT.
THE LEGAL PAPERS TO CHALLENGE GOTHAM'S SEIZURE OF THE MANOR ARE BESIDE YOU, MASTER BRUCE.
I'M NOT GOING TO SIGN THEM, ALFRED. THE CITY STILL HASN'T COMMITTED ENOUGH PLANNING OR RESOURCES TO ERECT A PERMANENT ASYLUM.
THE CITY WILL BE SAFER WITH THE INMATES IN THE MANOR.
I KNOW YOU'RE DISAPPOINTED.

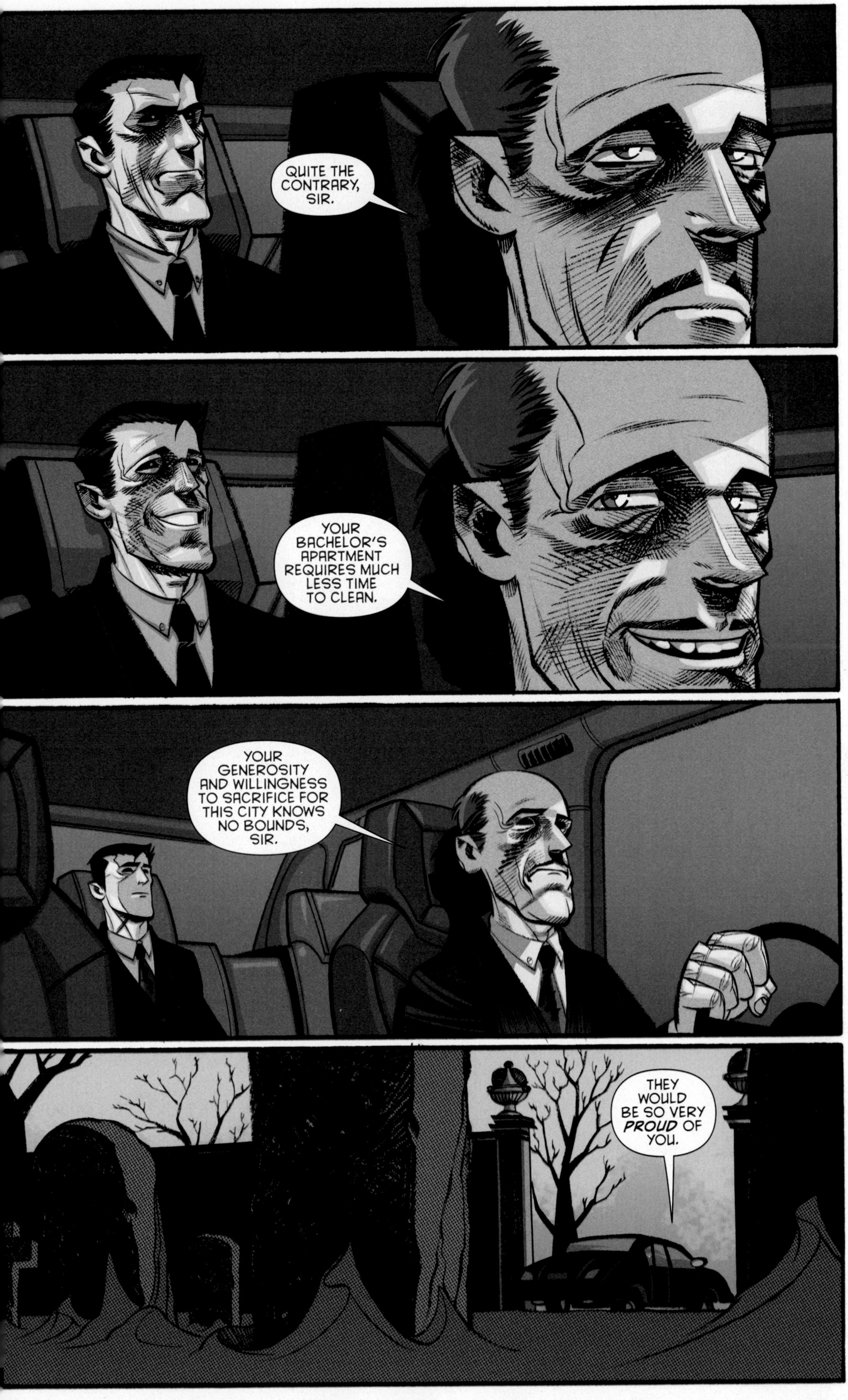
QUITE THE CONTRARY, SIR.
YOUR BACHELOR'S APARTMENT REQUIRES MUCH LESS TIME TO CLEAN.
YOUR GENEROSITY AND WILLINGNESS TO SACRIFICE FOR THIS CITY KNOWS NO BOUNDS, SIR.
THEY WOULD BE SO VERY *PROUD* OF YOU.

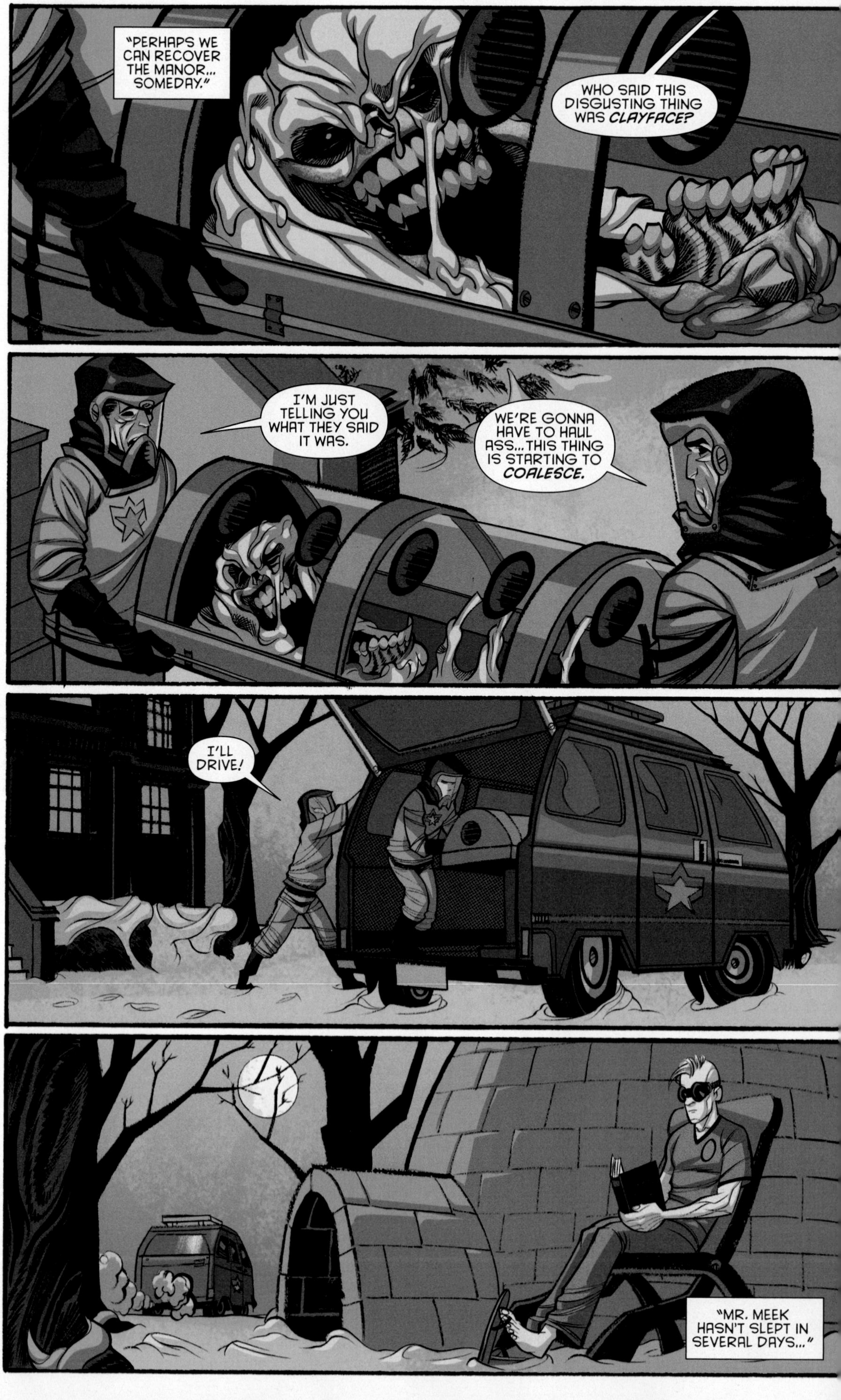
"PERHAPS WE CAN RECOVER THE MANOR... SOMEDAY."
WHO SAID THIS DISGUSTING THING WAS CLAYFACE?
I'M JUST TELLING YOU WHAT THEY SAID IT WAS.
WE'RE GONNA HAVE TO HAUL ASS...THIS THING IS STARTING TO COALESCE.
I'LL DRIVE!
"MR. MEEK HASN'T SLEPT IN SEVERAL DAYS..."

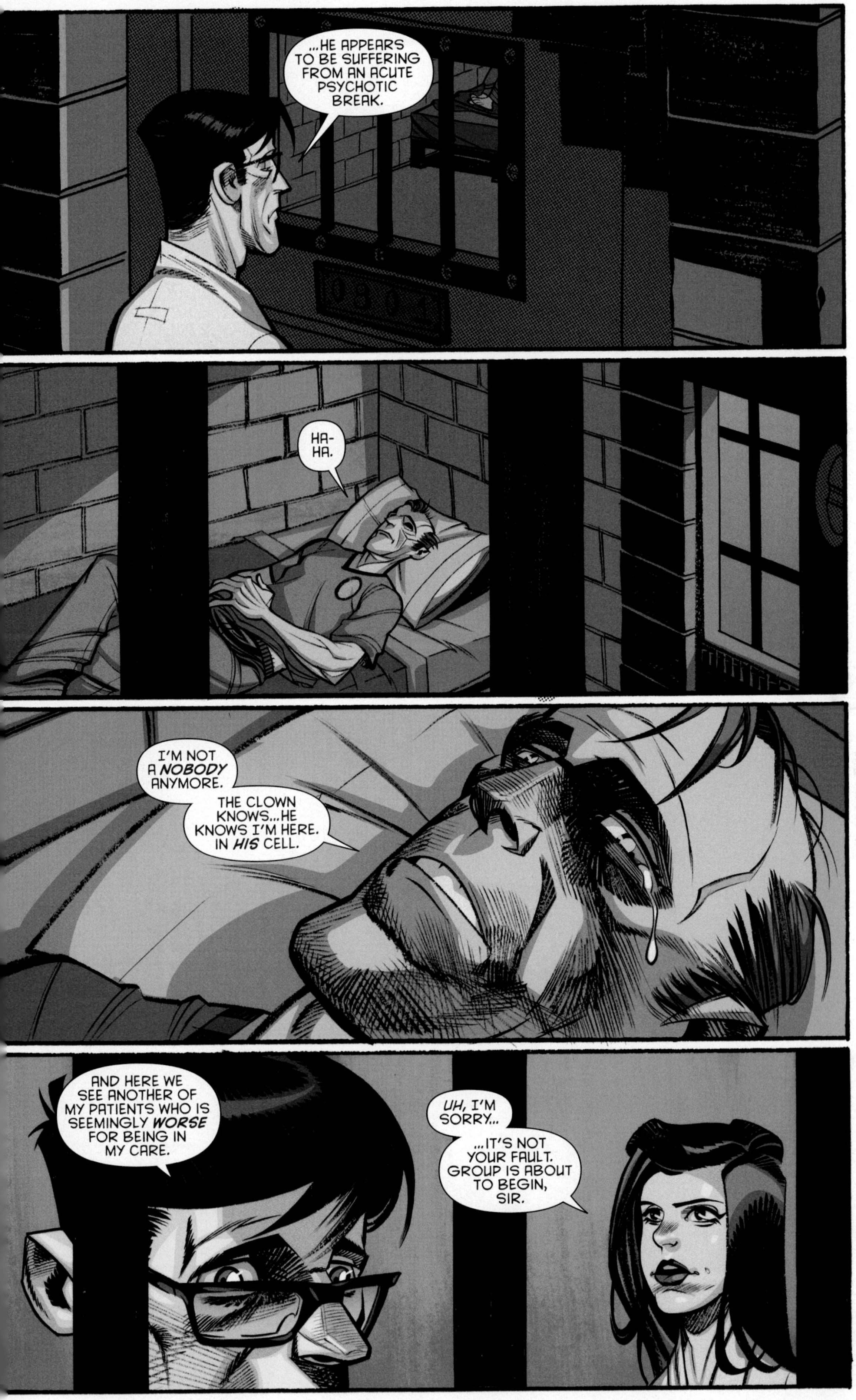
...HE APPEARS TO BE SUFFERING FROM AN ACUTE PSYCHOTIC BREAK.
HA-HA.
I'M NOT A *NOBODY* ANYMORE.
THE CLOWN KNOWS...HE KNOWS I'M HERE. IN *HIS* CELL.
AND HERE WE SEE ANOTHER OF MY PATIENTS WHO IS SEEMINGLY *WORSE* FOR BEING IN MY CARE.
UH, I'M SORRY...
...IT'S NOT YOUR FAULT. GROUP IS ABOUT TO BEGIN, SIR.

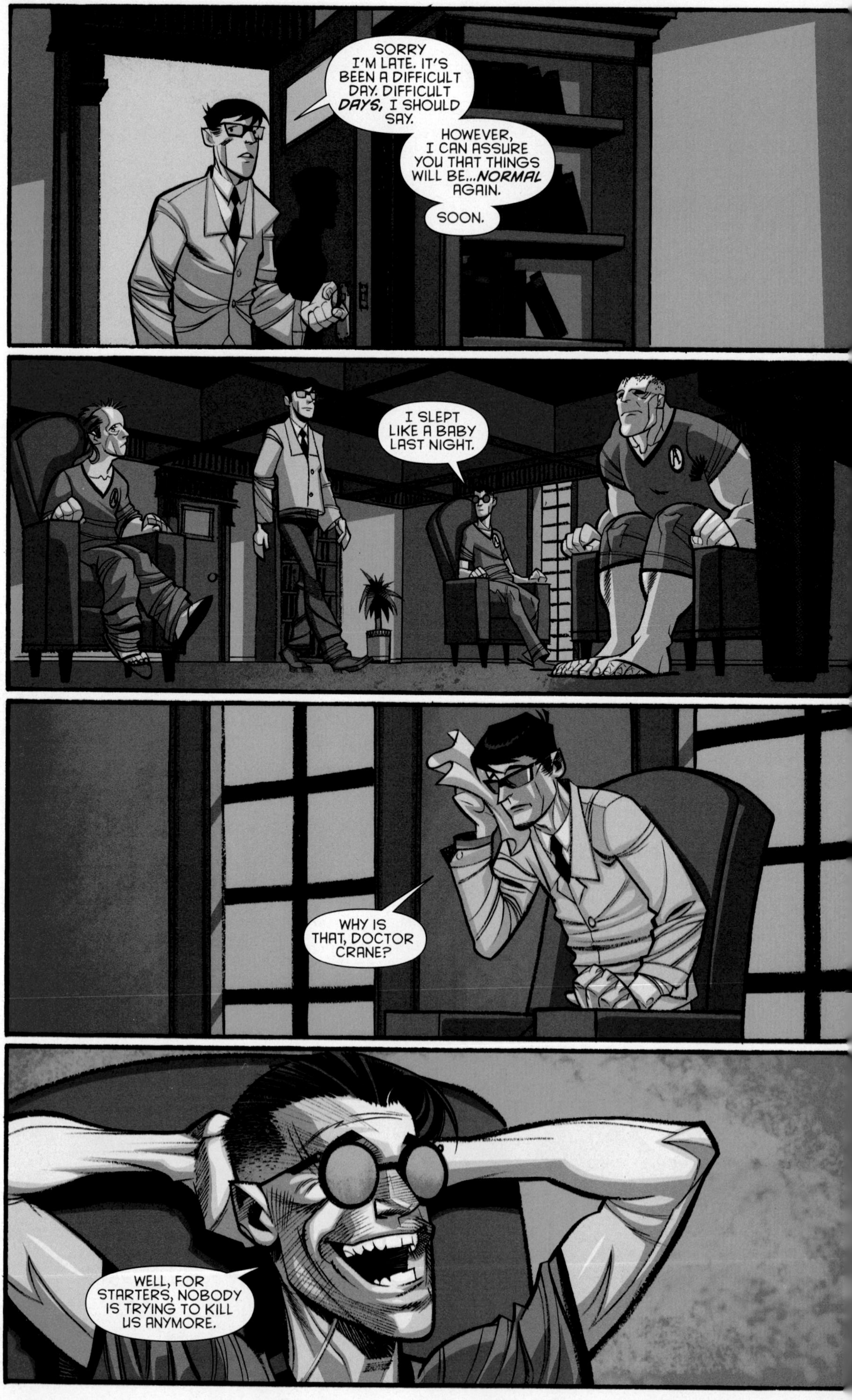
SORRY I'M LATE. IT'S BEEN A DIFFICULT DAY. DIFFICULT DAYS, I SHOULD SAY.
HOWEVER, I CAN ASSURE YOU THAT THINGS WILL BE...NORMAL AGAIN.
SOON.
I SLEPT LIKE A BABY LAST NIGHT.
WHY IS THAT, DOCTOR CRANE?
WELL, FOR STARTERS, NOBODY IS TRYING TO KILL US ANYMORE.

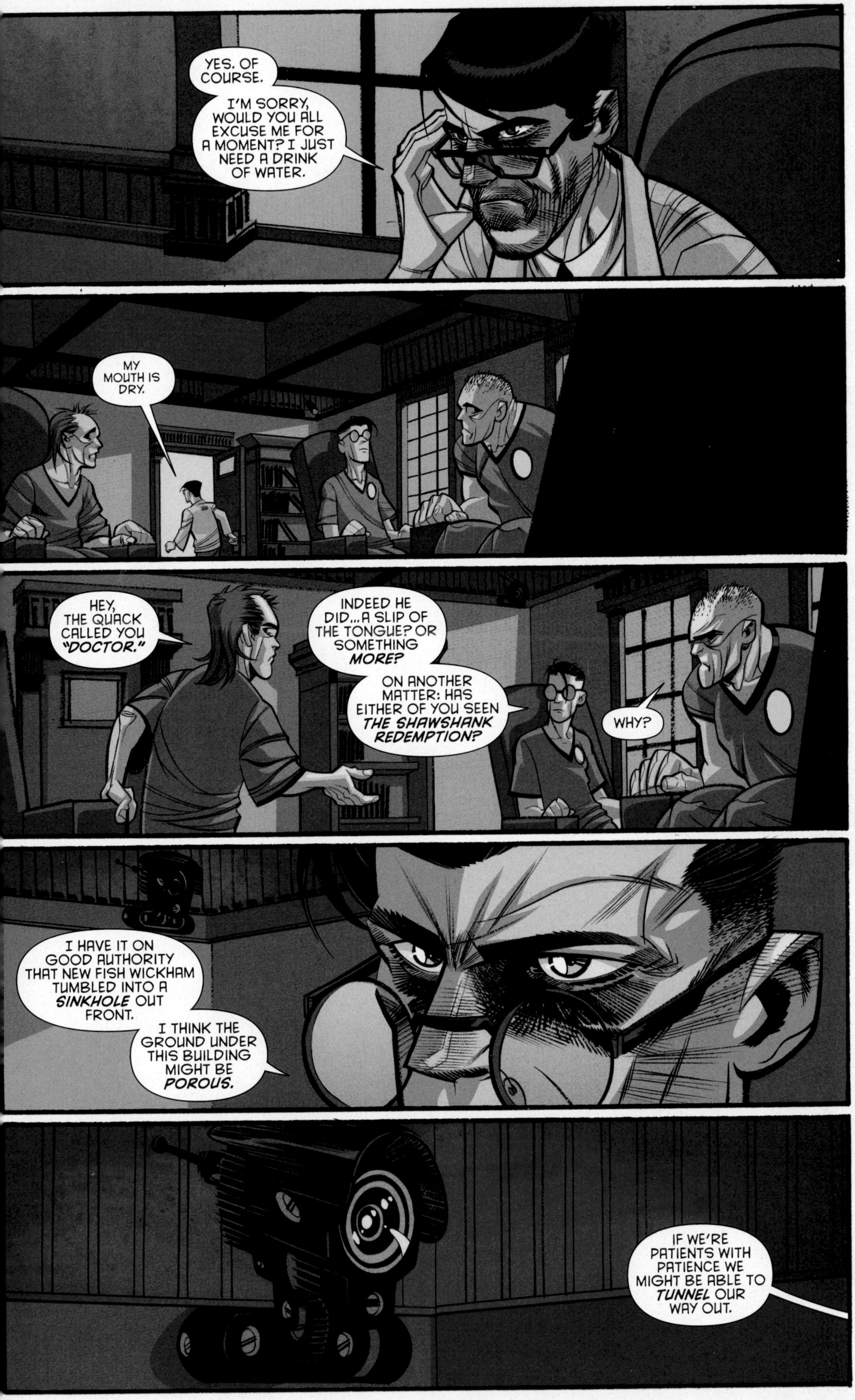
YES. OF COURSE.
I'M SORRY, WOULD YOU ALL EXCUSE ME FOR A MOMENT? I JUST NEED A DRINK OF WATER.
MY MOUTH IS DRY.
HEY, THE QUACK CALLED YOU "DOCTOR."
INDEED HE DID...A SLIP OF THE TONGUE? OR SOMETHING MORE?
ON ANOTHER MATTER: HAS EITHER OF YOU SEEN THE SHAWSHANK REDEMPTION?
WHY?
I HAVE IT ON GOOD AUTHORITY THAT NEW FISH WICKHAM TUMBLED INTO A SINKHOLE OUT FRONT.
I THINK THE GROUND UNDER THIS BUILDING MIGHT BE POROUS.
IF WE'RE PATIENTS WITH PATIENCE WE MIGHT BE ABLE TO TUNNEL OUR WAY OUT.

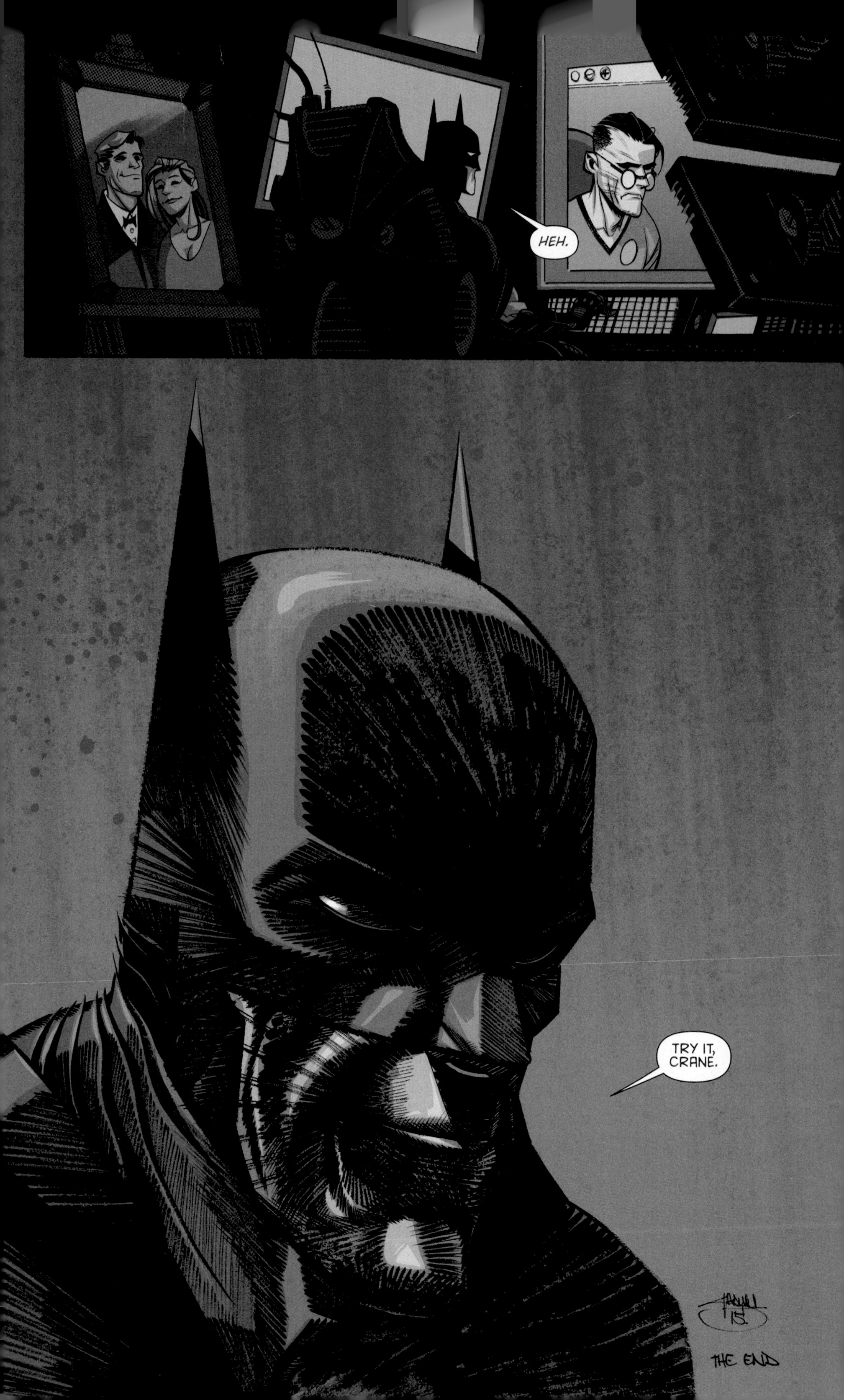
HEH.
TRY IT, CRANE.
THE END

CONCEPT ART AND THUMBNAIL LAYOUTS BY SHAWN CRYSTAL

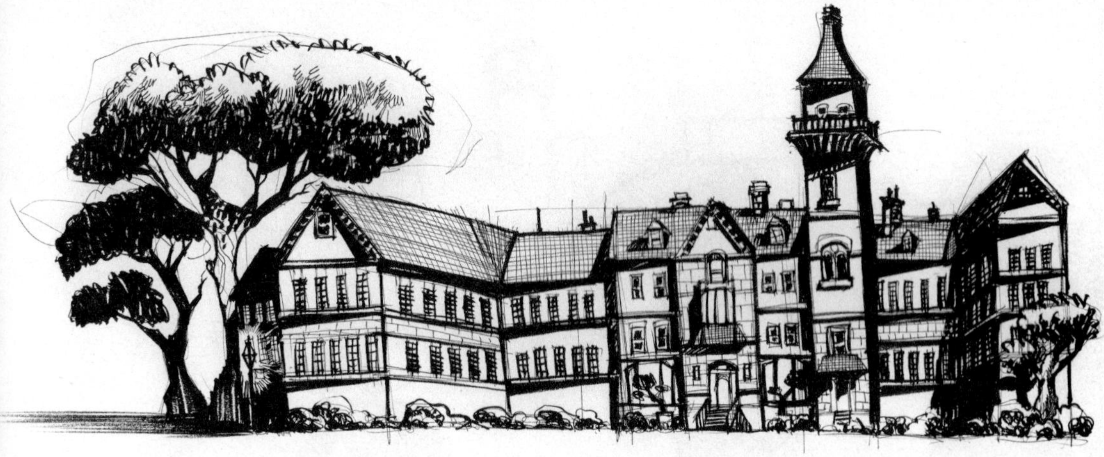

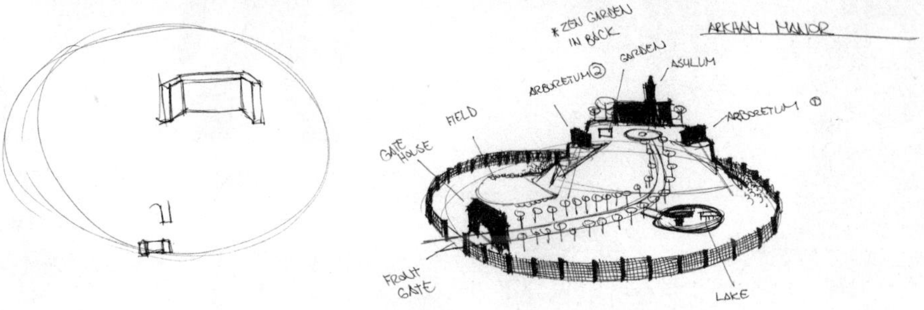

ARKHAM MANOR
*ZEN GARDEN IN BACK
ARBORETUM ②
GARDEN
ASYLUM
ARBORETUM ①
FIELD
GATE HOUSE
FRONT GATE
LAKE

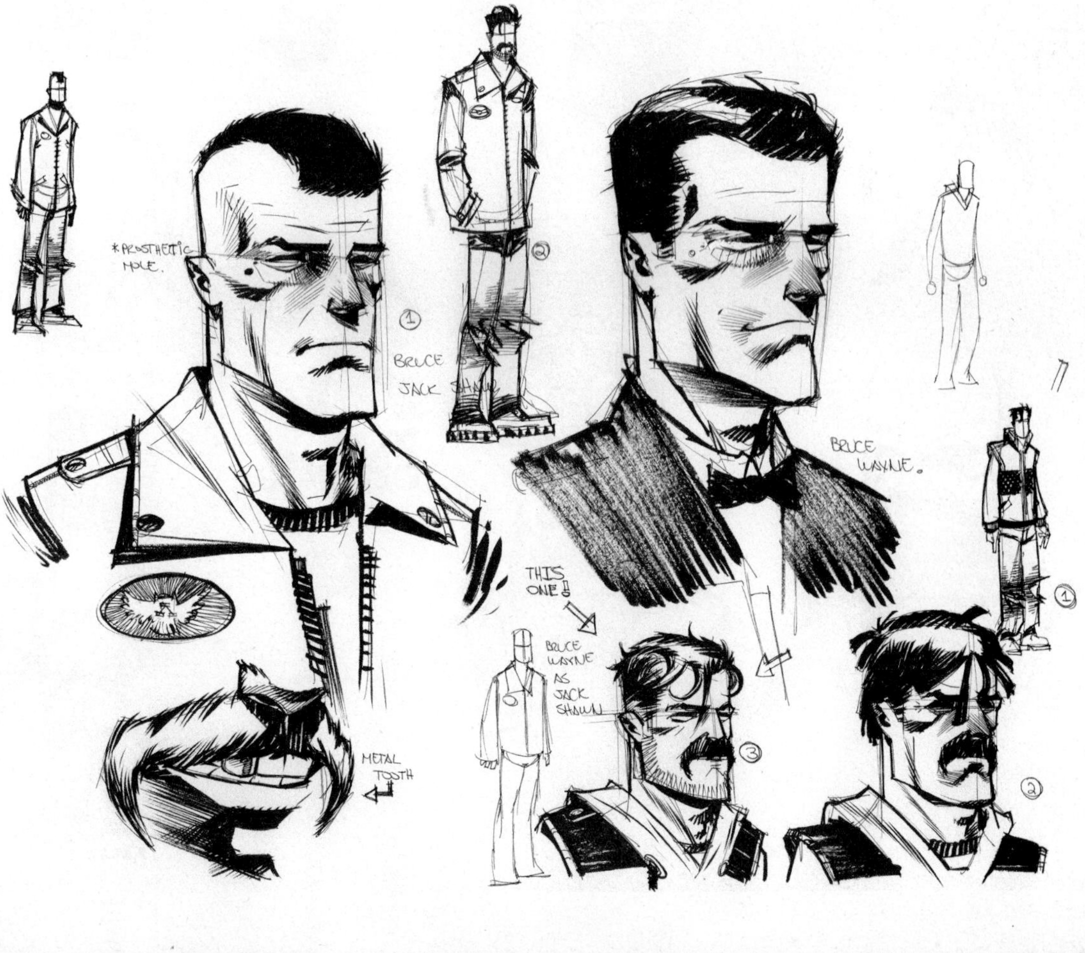

*PROSTHETIC MOLE.
①
BRUCE AS JACK SHAW
②
BRUCE WAYNE.
THIS ONE!!
BRUCE WAYNE AS JACK SHAWN
①
③
②
METAL TOOTH

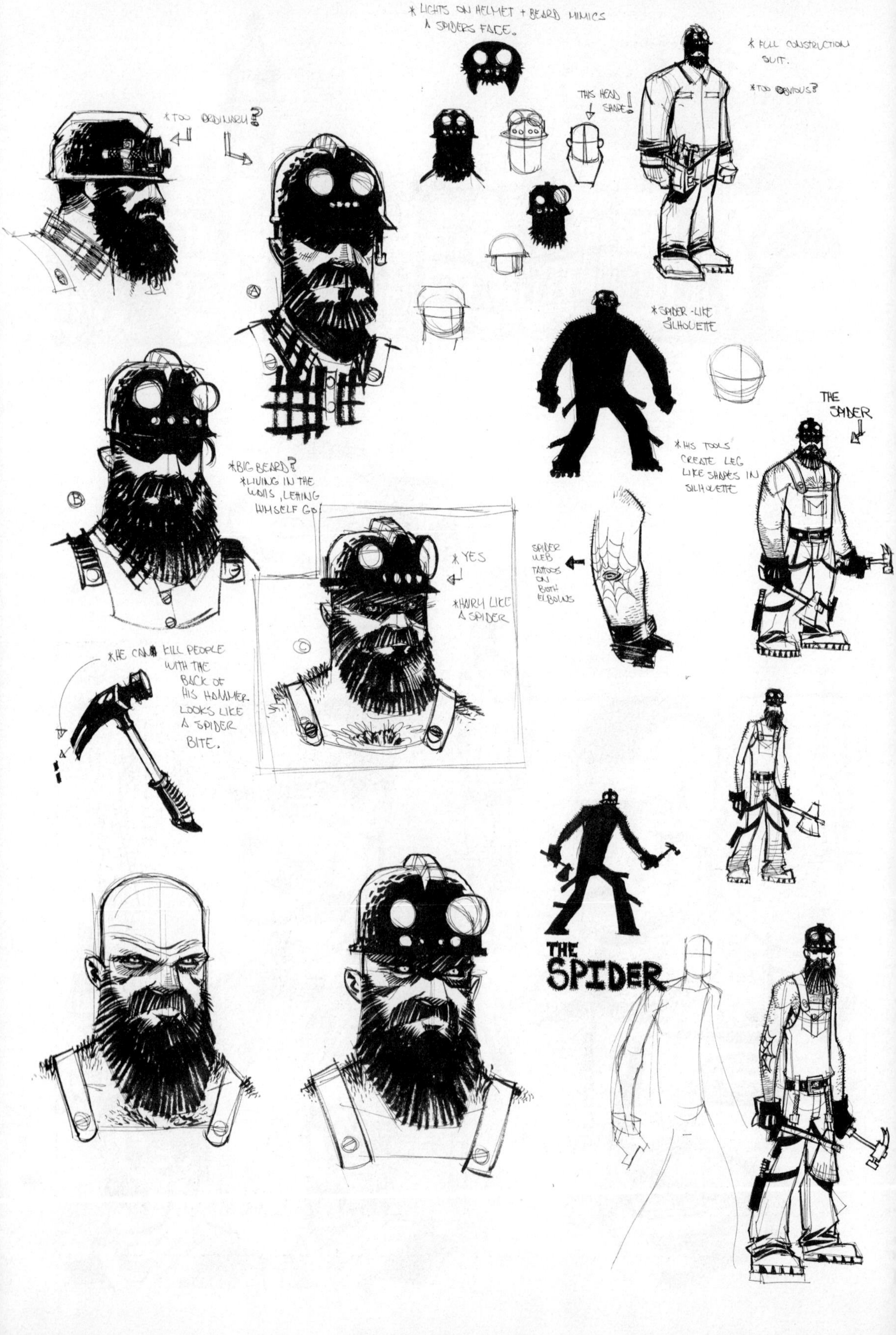

* LIGHTS ON HELMET + BEARD MIMICS A SPIDERS FACE.
* TOO ORDINARY?
THIS HEAD SHAPE!
* FULL CONSTRUCTION SUIT.
* TOO OBVIOUS?
* SPIDER-LIKE SILHOUETTE
* BIG BEARD? * LIVING IN THE WALLS, LETING HIMSELF GO.
* HIS TOOLS CREATE LEG LIKE SHAPES IN SILHOUETTE
THE SPIDER
* YES
* HAIRY LIKE A SPIDER
SPIDER WEB TATTOOS ON BOTH ELBOWS
* HE CAN KILL PEOPLE WITH THE BACK OF HIS HAMMER. LOOKS LIKE A SPIDER BITE.
THE SPIDER

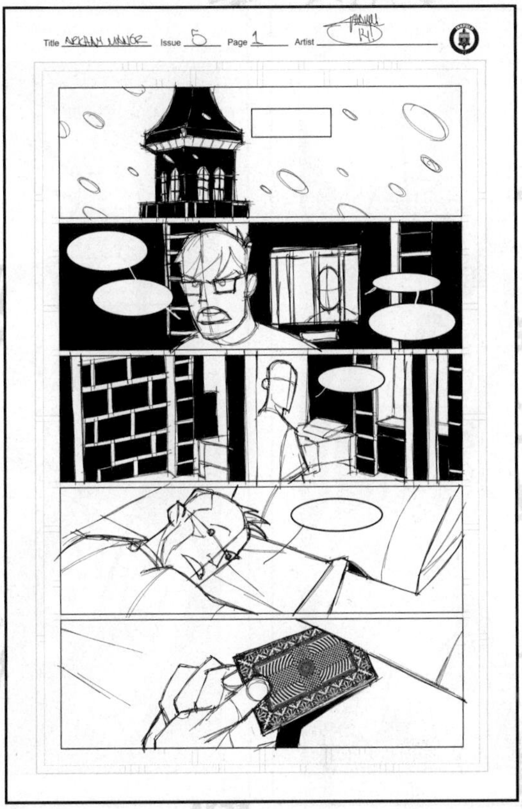
Title ARKHAM MANOR Issue 5 Page 1 Artist

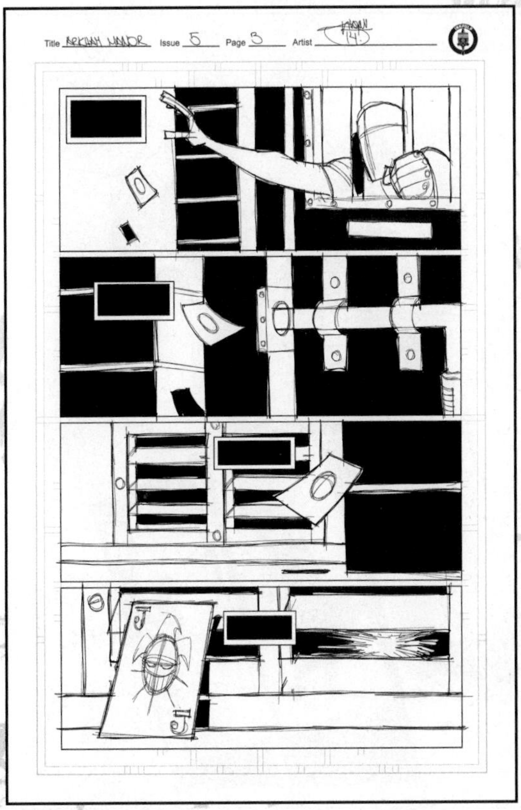
Title ARKHAM MANOR Issue 5 Page 3 Artist

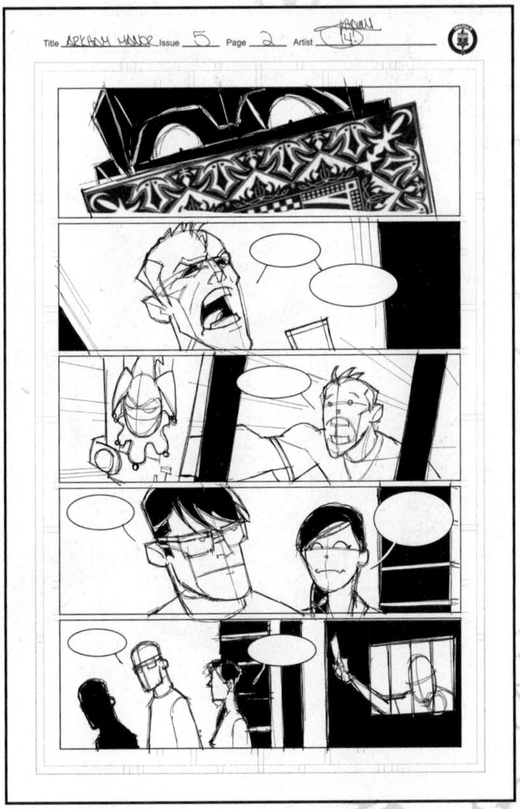
Title ARKHAM MANOR Issue 5 Page 2 Artist

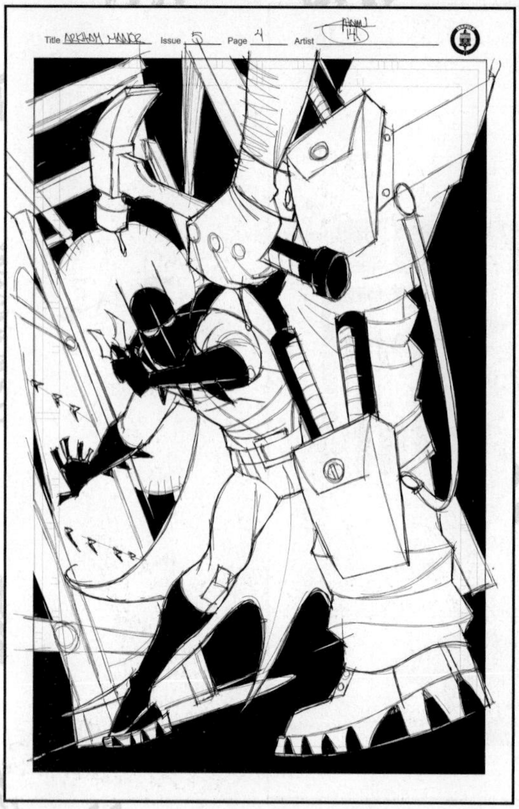
Title ARKHAM MANOR Issue 5 Page 4 Artist

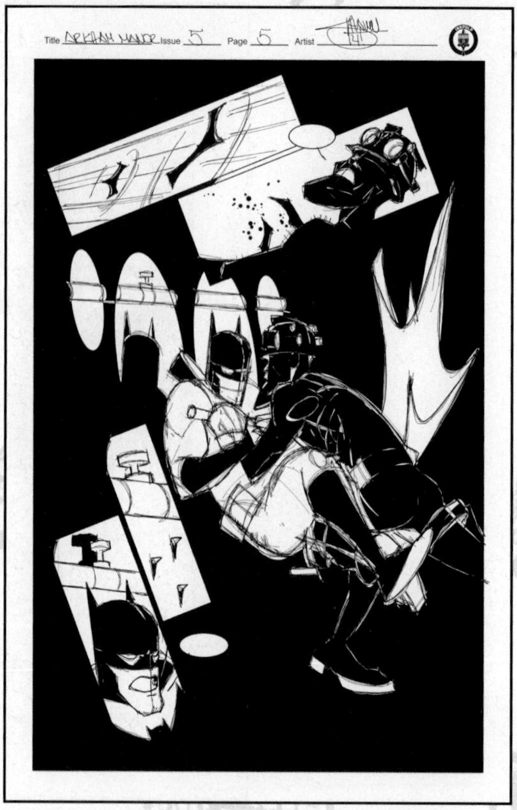
Title ARKHAM MANOR Issue 5 Page 5 Artist

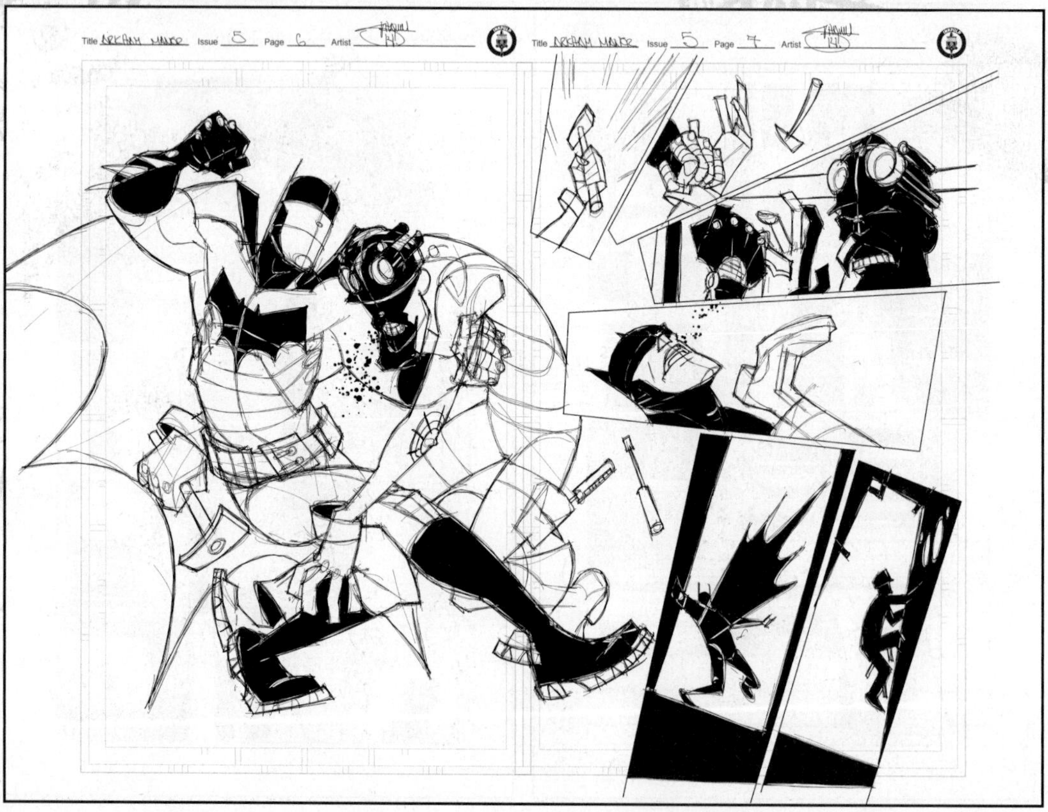
Title ARKHAM MANOR Issue 5 Page 6 Artist
Title ARKHAM MANOR Issue 5 Page 7 Artist

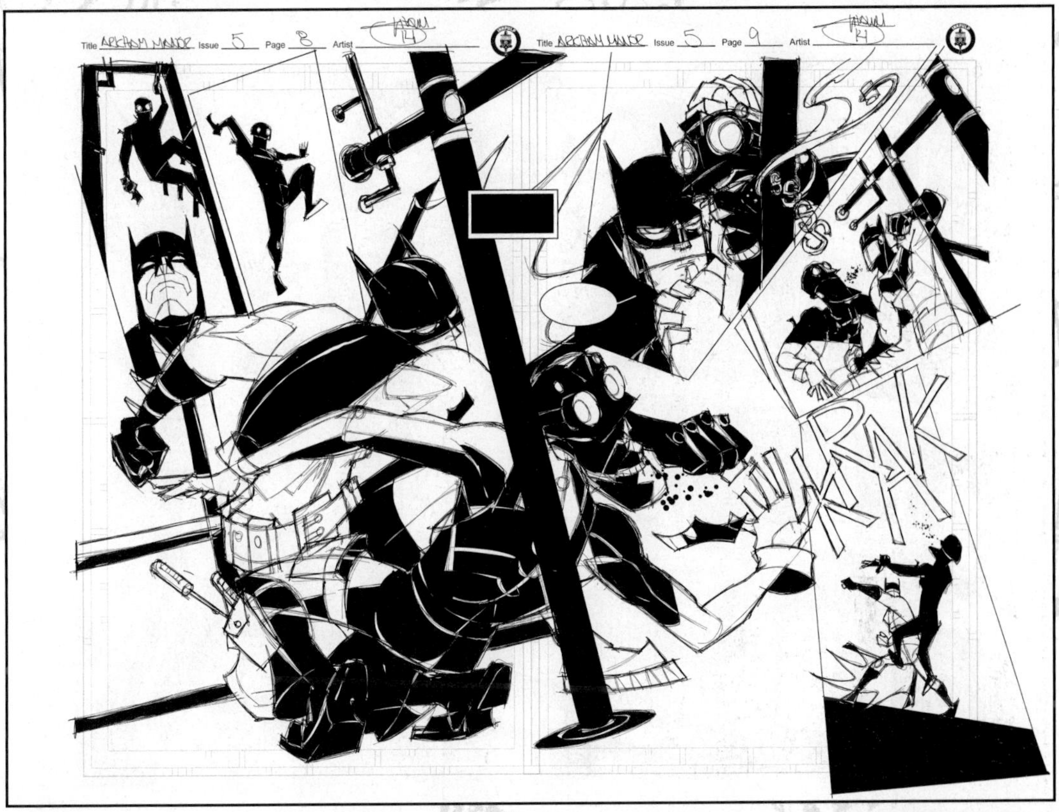
Title ARKHAM MANOR Issue 5 Page 8 Artist
Title ARKHAM MANOR Issue 5 Page 9 Artist

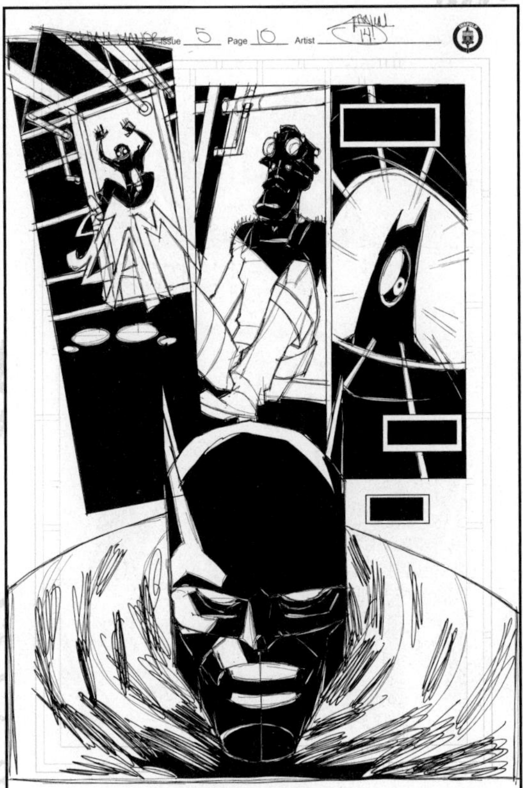
Issue 5 Page 10 Artist

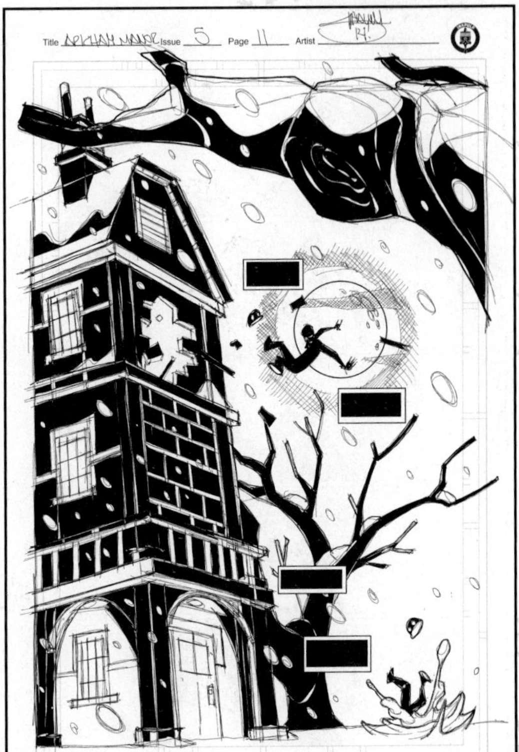
Title ARKHAM MANOR Issue 5 Page 11 Artist

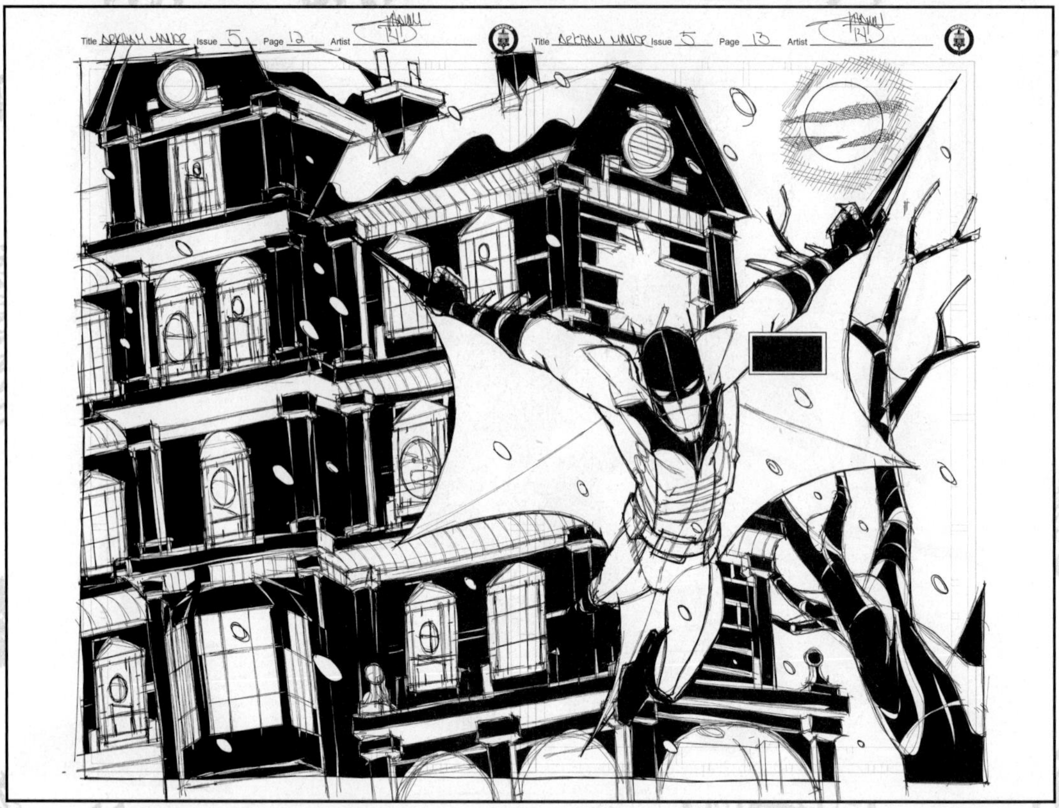
Title ARKHAM MANOR Issue 5 Page 12 Artist
Title ARKHAM MANOR Issue 5 Page 13 Artist

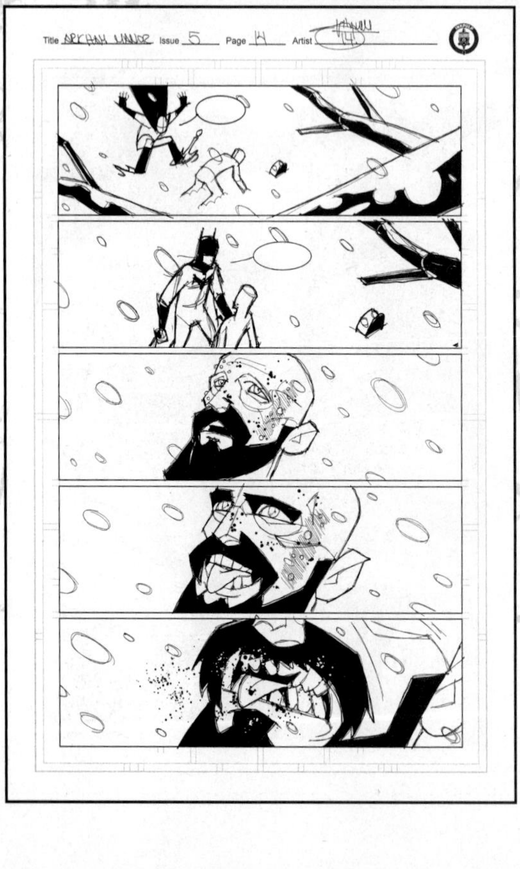
Title ARKHAM MANOR Issue 5 Page 14 Artist

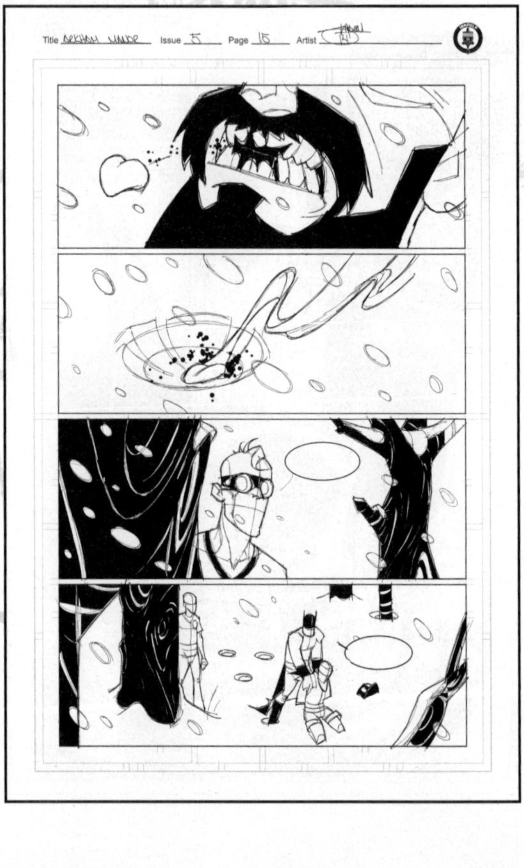
Title ARKHAM MANOR Issue 5 Page 15 Artist

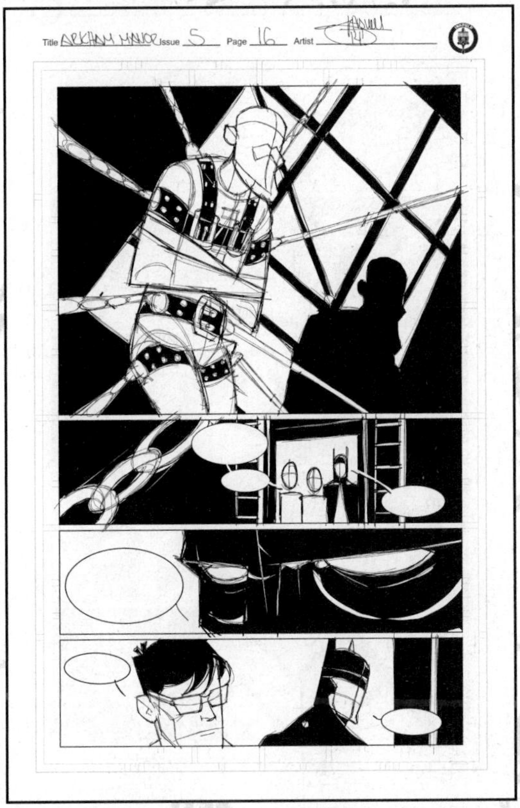
Title ARKHAM MANOR Issue 5 Page 16 Artist

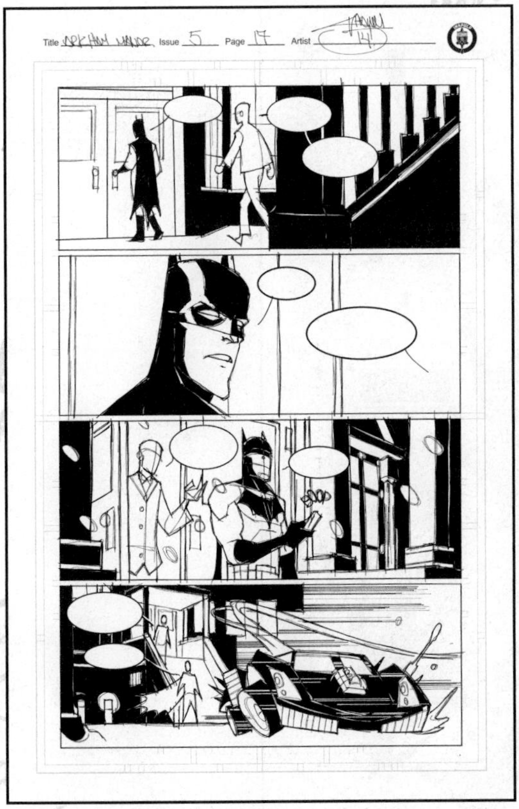
Title ARKHAM MANOR Issue 5 Page 17 Artist

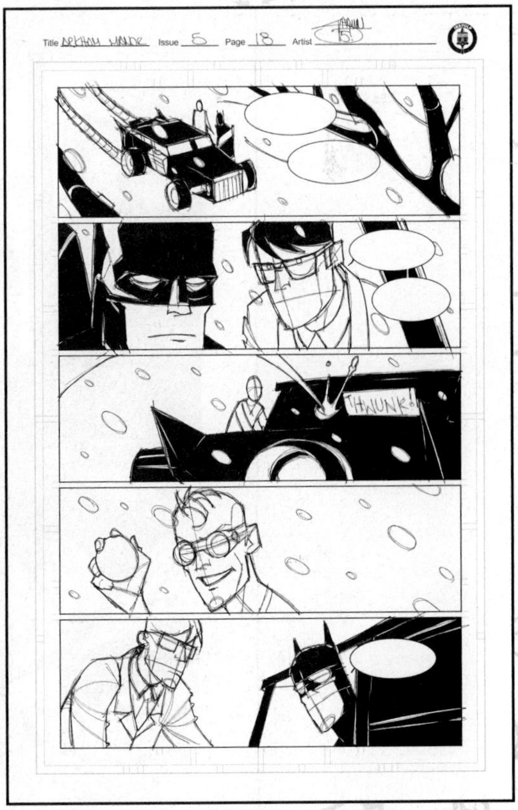
Title ARKHAM MANOR Issue 5 Page 18 Artist
THWUNK!

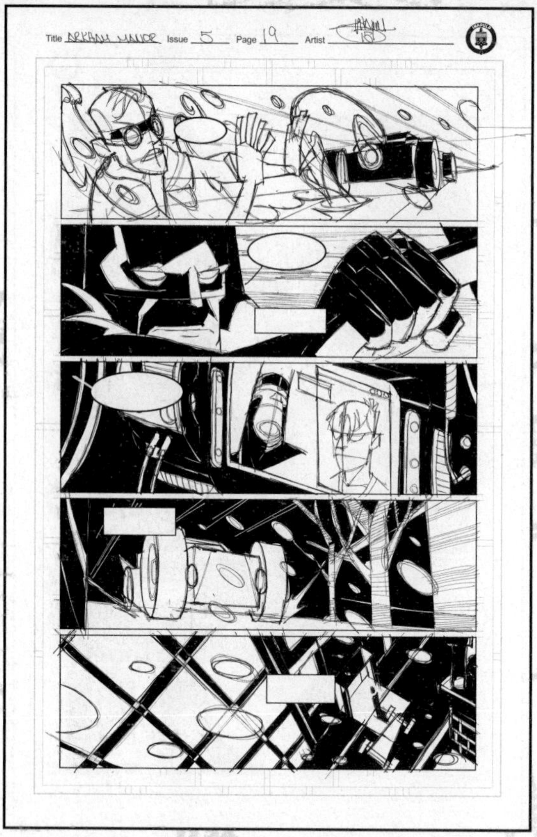
Title ARKHAM MANOR Issue 5 Page 19 Artist

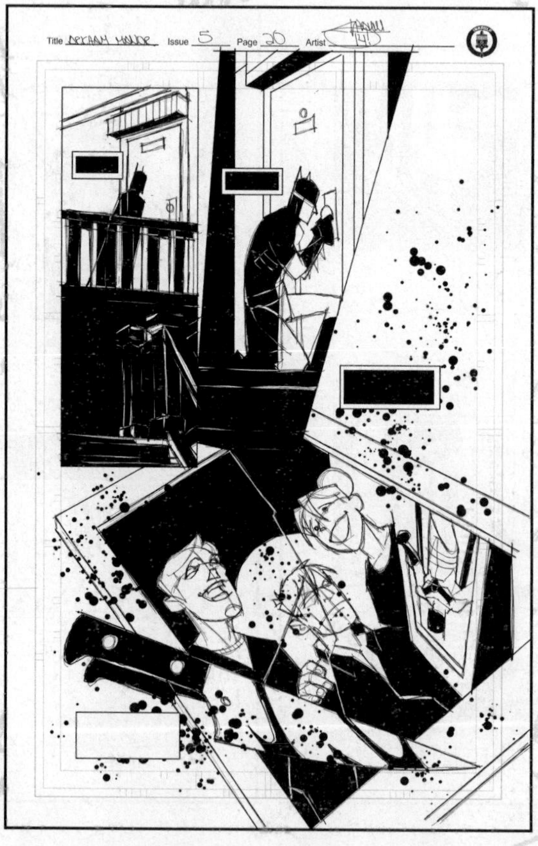
Title ARKHAM MANOR Issue 5 Page 20 Artist